*THE INSIDER'S
GUIDE TO
ANTIQUES, ART,
AND COLLECTIBLES*

Sylvia O'Neill Dorn

THE INSIDER'S GUIDE TO ANTIQUES, ART, AND COLLECTIBLES

DOUBLEDAY & COMPANY, INC.

Garden City, New York   1974

ISBN: 0-385-06747-x
Library of Congress Catalog Card Number 73–11701
Copyright © 1974 by Doubleday & Company, Inc.
All Rights Reserved
Printed in the United States of America

To Samuel David Dorn
in loving memory and gratitude

Preface

Many years ago a famous dealer in antiques, art, and curios said, "All collectors should be cynics," and that is more true today than ever. Not only do the unethical and dishonest plot to despoil the naïve and unwary, but honest and reputable dealers, auctioneers, and appraisers employ methods which the private person needs to know and understand to become more of an equal and less of a victim in the give and take of buying and selling antiques, art, and other collectibles.

Now that a reasonable standard of living for so many includes ownership of a collection of *something*, whether it be stamps, coins, Tiffany glass, Disneyana, Lowestoft china, commemorative plates, or any of countless variations on the theme of antiques, art, curios and hobbies, even larger numbers of people have a stake in understanding the economics, mechanics, and customs of a market in which they have invested varying proportions of their net worth.

A cultural revolution has brought new categories of collectibles on to the scene. In addition to art, the classic antiques, rare books, autographs, coins, and stamps, such items as barbed-wire fence, fruit jars, comic magazines, glass insulators, Kewpie Dolls, and Mickey Mouse watches are seriously accumulated. It has become as valid to collect some aspect of mass, or popular, culture, as of any bygone way of life. They now coexist side by side.

Suddenly the possibilities become fascinating and almost alarming. Certain comic books of the late 1930s sell for as much as $50 per copy. The first issue of *Playboy* magazine is quoted at $150 for a copy in mint condition. Mickey Mouse watches have brought $200 under the sales banner of Sotheby Parke Bernet. Avon bottles, which only lately "came calling," are now being sought by collectors who pay as much as several hundred dollars for a rare one. An epidemic of "limited editions" is compared to the tulipomania phenomenon of the seventeenth century.

"Collect for investment" has become a standard advertising headline. "Limited edition of 20,000" boasts an offering of plates. Bells, paperweights, ashtrays, spoons, mugs, jugs, jewelry, even plastic-boxed butterflies are sold in "limited editions," and it is implied their resale will enrich the owner when frantic competition by collectors to acquire the items will skyrocket the prices, which are seldom low at the point of issue.

Even for those who may buy on impulse when browsing, or who, like that Boston lady, "Never buy antiques, just *have* them," the problems of identifying, valuing, and eventually selling need to be examined in the light of economic reality.

Macy's may not tell Gimbels, but is positively garrulous when compared to what the professionals in the trade disclose about the business aspects of collecting. From the local flea market to the most prestigious international gallery, there is a conspiracy of silence about the mechanics of the trade.

This therefore is an attempt to redress the balance between the amateur and the professional. How some in the field use "price guides" to create new price "highs"; what pitfalls to avoid in appraisal; how to properly compute a speculative profit; the dangers of consignment; what markups prevail in various specialties; how to get a discount from a dealer; why to buy from, but never sell to, a picker is some of the information essential to the private person who wants a fair and fighting chance when dealing with those inside the collecting trade.

There is a large and excellent literature on collecting. It shows, tells, describes, explains, compares, catalogues, and even purports to price almost everything from rare autographs to zithers. What has been hitherto lacking is a lucid explanation of the inside mechanics of the collecting world.

With this guide, as the outsider becomes an insider, it is to be hoped that all aspects of collecting, an important source of pleasure and profit to many, will give pleasure and profit to even more.

Contents

vvvvvvvvvvvvvvvvvvvvvvvvvvvvvvvvvvvvvvvvvvvvvvvvvvv

PART II

Part I

⋙⋙⋙⋙⋙⋙⋙⋙⋙⋙⋙⋙⋙⋙⋙⋙⋙⋙⋙⋙⋙⋙⋙⋙⋙⋙⋙

Chapter 1

THE VALUE OF EVERYTHING

As an antique Chinese porcelain jar fetches over half a million dollars at auction, a museum pays more than a million dollars for an ancient Greek pottery bowl, and paintings sell for three and five million dollars each, the average citizen may be overwhelmed, possibly incredulous, even disapproving of such expenditures, but suspends judgment as to whether the prices were consistent with value, since he knows that he lacks expertise to determine that.

However, when a twenty-year-old rock-and-roll phonograph record originally selling for $.79 brings $100 and a pink pressed-glass butter dish that sold for less than a dollar during the depression brings $200, it boggles the minds of many, who find it disturbing to some private sense of proportion. They want to know how to account for assessments of value reflected in these prices, especially since their familiarity with similar items offers a paucity of clues.

Actually, value equations are the same for the divine and the ridiculous. They may not be immutable, but there *are* some long-established, stable value measurements. Unlike that Oscar Wilde character, we may know both the value and the price of everything we take the trouble to determine.

Not only can objective values be established with these components, but they offer sound basis for subjective response as well. Time, place, and culture, as well as personal standards, may put differing emphasis on the various elements, developing new and different relationships between them (and within each one as well), but in total they hold firm and fast as building blocks of value structure.

Age	Pedigree
Attribution	Period and style
Beauty	Quality
Collectibility	Quantity
Color	Rarity
Condition	Size
Fashion	Source and origin
Historical interest	Subject
Marks	Utility
Material	Workmanship

AGE

Whether considering antiques, art, books, coins, stamps, or wines, the question "How old?" is superseded by "Was it a good year?" Age alone is not a paramount factor in value considerations of collectibles. The importance of the age in reference to the character of the item forms the basis for this judgment.

Multiples of millions are necessary to place fossils into their proper time slots, yet some can be bought for a few dollars. A 500-million-year-old trilobite costs $3.50, exactly the sum quoted by a price guide for a 7-Up matchbook cover.

A Tiffany bowl or vase dating from the early twentieth century often is priced higher than the two-thousand-year-old Roman glass from which its design derives. Very ancient art, thousands of years old, seems comparatively low in value, if judged solely by price. Lovely two-inch-high Greek terra-cotta heads of about 300 B.C., broken from figurines, could be bought for about $10 a few years ago when many were sold under the auspices of the National Museum in Athens, because the collections already included countless better examples.

Book catalogues produce such strange bookfellows as a 1939 "Superman Comic" priced at $38 and an 1808 edition of Sir Walter Scott's *Marmion,* bound in calfskin and in sound condition, for $7.50. Obviously, age alone will not confer the value that brings high prices. It must be a coefficient of other attributes.

The late twentieth-century acceptance of mid-century material as "antique," and otherwise collectible, has been attributed to fast-paced psychological changes wrought by electronic and atomic technology. This may be a factor accounting for the speed of nostalgic responses to their own recent childhood by some people in the second and third decades of their lives. It used to take a longer while for unfashionable items to become old-fashioned; now only a decade's seasoning is required.

An obsession for shabby and "funky" clothing, as part of a youth rebellion against the commercialization of fashion, led into glorification of old-fashioned as avant-garde. Although Victorian styles were worn and copied, a particular chic attached itself to the styles worn from the 1920s to the 1950s. A generation that prided itself on its disinterest in history had difficulty in defining a perspective for its art and decoration as well, thus confusion is compounded, and the balance that time confers on judgment, suspended for many new categories of collectibles.

In a time of reassessment and reappraisal, there are some who are quick to grasp the changing trends and who turn them to their advantage; others resist or try to ignore them, usually as an emotional response in making a choice of values.

Yet for most objects, age remains crucial to the value profile, since placement in time is exactly what distinguishes and is responsible for characterizing it. Thus scientific tests are developed to verify and pinpoint the age of objects and to nullify the efforts of fakers who artificially age material to give it additional value and to price it accordingly.

In efforts to make objects appear antique, silver may be dulled, paintings filled with a network of cracks, and furniture distressed by being beaten and abused, as are metals. Glass is buried, carpets placed in animal stalls, ivory stained with licorice or nicotine, and in general, much effort employed to add the convincing aura of age to newer materials.

As individuals are said to be in the prime of life, or to enjoy their best years, so for certain objects there are especially good "circas." For each, there is a season.

ATTRIBUTION

When the Metropolitan Museum of Art announced that it had changed the labels on 15 per cent of its European painting collection, the general public was amazed; but the world of art considered the reattributions long overdue. It seems that experts had long questioned "The Old Woman Cutting Her Nails" as a work of Rembrandt's and "A City on a Rock" as Goya's, as well as many other paintings said to be incorrectly ascribed. What the layman wants above all is confidence in expert judgment, and whenever it is shaken, it comes as a surprise and shock. The experts know the difficulties of being absolutely sure of everything and take it for granted that there will be changes of attribution as knowledge is increased by research and scientific techniques.

Of course, the wealthy collector is even more dependent on authorities to guarantee the authenticity of a purchase, and not only fakes but incorrectly ascribed works drop sharply in price when downgrading changes are made. On the other hand, expert conclusions sometimes upgrade a work, with corresponding price increase.

Discovering "who done it," before buying or selling, may be the most lucrative of all detective work. Knowing who the maker is, no matter who it may be, adds some value. Neither Rembrandt nor Goya is too likely to cross the threshold of our private concern, but even in the less exalted realms of art or craftsmanship, the name of the artist or artisan lends value to an object. Having the name means you can check the rank and standing of your maker. Even if the item is the unsigned product of a traceable studio, shop, or factory, you are on the way to further enlightenment if you have that information.

The names of Fabergé, Tiffany, Cartier, and other famous jewelers add value, although it is well to remember that if the item merely originated in the factory workroom of the firm, it is less valuable than if it is the signed creation of an important craftsman in its ranks.

Handmade silver, whether antique or modern, is much esteemed according to the name of its maker, whether as hallmark or other form of signature. Yet connoisseurs differentiate quality variations under the same name and from the same hand.

Chippendale, Sheraton, Adam, and Duncan Phyfe are among the furniture makers to whom general styles rather than individual pieces are usually ascribed. If you are selling furniture, you are entitled to call your piece after the designer, but if you are buying, you would be wise to require proof if it is claimed to be of the period and made by him.

Overemphasis on the maker, rather than on the thing in itself, leads to snob, status, and fashion traps for the buyer. The best proof of the maker is in the "makership" as illustrated by the object.

BEAUTY

Although beauty rests in the eye of the beholder, there *are* standards of beauty for different things. Don't denigrate the value of a possession because *you* think it is ugly. Discover what is considered the standard of beauty for that object and be governed by it in valuing for sale. Just as ugliness is a form of beauty in bulldogs, so each thing has its own kind of perfection.

Stamp collectors ardently seek reversed or upside-down printing errors, finding beauty in the subtlest deviations.

Proof coins are generally accepted as the epitome of beauty, whether copper, silver, or gold. On the other hand, there is an Association of Mint-Error Collectors, who choose to see beauty in imperfection.

Some find beauty in the stark simplicity of Shaker design, others in the winding ornate lines of the Rococo style. Connoisseurs of old silver prefer the patina which is more satiny and has greater depth, to the more obvious attractions of a brilliant shiny finish.

There are endless variations of these standards, many of them changing with fashion and new developments in collecting trends. Beauty is a paramount ingredient of value, but can never be taken for granted.

As businessmen often disclaim aesthetic judgment, bowing to the customers' preference, so most dealers in the fields of collecting reserve their private opinions as to beauty, allowing customers to bestow the accolade where they will.

The expletive description, "beautiful," may be banal, but those who confer it rarely find it boring. It is often applied to objects for which other adjectives would be more appropriate, and through some misplaced courtesy, is rarely refuted.

However, beauty as an extension of the idea of perfection, or a reaching for perfection, or perfection itself, is a constant value factor. What changes is the ideal.

COLOR

Canton blue china, blue and white early Della Robbia, Staffordshire transfer blue, Wedgwood blue and white jasper, Renoir's blue grass, Picasso's blue period, the utter, unforgettable blue of Bristol glass offer but a small sampling of just one color's place in the value spectrum.

Spinach green for jade, cranberry red for glass, "Imperial" yellow or delicate peachblow for Chinese porcelains, and Pom-

ANTIQUES, ART, AND COLLECTIBLES   9

padour pink for Sèvres are some other hues which are fast colors indeed, made more so by the passage of time.

Old Waterford glass, produced in Ireland in the eighteenth and early nineteenth centuries, contains a hint of steely gray that is so subtle, it can hardly be called more than a tint. Yet this greatly increases its appeal for collectors, as it lends authenticity and "presence."

Dark backgrounds prevailed as the standard for painting until Impressionist light flooded and overcame the older tradition and, ultimately, raw color overwhelmed almost all canvas.

Patina, which combines finish with color, enhances the worth of wood and metals. Stamps, coins, carpets, and jewels also have their places on the value color palette, achieved through generations of choice and chance.

Whether it was the only color, the best color, the costliest, the rarest, the most popular color, or an historical personage's favorite color, somewhere along the line discriminating taste pronounced a verdict which was accepted, making a certain shade or hue especially desirable. Additional appeal may be conferred as contemporary taste cycles emphasize pastels, brilliant tones, or, as recently, the "natural" palette. Then these are extrapolated from the storehouse of the past for additional, if sometimes temporary, emphasis.

In search of the profits which colors add to price, generations of restorers, repairers, and unscrupulous vendors have "doctored" both copies and originals, to achieve the colors collectors may be seeking. Color is a great tempter, leading to many mistakes. In looking for the "right" color, it is prudent to make sure that everything else is also "right" about the object.

There are some art experts who prefer to study the black and white photographs of a painting, believing that in this way the bare bones of a work are exposed to study, without the distractions of color to obscure forms and balances. Others, claiming that the color of a work is intrinsic to its form, try to blank out the shapes and see only the colors.

Experts of both persuasions make it a point to avoid judging colors of any object in fluorescent light, since it distorts both colors and tones.

COLLECTIBILITY

Pioneer typewriters, washing machines, and ice boxes are now included in lists of collectibles. The Campbell Kids, Kewpie Dolls, and Mickey Mouse cavort into serious collections. Pot lids and paperweights, postcards and pipes now join papier-mâché, political campaign buttons, and photographic and phonographic "antiques" under the letter *P* in price guides for collectors.

Add to them children's jumping jacks, tops, high chairs, postcards, movie posters, and radios; somebody wants them, collects them. Presto! they are collectibles. The variety is indeed endless, and now there are those who collect catalogues of items that collectors collect!

A new industry manufactures "limited edition" so-called "investment" collectibles. Assortments offered range from silver medallions at $10 to glass vases at $1,400, with some items at even higher prices.

Where royalty once collected state carriages, a breed of automotive buffs collects old automobiles, some of which fetch tens of thousands of dollars when sold at "antique automobile" auctions. Incredibly, military vehicles are being privately collected, with Sherman tanks especially appreciated.

Aspects of collectibility stressed by insiders require that subjects in a category be fairly plentiful, or at least generally available. If they are exceptionally scarce, there will be no momentum for a market, and dealers and those who collect with a view to sales and profits are largely concerned with this.

To become a popular collectible, an item should be easily identifiable, with not too much study required for its differentiation from other wares, nor within the framework of its own category. Preferably it should not be easily or cheaply reproduced.

Items that must be collected in series offer themselves as ideal subjects. Nothing is more addictive than the filling out of a series; it seems to carry its own compulsions. However, the drawback of being trapped by the need for missing units, and possibly being held up for an exorbitant sum for the rarity, makes blackmail seem an innocent enterprise. Insiders are careful to avoid disclosing great anxiety for certain items, to avoid artificially enhancing the value of such a necessity.

For years French-print dealers were amused by a fervent collector who spent a lifetime looking for a poor-quality etching by Callot. It was the only work by this artist that his collection lacked, the only appeal it had for him.

CONDITION

This is an aspect of value superseding many others. It is hard to imagine what item could be considered for acquisition or sale without reference to its condition.

Furniture more than a third restored drops sharply in value, and there is a constant duel between the restorer and the expert to discern the proportion of the former's contribution to the whole.

Clocks and watches not in running condition, but with all their parts intact, are in a different (and much better) value bracket from those with missing parts.

The value of paintings responds very sensitively to the element of condition. This is a matter for experts and X rays when it comes to masterpieces, but even in modest decorative art, it is an important consideration. How well a painting is cleaned, whether it is overpainted, and the condition of the canvas and paint itself will play a large part in the assessment of its value.

Electroplating an old piece of Sheffield to cover the "bleeding" copper may please the eye of an amateur, but it will neither fool nor please the dealer or collector who can easily spot it by the bright finish lacking patina, a minus on the value scale.

Condition is "all" for the coin collector. Prices are quoted according to an ascending scale which starts with "fair" then goes to "good," "fine," "uncirculated," and "proof." Delicate variations such as "very good" or "extra fine" are common. A three-cent silver piece, minted 1855, is quoted as follows:

Good $12   Fine $30   Uncirculated $150   Proof $850

Charles F. French, the American numismatist, advises against cleaning badly worn coins of any kind. He points out that it is a waste of time, and cleaning a coin that is in a condition inferior to "very fine" will not improve it.

Charles Hamilton, the well-known autograph dealer, warns that "any self-sealing type of adhesive tape will badly stain and may ultimately destroy the document upon which it is placed."

Since the most common technique for the buyer who wants to denigrate the merchandise offered is to point out any flaw in its condition, it is important for the seller to know the value aspect of the condition of the wares to be sold.

Experts advise that the owner who plans to sell should never try to repair or restore any old or fine piece without carefully checking to make sure that the value is not being destroyed rather than enhanced.

For some reason, pottery that has suffered breakage or chipping, and requires some restoration, will not be written off by collectors to the extent that porcelain which has been repaired will be reduced in value. Perhaps it is the very vulnerability of porcelain that makes its perfection an asset of its totality. Glass is equally depreciated in value by any flaws.

Disguise of poor condition is the reason for a never-ending vigil that all who collect must keep, to avoid acquiring imperfect material. More dangerous than the outright fake, which may signal its falsity from a distance, the skillful restoration covers its secret well.

The best school for spotting restoration and repair is the studio of the restorer. Most in this profession are privy to the secrets of the trade for which they work. Usually they receive the objects to be worked on, in an anteroom, apart from the working area. This is to keep clients from knowing what is being done to transform the imperfect to seeming perfection.

The smart insider has a restorer for a friend and access to his studio to observe work in progress, especially on the merchandise of others.

FASHION

Experienced merchants say that fashion, whether in the cut of clothes or the color of carpeting, is the result of sales promotion that has been successfully timed. Dealers in antiques, art, and collectibles agree, although most of them do not originate trends but either follow propitious circumstances or their more aggressive colleagues who initiate fashions.

Political, anthropological, and artistic trends seemingly dovetailed when a famous collection of North American Indian artifacts and crafts fetched astronomical prices. A basket from the Green sale brought $6,100, hide robes and dresses, along with blankets and robes, were bid to thousands for individual pieces. Seemingly overnight, American Indian art was "in." However, the almost simultaneous appearance of museum and gallery exhibitions, books, articles, and department store advertisements told insiders that the American Indian had not received the accolade of fashion by any accidental means.

There are many variations on fashion promotion as it relates to collecting. Some are based on events such as the Fisher-Spassky chess duel. It had been anticipated by manufacturers of chess sets and publishers of books on the subject, but it was hardly underway for commercial wares, before antique dealers found it was stimulating interest in the purchase of old sets. Scouts and pickers were alerted, better prices paid, advertisements placed. Soon vintage sets were brought out of closets, restored, repaired, and sold for good prices. Sets were brought into shops, offered for sale when owners saw price tags indicating their desirability. Decorators used fine chess sets in room settings and window displays; buyers were tempted by the assortments. The fashion cycle for chess sets, based in this case on a cultural event, had taken off.

Although there had been a growing market for oriental objects prior to the Nixon visit to China, the growth was accelerated by the event, especially since traders got modern merchandise to promote along with some nineteenth-century antiques the Chinese government now allowed to be exported. In addition, a splendid exhibition of ancient Chinese art from recently excavated tombs was sent abroad, engaging the international interest of collectors and scholars in Chinese art. Chinese coins and stamps were also enhanced in value by the same wave of interest.

Social developments and economic forces also play a part in making collectibles fashionable. Greater awareness of the environment has been manifested in many ways, few more direct than the increased interest in minerals, fossils, and shells as collectibles and decorations. Small animalier bronze figures and small equestrian sculpture have always been appreciated and valued according to artistic criteria, but dealers report that, more recently, buyers have been acquiring them for their fashionably naturalistic features.

Fad, fashion, or staple collectible are appellations that only time can fully establish. In general, those who have items to sell are wise to do so in a period when interest in them is rising. The delicate matter of waiting for the crest is a chancy one, and fashion ebbs quickly.

Manipulating fashion for profit in collecting is inherent in the merchandising system of antiques, art, and collectibles; it has been done over the centuries. Today's techniques include radio, television, newspaper, and periodical presentations. "Limited Editions" are touted by politicians and socialites, quilts by artists, prints and graphics by movie stars, paintings by critics who have an economic stake in them. With interior design timed into ten-year cycles of style obsolescence, only the very rich

can afford to follow the leaders, the rest of us are well advised
to choose the object, not the fashion for it.

Paul Revere was a fine silversmith who sometimes rose to
great artistry in his work, but it was Paul Revere the patriot
whose simple six-inch silver sugar tongs fetched $5,250 at auc-
tion. Association with famous names as creators or owners, or
with historical events, is a powerful value inducer.

The 1930 Graf Zeppelin issue of a set of three airmail stamps,
totaling less than five dollars at face value, were listed at well
over a hundred times that amount in stamp catalogues, another
example of historical appeal, this time on a note of tragedy.

A morbid fascination with prominent criminals, Nazi souvenirs, and similar unedifying subjects has created a market with
a special set of macabre values which the *cognoscenti* appreciate.
It is a limited market, but a thriving one.

A lock of Napoleon's hair, Marie Antoinette's handkerchief,
or Washington's shoe buckles can thrill thousands in museums,
and when properly authenticated, bring high prices from private collectors who want the satisfaction of owning such
personalized contacts with greatness.

Vagaries of history may create some strange value phenomena,
as when the letter of a general who led the battle is less
valuable than that of a simple foot soldier who reveals some
hitherto unknown crucial strategic fact.

The scandals connected with the sale of stamps and some
other souvenirs of moon trips indicate the values put on historical events of this magnitude. Those who paid large sums
gambled that if future trips to the moon become commonplace,
mementos of early trips will be valuable as relics of the pioneer
period. If future trips are rare, then the material from the
early voyages will gain even more in value.

Dealers and collectors currently seem much more aware of
the possibilities inherent in historical interest as a source of

future value. With this alertness, more profits are garnered at earlier stages while events are still news rather than history.

MATERIAL

Gold snuffboxes, silver plates, silk carpets, enameled Easter eggs, semiprecious stone vases of malachite and lapis lazuli, crystal chandeliers, and precious jewels are among the treasures given value by the materials of which they are made.

Ivory, bone, and tortoise shell, once considered in the semi-precious rank, still give additional value to the objects they constitute. Furniture made of Amboina, palisander, and similar rare and costly woods is usually superbly made just because of the precious materials.

Until the early decades of the twentieth century, collecting was the prerogative of the very rich and the upper middle class. With the exception of a few with scientific or artistic bents and who collected natural wonders and art, the majority accumulated treasure that was in itself a permanent form of wealth. Silverware, gold coins, articles of "vertu," carpets, tapestries, and furniture also had the additional attraction of acting as a hedge against inflation, always the particular bane of those with much money that might be devalued. For many, collecting was a more cultured and sophisticated form of the French peasant's hoarding gold under his mattress, with the added appeal of offering social status as well.

However, there are less costly materials which also add value, although in less obvious form. Antique steel furniture, iron mechanical banks, tin trays and biscuit boxes, jet jewelry, and old crewel bed hangings add to a total entity which derives its value from being the right material for the right object.

More recently, a fascination with our own development in terms of social history and a sense of nostalgia about our recent past have changed the value quotient relating to intrinsic material values, giving us the "new antiques" of paper, base metals, and cheap plastics.

Yet, whenever there is a run on the dollar, a threat of devaluation, higher prices of gold and silver on the bullion market, or news of inflationary price rises, many private individuals still buy art, antiques, and collectibles with an eye to their material content.

MARKS

Those who live by marks are often defeated by them, making victims of themselves in their anxiety to indicate value by such means. This is especially so when marks are more highly rated than other value aspects of an object.

Many marks are purposely confusing. One such victim is the "beehive" of the Royal Vienna factory of Austria, actually a shield either incised or in underglaze blue, used from 1744 to 1864 by the original factory. This was not only much copied in Europe, but, as used by the Wheeling Pottery Company of West Virginia about the turn of the century, was often mistaken for it and still is. Meissen, Capo di Monte, Chelsea, and Wedgwood are among the other famous marks too often the targets of fraud.

The great English silver hallmarks are less often copied in Britain, perhaps because of the grave legal penalties for doing so, but they are sometimes "imitated" by manufacturers in other countries who produce something that looks like an imposing English hallmark.

Not all marks are intended to identify the object as to maker, factory, date, material, quality, or place of origin. Some show the name of the seller or retailer, others show the factory designation for shipping destination or serve to define position in a set or group. The study of marks is an important contribution to knowledge about any ware, in addition to its price-value importance.

No expert, authority, scholar, or dealer of any experience considers the mark or signature to be other than a confirming piece of evidence in establishing the identity of a piece. However, clear, authentic marks make a piece more valuable than one comparable, but unmarked or unsigned. If properly supported by every other characteristic of value, they will crown the piece, giving it the star appeal that breaks records and the hearts of those who yearn, but underbid.

Splendid "bibles" of marks serve the earnest seeker for knowledge and the speculator alike. It is a great and joyful experience to find verification in such volumes as William Chaffers' *Marks and Monograms on European and Oriental Pottery and Porcelain,* or Sir Charles James Jackson's *English Goldsmiths and Their Marks.*

PEDIGREE

"Who had it last?" is a game which may require a large forfeit, especially if the antiques, art, or collectibles in question should prove to have been stolen. In that case, the objects go back to their true owners and the money paid for them is irretrievably lost, should the recipients have dissipated or otherwise placed it out of reach.

Tracing the object in terms of ownership for a secure title is not the only reason for wanting to know its history. There are other facets to pedigree and provenance. One is authenticity. The presumption is that if we know where it has been, we have a better chance to discover what it is.

Sotheby Parke Bernet auction galleries offered a gravy boat made by Paul Revere, who gave it as a wedding present to a couple whose descendants, having kept it since then, decided to sell it in 1972. The price of $26,000, which it fetched, reflected its impeccable pedigree, as well as the other confirming value factors.

A painting, traced from the collection of Charles I to Cardinal Mazarin, Louis XIV, Philippe Egalité, and finally to a Rothschild, could be said to incorporate its pedigree into its value. The paperweight that comes from a famous collection formed by a great expert will have more value for having been in possession of a person whose taste and judgment is admired and respected.

Inscriptions, monograms, and coats of arms, which indicate that objects sojourned in specific households or institutions, are also part of the pedigree, and as they add prestige, they add value. However, they can also tell tales out of school, reducing value. No matter how rare, books marked "Property of Public Library" disenchant a collector.

Objects that are described in old documents, such as inventories, marriage contracts, letters, or auction catalogues, may carry a confirmation that increases value. On the other hand, the description has sometimes spawned an object to fit it (an old trick with European fakers).

The name of the owner of an object is part of the pedigree that goes along with it. In recounting the difficulties of Russian emigrés in France in the 1920s, Romain Gary tells how his mother acted as saleswoman for jewelry that had supposedly belonged to a grand duke, but actually was supplied to her by a local jeweler, out of his stock.

Especial weight is given to the actual site and circumstances of a find when antiquities and ancient artifacts are in question. Archaeologists point to the importance of careful excavation so that each piece found can be placed in its proper context in relation to a culture and civilization. When objects are illegally excavated, much more than material objects have been pillaged; facts and values accruing from them have been destroyed. Although great museums, collectors, and dealers may mouth pious platitudes, they actually encourage bootleg digging by paying huge sums for precious finds which, no matter how seemingly valuable at million-dollar prices, are less valuable than they might be, were the pedigree known.

PERIOD AND STYLE

No period is pre-eminent for everything made within its time span. Queen Anne silver, Rococo porcelain, Etruscan jewelry, Art Nouveau glass, and mid-Georgian furniture, each rose, above other kinds of objects made at the same time, to a pinnacle of preference. Conferred by the judgment of critics, art historians, dealers, and the accolade of collectors' taste, it is usually confirmed in the marketplace.

The vocabulary of period and style is undoubtedly an important element in the market value of antiques and collectibles. Calling it "a walnut table with cabriole legs" is a start. "A French provincial table" is an improvement, but if you say "Louis XV, country style," you have maximized the value elements of period and style. Design books are plentiful and period guides are easy to follow. If you sell an "old chest" to a dealer and he resells it and prices it as "American Sheraton, serpentine, reeded, veneered, circa 1810," you are literally paying for your oversight.

It is only after you can recognize the different styles of Windsor chairs that the oldest, finest, or rarest comes into focus. Most who bother to learn can name a style and its period by the general profile a piece presents. A few go on to study detail and fine differences. This effort is always repaid with interest.

All antiques, art, and collectibles belong in some period slot and can be so described. If an object is authentic and dates from the period of its style, its value will be so much the greater. If it is only in the style of a period, the value will be less, but even so, some value derives from its virtue as a copy. Victorian versions of Gothic, Renaissance, or Baroque styles are now collected as a special genre, in themselves worthy of interest.

Decorations, art, jewelry, furniture, and even clothing, in the naturalistic Art Nouveau style of the late nineteenth and early twentieth centuries and the "moderne" Art Deco style of the 1920s, have become established on period and style charts during the past decade. Many unsophisticated folk see them still as dated and unfashionable, not realizing that these styles have matured into recognized new categories in recent times. While art critics and scholars write books and articles, galleries assemble exhibitions, and connoisseurs form collections, the uninformed private vendor may let valuable possessions slip through unwary fingers.

QUALITY

Dealers and collectors, like butchers, use the expression "prime quality" to describe the very best. For the investment-minded in the collecting trade it is an invisible label indicating that even under poor selling conditions in the market, the article of prime quality will usually find a buyer and probably at the best price obtainable at that time.

Quality is a kind of charisma that results from a confluence of the value virtues. It may appear in anything from postage stamps to heroic sculpture, from an Egyptian scarab to a sulphide marble. It may combine rarity with workmanship and impeccable marks, or it may stem primarily from subject matter, color, or age. It will have many plus factors and none that are minus.

Because quality is often associated with great simplicity, it may be unperceived by the inexperienced eye which connects quality with ostentation. Certainly in coins, stamps, books, furniture, carpets, silver, glass, ceramics, and art, it is a matter for expert opinion. If you have any doubts, before selling a possession, get an expert opinion, or you may be throwing away your lottery ticket without verifying the winning number. Because quality integrates so many aspects of value, it is the greatest of all its components.

QUANTITY

Just as the total value of a collection exceeds the sum of its parts, so there are combinations of numbers which increase the values of certain objects. This aspect of quantity is a different consideration than the matter of rarity.

Pairs of decanters, lusters, salts and peppers, vases, urns, compotes, bracelets, earrings, and andirons, are among the obvious combinations.

Silver candlesticks and vegetable servers in sets of fours will also improve value in greater than quadrupled multiples of one.

Matched sets of luggage, certain units of furniture as suites, complete sets of books, complete sets of coins, and sheets of stamps are more valuable when ensembled.

Dining room chairs in units of at least six; plates, cups and saucers, glasses, goblets, napkins, and silver flatware are also obligatory "by the dozen," to be properly numbered and desirable.

You can be sure of one thing. If you split the pair, break the combination or the dozen, someone will come along to tell you how much more you would have been paid for the unit intact.

When a set of the first five editions of *The Compleat Angler,* by Izaak Walton, brought $11,040 at auction, it was a "compleat" set indeed.

RARITY

Rarity is not enough. Someone has got to want the treasure, or it isn't one. And anything so rare as to have few or no collectors will lack demand, the other side of the coin.

Yet rarity in proper proportions is very high on the list of ingredients in the value recipe. It means, principally, that there will be enough competition to acquire the few available examples of a rarity and that the price will reflect it.

The need to fulfill the scope of a collection is the basic component that encourages such competition; not far behind it is the ego satisfaction that comes with being one of a few to possess a rarity. The British Guiana one-cent magenta, which was even lacking from a king of England's collection of British stamps, was sold at auction in 1970 for $280,000; indeed an indication of the power of rarity.

Knowing what to do with a rarity, and how to establish its value, may pose problems for the private vendor. The first step is to probe authenticity, the second, to locate and establish the relationship to identical or similar objects elsewhere in the world. One country's scarcity may be another country's surfeit.

Greece and Italy are particularly rich in ancient Greek vases, while other countries lack a sufficiency of great examples. Yet those which are excavated in Greece and Italy are considered national treasures and may not be legally shipped out. Similarly, Latin America is rich in pre-Columbian materials, much coveted by other countries. Yet in a praiseworthy effort to keep archaeological evidence intact, it is necessary to embargo valuable items. Thus, there are artificial rarities, which enhance value geographically. The illicit traffic in such goods is a sad matter —the outcome of an artificial scarcity.

Dealers with great rarities to sell may decide to sell at auction or, if preferring to sell to a private clientele, may first contact one leading collector who has the means to pay the top price the dealer will ask. If this doesn't go through, the dealer may approach several collectors to bid for the item privately, by passing the word that such an item is available, then discovering from each what price he would be willing to pay. If the dealer who has made the find does not have the proper clientele for the rarity, he may offer one who does have such customers a chance to buy a share in the item, so that each will profit in proportion to his investment.

SIZE

To put it in a nutshell, fine things in miniature have a special fascination, and very often diminished size increases value.

Tiny books, minuscule tea sets, and similar objects in silver and porcelain; fine small containers such as vinaigrettes, etuis of all sorts; all the precious small boxes of gold, enamel, and jewels, under the heading of "vertu"; and charming model or miniature furniture, sometimes known as "sample furniture," are among the morsels of great value. Hardly anything is rejected because it is too small, but unwieldy size makes many a sale more difficult.

A finely carved, huge Elizabethan paneled room was purchased in 1965 by the Metropolitan Museum for $5,250. Compared to the price of $25,000 for a normally proportioned elegant eighteenth-century bookcase, it was a bargain. The point was that its very size militated against there being many buyers for the room, thus it was literally a very big bargain.

Most things have a "right" size consistent with their purpose and design. Don't overlook this value factor when you "size up" your possessions for sale.

SOURCE AND ORIGIN

Whether or not you can sell refrigerators to Eskimos, you can certainly sell English Georgian silver to the British and Holland Delft to the Dutch. Italian dealers come as far afield as the United States, looking for antique Italian silver for which highest prices are paid in Milan and Rome.

The interest in American painting of the nineteenth century reaches its peak in the homeland. A marine painter, Robert Salmon, has enjoyed a good reputation in England where he lived until he emigrated to the United States in 1828. However, his painting, "View of Boston Harbor," sold for a record $62,-500 in a sale in New York. None of his excellent English marine views had ever, in any country, reached a figure of this magnitude and, according to good authority, probably never will. As an American painter, his American scenes bring highest prices in the United States.

Returning antiques are not coals to Newcastle. Mission furniture fetches higher prices in California, ante-bellum Victoriana in the South, fine Colonial antiques in the Northeast. The pride of place is a valuable pride.

In still another aspect, international esteem accrues to many wares on the basis of place of origin. French eighteenth-century furniture, Venetian glass, English silver, German armor, Russian icons, Chinese porcelain, and Japanese lacquer are a few of those recognized by collectors as claiming some credits on the basis of birthplace, albeit requiring reinforcement for other virtues.

SUBJECT

An experienced auctioneer notes that bulls sell better than cows, and roosters better than hens. He finds that dogs are powerful sales magnets and observes that race horses bring higher prices than cart horses.

He's not a farm auctioneer, but an art auctioneer; and he doesn't mean the live animals, but the paintings, sculptures, and other representations of them.

The fine hands of Italian art fakers have for centuries been changing subjects from the originals to more appealing ones on coins, medals, bronze bas-reliefs, and even paintings. In art galleries they tell you that flowers sell better than still-life subjects, portraits are hard to sell unless the sitter is well known, and nudes sell better in sculpture than in painting. Snakes have great sales appeal, and so do insects, as any jeweler will affirm. Cupids and "cute" subjects sell much faster and at higher prices in antique shops than dour subjects.

Apparently there is value for many in gaiety. And yet, the abstract expressionist period in twentieth-century painting, which could be credited with some of the most morbid motifs in all the history of art, enriched both artists and dealers within a short period.

Subject relates to value in many subtle ways, as well as the more obvious. Preference for subjects in various media depends on rarity, fashion, historical interest, and maker or artist, in a value quotient tested in the crucible of demand.

UTILITY

For a long time the left-handed mustache cup was at best a curio and, for many a joke. When mustaches returned to fashion, the value of any mustache cup as a collectible was enhanced by utility, as many luxuriant mustaches enjoyed the support of this specialized and practical device.

Nor is it necessary for an item itself to be used, as long as its purpose catches the contemporary taste. The return of the clean-shaven to the ranks of the stylish may again revise the position of mustache appurtenances, but by then, some other "useful" item will have rewon a position in the front rank of collectibles.

Decorators, a powerful force in the antiques and collectibles market, set high value standards on objects they can use in room design, often setting off trends. Old trunks as tables, quilts as wall hangings, and clock cases as miniature display cabinets are among items that have gained value through their decorative utility.

If you have an old bellpull to sell, don't be discouraged by the shortage of maids and butlers to be summoned by potential buyers. Bellpulls are being used to serve as margins for picture groupings.

In general, hold back from selling until you have established the utility of your wares, and try to profit from its support to value.

WORKMANSHIP

The craft or skill with which an object is made literally holds it together to survive to be collected and appreciated. Durability guarantees existence and, as it reflects in condition, is also a value constituent.

Workmanship consists of the techniques of creation. Carving, casting, molding, brushing, engraving, and stitching are a few of countless processes that could be mentioned in this connection. Not only the arts and crafts but products of commercial manufacture are judged by how well they are made. Fine workmanship alone is not sufficient to make an object valuable, but poor workmanship is an unlikely contributor.

Handmade items are not always well made. However, those that exhibit fine workmanship are increasingly valued in the market. Outstanding hand-knotted oriental carpets, hand-sewn quilts, hand-woven textiles, and hand embroidery are more generally appreciated and collected as standards of workmanship decline and labor becomes more costly. Delicate reticulation and hand painting on ceramics and glass that is finely engraved, etched, or otherwise ornamented are more expensive in modern manufacture and more prized in older wares, partly for that reason.

As mechanical and automatic industrial techniques are responsible for most present-day production, there is an increasing nostalgia for fine craftsmanship that personally relates the thing to the maker and shows that relationship to the owner. Early American and English antique silver are especially collected for those signs of craft that show the hand of the maker. This is true of elegant Georgian furniture and of plain country furniture too. Fine French furniture which was made like fine jewelry, and where workmanship and design were blended in the highest degree of perfection, is the most valuable of all.

∿∿∿∿∿∿∿∿∿∿∿∿∿∿∿∿∿∿∿∿∿∿∿∿∿∿∿∿∿

Chapter 2

BUYER TAKE CARE

Not all antiques, art, or other collectibles are acquired by purchase. Some are inherited, some come with a marriage, some with a house, some as gifts, some as souvenirs of childhood, others are byproducts of a period or style of life, since altered.

Those that are bought, however, have a special distinction, in that they are exchanged for money in a conscious evaluation of their worth. Every purchase involves a choice and a decision which time will assess.

Generally, it is agreed that buying is easier than selling. Certainly it seems that there are more offers to sell to, rather than to buy from, the private person. But if our buying is qualified to signify purchasing desirable antiques, art, and collectibles of value commensurate with price, then neither is easy.

The temptations to buy are besetting for those inclined to collect. Treasures beckon and lure the easy mark with the open hand and the tightwad with the rusty purse. With hardly anything at all now available for small sums, almost every purchase carries some financial consequence. Skillful buying, the keystone to the good collection which grows in stature and value, becomes more and more essential. Before the days of price guides and national collecting journals, when "finds" and "sleepers" turned up more often, a small expenditure might produce a great treasure. The odds for this are now less than for success in a lottery, but someone wins every lottery, and collectors are optimists by nature. Every purchase renews hopes for a bonanza.

How then shall the private buyer conduct a search balanced between excessive caution and careless confidence? As a first step, awareness of one's own characteristic strengths, weaknesses, and motivations is indicated. Dealers size up a prospective customer by buying style. Before going on to beware of others, the wise buyer will become aware of self.

Why are you buying?

Have you ever stopped to check your precise reasons for making the purchase of a collectible? Do you know exactly why you want that particular item? Have you weighed the factors of quality, rarity, age, condition, color, material, maker, subject, size, or workmanship against the price? Do you buy on impulse just because something seems to be a good buy? Do you buy sometimes because an item is *sold* to you? When you buy because you believe the item to be a good investment, just what do you know about the prospects for its resale?

Do you sometimes buy, just because you are on a holiday and happen to have some money to spend? This combination often creates a euphoria in which those who enjoy the sense of power and pleasure that the purchase of a collectible evokes will almost demand that it be appeased. No one who has seen a group of eager tourists descend on a native bazaar, or been in the Clignancourt flea markets in Paris on a Sunday morning, will gainsay the strength of the urge.

Buying out of boredom is another variation expressing compulsion, and rainy days at resorts make for happy merchants. Even seasoned collectors can succumb to this kind of atmospheric pressure, abandoning discretion along with standards.

Exploring new territory, finding new dealers, seeing a wider assortment, noting local emphasis and variations of price are fine activities for collectors, but they also present certain drawbacks and possible dangers. Aside from the obvious tourist traps offering banal or bizarre souvenir material, the average dealer, who sells to a transient customer in what the trade calls a "buying frame of mind," is not pressed to offer either the best of merchandise or the lowest of prices. Unless our buyer is dealing with a most reputable establishment, or possibly a dealer who has that day taken a secret vow of honesty, the temptation to stretch the description, overlook flaws, and claim unproven virtues is rarely resisted. Items touted as "embroidered by blind nuns under water" have intrigued cruise passengers since the crusades, and "handmade Persian rugs," machine-produced in a Brussels factory are sold to credulous vacationers in Maine and Morocco.

Thus it is up to the buyer to avoid confusing a souvenir with a valuable collectible. The souvenir may be bought happily and heedlessly, the serious purchase more seriously and carefully so that it will give pleasure as a joyful remembrance, not disappointment as a souvenir of credulity.

If the amount involved is a considerable one, safety measures include checking the responsibility of a dealer with a consul, not a concierge. Local friends and business connections may be helpful, although here, too, the commission could be a factor in the recommendation. Since a minimum commission of 10 per cent is included in the price you pay when brought in by a guide or "friend," you can always start out by demanding this discount because you have come in "without recommendation." In addition, experienced buyer-travelers claim that offering half of the price asked is too much in any bazaar-type situation, and often in others as well. Demanding another discount for cash, as an alternative for credit cards, is recommended for items to be taken along; those to be sent are usually better charged, so they may be traced if lost.

The canny buyer on an off-season vacation may find a resort antiques or specialized collectible shop, which is not only open for business but eager to make a sale by offering off-season prices. If you size up the situation, giving the dealer's anxiety to sell priority over your anxiety to buy, you will have conquered the souvenir syndrome.

In general, just as the experienced traveler tries to eat in restaurants where the local residents dine, so the wise buyer-collector prefers the shops having a bona fide residential clientele.

The "bargains only" buyer, who is forced to this role by limited finances, must look farther, search harder, and generally settle for less than hoped for; but the arduous rounds of the hunt often produce a seasoned and experienced individual, whose collection may be meager, but whose knowledge is not. If prosperity smiles at a later date, the rewards are many, for this collector has a good sense of values and much pleasure in the art of accumulation.

There is another species of "bargains only" collector, sometimes of substantial means, a type which never graduates from the category. The goal is for a personal victory, in which out-negotiating the seller supersedes the other elements in a transaction. It is stronger than the urge to possess beauty, create perfection, or to develop a harmonious series which will make some statement of value as a collection. Lacking the instinct to be fastidious, few of these bargain hunters collect prime material of the kind that greatly increases in value, while giving great satisfaction in ownership. Some will buy only flashy objects that look like a lot for the money; others insist on important names and makers, but settle for their secondary output or outright fakes. Still others buy large quantities of low-priced items, thereby dissipating goodly sums in small driblets.

These buyers are the most susceptible to being cheated and swindled. They buy the $2,000 "Picasso" which they are assured is worth $25,000; the "precious" jade ring for $50, said to be selling elsewhere for $500; and the "perfect" Dorothy Doughty birds for $3,500 which were supposedly auctioned the previous week in London for $20,000. They literally ask to be victimized, because they are depending on the seller, who knows the value, to make them a gift of the difference between that and the price. They refuse to face the only reasonable explanations: poor condition, well disguised, outright fakery, or a questionable title to the merchandise.

There *are* purchases made for a fraction of an item's true value, but this is the result of a seller's ignorance. However, the variation of the confidence game, wherein the buyer is led to believe he is outwitting the seller, is common in the collecting field. It is an old trick to plant a reproduction or fake and allow the buyer to "steal" it at a price much greater than it is worth, but much less than the normal price of an original. Perpetrators of this type of trick are careful not to say that the item is authentic; they often cleverly admit to some doubt. Sometimes they naïvely "intend" to look it up, so the buyer grabs the item beforehand. In other cases they pose as uninformed, allowing the buyer to make the wrong assumptions.

These bargains are so irresistible to the seller that they bear repetition. Suspicious souls watch for a "replanting" after seeing such a purchase made. It may be only a matter of hours, if not merely minutes, before a replacement appears.

Dealers are always happy to welcome customers whose interest in bargains leads them to buy cracked, broken, torn, stained, dented, repaired, or otherwise imperfect wares. Every establishment has its quota of casualties to recycle. Coin, stamp, toy, and print collectors are among those who will fill in with pieces in poor condition, pending their replacement with superior material. It is interesting to note that the temporary owners do everything possible to repair and restore such wares but replace them as soon as they possibly can. Then the flawed piece may make a re-entry into the market in its restored or reconditioned state, very often to a guileless buyer who mistakenly accepts it as perfect.

Buyers, who, for whatever reason, are in the market for imperfect objects, are wise to let it be known. There will be less temptation for vendors to fool them, and they should trade advantageously, paying the same poor and imperfect prices they can expect to receive when making an honest sale themselves.

Dangerous to themselves are those who never want anything unless someone else has staked it out. Experienced dealers know how to spot such a customer and artfully create a situation in which there seems to be a competitor who has "just placed a deposit," put the item on reserve, or otherwise contemplates its purchase. Like a suitor who stands in jeopardy of being jilted, the prospective buyer now finds the prize becoming even more desirable. Should the item become easily available, it will lose its magnetism, and the buyer will tend to withdraw. The dealer knows that this type must wrest the treasure from a competitor and somehow manages to let it happen every time.

Bidders of this disposition are an auctioneer's delight, as each succeeding bid enforces both desire and determination. Because of them, some dealers and collectors bid anonymously or with secret signals. Having determined that someone of standing wants the item, this type of buyer feels secure in the belief that a lot must be desirable and worth having. Of course, there is always the possibility that the greedy follower is bidding against the real owner. Dealers usually drop out after a price is no longer in a range for profitable resale, but occasionally, out of pique, will force the price to astronomical heights, designing a pyrrhic victory for the determined winner. This kind of buyer is also the perfect victim for the "shill" whose function it is to push the bidding to a high price and then drop out of competition.

Impulse buyers and compulsive buyers, acting under the pressure of their own powerful urges, often overlook such simple and sensible precautions as measuring the size of an item to be sure it will fit into a particular space, can be stored, moved, or otherwise avoid becoming a white elephant. Carelessness in checking marks, labels, dates, and condition is another corollary of haste and anxiety, resulting in disappointment.

The rising number of thefts and burglaries of collectibles requires that buyers verify the source of their purchases. Not only embarrassment, but loss of the goods results when they are traced. It may take a thief to sell stolen goods, but it needs a fool to buy them unawares. Proper bills from a dealer and identification of the private seller are prudent measures taken by veteran buyers.

Are you a pushover for an obsequious seller? Accepting personal compliments instead of requiring hard facts about the merchandise can be a costly luxury. A low threshold for fast-talking salesmanship makes for a sorry buyer. The self-proclaimed authority is best checked through others in the trade. In general, dealers of integrity tend to be low-key individuals. A flamboyant, high-pressure-selling style alerts most experienced collectors to be wary.

Although the genteel, old-fashioned, scholarly, and soft-spoken ambiance of carriage-trade collecting has long since been challenged by a more raucous and commercial tone, it can still be found. Buyers and collectors gravitate to the atmosphere they prefer. Whoever wants to be treated with courtesy, requires merchandise to be fully identified and clearly priced, and appreciates informed advice in collecting can still find those who offer such amenities; after all, the expression "carriage trade" refers to the buyer, not the seller.

If you often ask "How much for the whole lot?" you will probably have a lot of whatever you have been asking about. Reckoning that lower prices are obtained through quantity purchases, private "wholesaler" buyers will take the risk of unloading the material they don't want, to get bargains in the rest. The trick is not to end up with more than you bargained for and being stuck with it. This is the way that many collectors become dealer-collectors, so it turns out all right for some in the long run. Others ruefully point to pieces for which they overpaid on the way to a bargain that didn't materialize because they couldn't profitably dispose of the whole thing.

Buyers with the gargantuan appetite for acquisition of a William Randolph Hearst are limited by ways as well as means for such enterprises. Because of a lack of discrimination and purpose in his buying, his warehouses bulged with accumulations rather than collections. However, even on a modest scale, it is worth while for a buyer of antiques, art, and collectibles to analyze direction and goal. Magpie assortments may be useful in making a home into a nest, but make sure that's what you intend.

Shoppers who buy labels, and then only incidentally the product, are also to be found acquiring antiques, art, and other collectibles. With marks, makers, and signatures as their principal goals, they are usually name-droppers as well as label buyers. Rarely completely conversant with the true value aspects of their quarry, they are easily spotted by observant dealers, who note both use and abuse of terminology. It is a mistake to be a name-dropper when collecting. If you know, you needn't say. It serves no purpose except to alert others as to your ignorance if you should be mistaken.

However, the status buyer, who is willing to wade in and learn the values as well as prices in any field of collecting, can go on to overcome the handicap of the original motivation. Such individuals, whose intelligence and capacity to absorb information are stimulated by the excitement and incentive of the financial aspects of collecting, make shrewd buyers. Starting out only to impress others, this person will often develop into an informed, keen, and sensitive collector.

The most vulnerable buyer seeks to become "somebody" by buying a whole collection at once, mistakenly perceiving "the collection is the man." Ironically, something of its value will always evade the purchase of a complete collection, even if it turns out to be worth the money.

Are you the sort of person who finds it embarrassing to require that a vendor write out and sign information given verbatim? That kind of diffidence may be costly to you. Overcome any shyness you may feel and suggest the best place for the guarantee is on the bill, under the letterhead.

Do you carry pocket guides of marks? Some collectors stash larger volumes in the car, but in many cases the slim, convenient pamphlets and booklets with marks of silver, pottery, china, and glass are useful aids. The buyer who follows through on facts, figures, and dates, and who indicates an interest in accuracy, will win the respect of a dealer who may automatically become more exact and careful in making claims to such a customer. Some buyers will even ask to see the dealer's reference books to make careful comparisons. This is often done when high-priced rarities are under consideration.

There are however, some who, believing that openly consulting such guides is a public confession of ignorance, avoid it, on the assumption that they will then be more likely to be cheated.

Whatever the decision about carrying guides to marks may be, and it is a personal one, there should be no doubt about the matter of publicly consulting price guides when buying. This is a mistake! Since price guides usually list the high retail price, it is an encouragement to the vendor to go and charge likewise. It also inhibits the buyer from bargaining for a better price, although the seller may be able to profitably sell for much less. Nor is the fact that price guides show prices for mint condition exactly helpful to the buyer who may be interested in an item that is not necessarily absolutely perfect.

The buyer, who does not attempt to probe a little, will never know if an effort to soften the price would have been successful. One veteran of over thirty years of collecting claims that after examining the item and noting the price, her ingenuous question "Is there a discount for buying?" has produced lower prices more often than not.

On the other hand, an aggressive demand for a lower price may result in an unco-operative response. Some dealers react resentfully and stubbornly to the implication that their prices are unreasonably high. The buyer who observes and appraises the personality of the dealer will often find it remunerative to do so. There is some margin for discount in almost all retail prices. The problem is for the buyer to help the dealer recognize the desirability of allowing it. Among the advantages are the addition of a steady client, the purchase of a large enough amount, and the sale of slow-moving merchandise. In any case, the observant buyer who watches for an appropriate opening can sometimes be persuasive on the first count alone.

In addition to attractive prices, some buyers seem to get favored treatment in the choice of merchandise offered to them. Do you try to cultivate dealers by a friendly manner? Do you bring in newspaper clippings, articles, or books of interest? Do you recognize and act on the value of being considered a regular customer with a degree of loyalty, rather than an inconstant or transient one?

The naïve buyer need not deal with dishonest sources to be cheated or to find, too late, that things are not as they seemed when purchased. Dealers of good reputation and respected integrity will always honestly answer direct questions that are put to them. But even these will rarely volunteer information adverse to the merchandise under consideration by the buyer.

If you don't ask whether the monogram on a silver teapot is the original one, or whether it replaces an earlier one which was erased thus making the silver at that point dangerously thin, the likelihood is that you will not be told. Yet this dealer may be one who would never misrepresent the facts. If you should ask about the monogram, you would be given the correct answer. But if you don't ask the right questions, you won't get either the right or the wrong answers.

Care and patience in the examination of goods under consideration for purchase cannot be overemphasized in any area, whether it be art, antiques, or other collectibles. Not only fakes and forgeries but restorations and imperfect and undesirable items look better to those in a hurry. If you take the time to ask the right questions, you may get the right answers.

There *are* circumstances when there is no happy alternative to a hurried decision. It is always amusing to see the participating dealers on the first, or setting-up, day of an important antiques show torn between arranging their own displays and watching their colleagues unpack. Very often husband and wife or partners will take turns at arranging their own merchandise and scouting neighborhood booths, so as not to miss the possibility of making a fortuitous buy before the public is admitted.

Part of this is the natural curiosity that informs all who are dealers, collectors, antiquers, and hobbyists. They are confirmed optimists who constitutionally hope for the lucky find. The dealer is, of course, comparatively expert in buying under pressure, but it is not unusual to hear complaints that the hasty purchase was not all it was thought to be, even by the experienced.

An American dealer, visiting London's outdoor Bermondsey market for the first time, made the rounds of the scouts, pickers, and dealers disgorging their vans in the foggy dawn. He merely noted the items of interest, intending to inspect and purchase by a little later and better morning light, only to find that earlier birds had gotten away with the desirable goods by eight o'clock when he returned. On subsequent successful visits, with flashlight in hand, he made his purchases on the first and earliest circuit. In addition to magnifying glass, tape measure, and notebook, he recommends that buyers carry flashlights "for buying in the dark."

Sometimes the buyer-collector is also in a situation where there is no alternative to a quick and risky decision. If the person feels qualified by knowledge and judgment to hazard a limited sum on such an "opportunity," then it may be justified. An inexperienced buyer is taking an even greater gamble and, since it is better to be lucky than smart, had better be lucky.

Are you prone to follow current fashions in the collector's marketplace? This makes you vulnerable to every weakness of the overanxious buyer who is susceptible to promotion and pressure and thus is easier prey for the unscrupulous. The most prudent buyers and successful investors are those who buy against the tide of fashion, choosing items of individuality, quality, or social reference currently in low esteem or disregarded. Such diverse and formerly unfashionable material as American Indian baskets, fancy cut glass, Federal furniture and quilts have been rewarding to those who prudently purchased them avant the garde.

Yet no matter how skillfully you buy, how splendid your bargain, none of this is turned into investment profit until it has been successfully sold. At this point, we must reverse our field as the buyer becomes a seller.

‹‹

Chapter 3

AS A SELLER, BEWARE

"Buyer beware," the "caveat emptor" of ancient Rome, is no less urgent a warning today, than when it originated. Certainly, in these days of consumer consciousness, it is an idea whose time has come.

"Seller beware," or "caveat vendor," may thus appear to be a superfluous caution in behalf of those whose business is selling. They seem quite capable of defending their interests, whatever the merchandise in question.

But sometimes a different perspective is required. When a private individual wishes to sell a valued or valuable possession, then the frame of reference changes. Then it is indeed the seller who must beware.

Confronted by professionals experienced in trading both as buyers and sellers, whose livelihood is to buy cheap and sell dear, an inexperienced private seller enters unknown territory.

"What is it? How much is it worth? How do I know I'm not being cheated? Where can I find out? How be sure about the appraiser? Where can I sell? How do I know I'm not being cheated? Should it be auctioned? Or perhaps donated for the tax deduction? How do I know I'm not being cheated?"

When great museums, such as the Metropolitan Museum of Art, seem to be at a disadvantage when selling their treasures, private individuals are not likely to be charged with confidence in bringing their antiques, art, or collectibles to market. Nor are they wrong in their trepidation. If the mighty prove so inept, what hope for lesser folk?

This is not to say that all dealers, auctioneers, and appraisers are not honest. Many of them are. However, unless you have the knowledge and standards by which to judge, how can you tell which to trust, and in what circumstances?

In general, one hesitates to advise sellers to be suspicious, but it has been well said that not to be a little paranoid is entirely crazy. Whenever you dispose of private possessions, be they heirloom, antique, collection, or household overflow, you are vulnerable to being underpaid, if not cheated, unless you learn something about the area into which you are venturing. The first step is understanding your own position.

Why are you selling?

Make sure that you have a valid reason and won't later regret what may be irrevocable.

Try to avoid selling under pressure. The old saying that every great buy is a poor sale originated when a seller needed money fast. It may be wiser to borrow the money, perhaps even by pawning your treasure, rather than to sell it in haste and for too little.

When sad, neurotic Mary Todd Lincoln thought herself to be in straitened circumstances after the death of the President, she tried to sell her clothes and jewelry through a firm of commission agents. After promising to raise $100,000, these gentlemen crowned a fiasco by sending her a bill for $800 which the frightened woman paid. Most historians agree that her affairs were really not in such bad order as she thought.

A singular example of a successfully postponed sale is that of Rembrandt's painting, "Aristotle Contemplating the Bust of Homer." When Alfred Erickson, the advertising tycoon, bought this masterpiece from the art dealer tycoon Duveen, in November 1928, he paid $750,000 for it. By 1930, the collapse of the stock market forced him to raise money by disposing of this picture. He prevailed on Duveen to give him $500,000 while "holding" it until he could rebuy it. This he did in 1936, for $590,000.

Because Erickson had analyzed his need to sell, he was able to make an arrangement that saved his prize and brought him joy for the rest of his life. When his widow put the painting up for auction in 1962, the Metropolitan Museum of Art bought it for $2,300,000. Both Erickson and his estate profited from his astute judgment.

Not every forced sale involves so considerate a "buyer" as Duveen in this case. Most art transactions, on whatever price level, put the objects forever beyond the reach of the seller. Unless the item is one easily replaced, it is best to think carefully before selling. Certainly, being absolutely sure that you want to dispose of the painting, curio, stamp, coin, carpet, or Coca-Cola tray is a sensible first step.

An avid collector of Coca-Cola material might be as reluctant and unhappy as Erickson if he had to sell his 1904 "Nude" multicolor, lithographed tin tray, even at a $350 going price. Nothing is more futile than vain regrets, nor more tedious than the "I shouldn't have sold" story, whatever the object so mourned.

Successful private selling is best done by advance planning. Obviously the move should be anticipated whenever possible. The more time you have to sell, the better chance you have to get a better price.

If you expect to retire within a few years, start now to take stock of your possessions. That large segment of the population leaving lifetime homes, to move to retirement communities all over the nation, leaves an overly generous quota of profits to dealers who buy their possessions.

Too often the impulse to keep a few mementos and to dispose of the rest of the household in one quick sale is a mistake. If time is taken to list the items, to check the values and prices, there may be some pleasant surprises in store.

A Remington "Straight Line" pocketknife in mint condition, is listed in one price guide at $75 retail, a Donald Duck Ingersoll wrist watch at $175, and a box of three Mickey Mouse handkerchiefs at $20. While some pocketknives are worth much less, and other Disney items are not as rare or costly, it is worth while to sift the contents of cellars, attics, and closets, and then to compare them with lists of the "new antiques," or nostalgia collectibles.

Although, as we shall see, the chance of getting the listed retail price is not in the private seller's favor, trying to get a fair share of it is a worth-while effort.

Statistics indicate the average American executive moves about fourteen times in his life, involving young and middle-aged groups in disposal of possessions in relation to the moving cycle. People who have to pay their own moving bills often choose to sell rather than to ship at high prices and risk destruction of fine and fragile objects.

Adding further to the volume of private possessions constantly flowing into the sales stream, are fine china, crystal, linen, silver, and bibelots. In many homes entertaining becomes simplified and curtailed, with the scarcity of household help available, and there are fewer facilities for, as well as diminished interest in, the care of precious household goods.

The interior designer or decorator, whose new plan calls for disposal of old furniture, decorations, and even collections, also contributes to the cycle of redistribution. Redecorating is a classic reason for selling. In general, change of taste and requirements for more or less space are major factors in the sale of used homefurnishings.

Fashion changes are often responsible for the private sale of jewelry, both semiprecious and precious. And when the styles in furs, expensive evening bags, and costly cosmetic containers change drastically, the outmoded items appear on the market to be resold.

In many of these cyclical changes, both personal and domestic, the items can be sold to much better advantage when they have been out of style for a long time. Then they are viewed with nostalgia, or with a fresh eye as to their aesthetic appeal. In the 70s, the fashions of the 20s, 30s and 40s have gained in price as collectors gain perspective.

The ever higher costs of insurance, combined with fears of theft, burglary, and other forms of loss, are growing factors in property disposal. As more and more families enter the two-home category, there is a hesitancy to leave valuables in whichever residence is untenanted. Increasingly there are situations in which it is considered poor judgment to wear costly jewelry, even when insured. In certain sections of the country it has become almost impossible to obtain insurance coverage for jewelry, and owners prefer to sell rather than to be uninsured.

Ancient man had the solution to some problems which defy his modern counterpart. He knew how to take it with him. Cherished possessions went into the tomb or grave, and unless grave robbers brought them back into circulation, there they stayed.

With the certainty of the horrid combination, death and taxes, not only did the deceased have to decide, but executors and heirs are further required to make decisions regarding estate disposal. When the estate is very large, high taxes may require that all or part be sold to raise the government's share, which must be in cash. Sometimes the widow or widower who helped to create a collection must sadly participate in its dissolution to satisfy the tax collector.

Often heirs prefer money to inheritance of objects. Estates that vary from millions in value, of art or other treasures, to modest bequests of jewelry or other collectibles, are all subject to such conversion. Choosing cash, heirs sometimes easily give up much value for little money. Whether grieving or glad, heirs are advised to carefully evaluate all offers to buy.

Heirs who quarrel over objects in an estate are well known in literature and life. Approaching their declining years, individuals who wish to avoid family friction will sell their valuable possessions to forestall problems of this kind.

Treasures and collections are often sold in anticipation of death by owners who want to ensure continued care for their possessions. Many collectors are so emotionally attached to particular objects that they want to see them sold to new owners who will also cherish them.

Other collectors, equally attached, prefer to bequeath favorite possessions to museums. However, if the donors do not carefully make the correct legal provisions, museums may, like some heirs, prefer the cash, putting the bequest on the market, despite the owner's intentions.

In general, easy come, easy go refers to the undervaluing of material that was neither collected nor paid for by the seller. Shrewd buyers and experienced dealers are aware of this weakness, finding it profitable. Greedy sellers do not necessarily sell to best advantage.

Selling a precious possession, because it is the only way to get the money to buy an even more desired one, can be a better move than making a disadvantageous barter. Even experienced traders tread warily in making exchanges, rather than buying or selling. Trading collectibles makes horse trading seem child's play. The inexperienced seller has enough of a problem to get a fair price without the handicap of trying to come out ahead in a barter or swap.

Culling a collection to sell acquisitions of lesser quality, or duplicates, can be turned to especially good advantage when the collector has a reputation as an authority. On the other hand, even better material, but from a lesser source, will require a struggle to make the same price. Who sells is as important as what is sold.

For those who are selling to realize on an investment or speculation, the wisdom of the original purchase now receives its acid test. It has been said that whenever a collectible is sold as an investment, it is already too late to buy it. This is the time to unload. The proof of a good investment is in the selling, and that, like any other such sale, depends on knowing where, when, and how to sell; subjects requiring consideration, as we shall see.

Changed or improved taste and standards can transpose earlier acquisitions into unwelcome boarders, delinquent in paying for their keep with the compensation of pleasure. Usually a combination of sentiment and frugality precludes their being given away, in which case they are pushed up to the attic or down to the cellar in the vague hope that they will some day appeal to children or grandchildren. This rarely happens, but the passage of enough time can develop a revival of interest in the discard.

The alert seller recognizes the signal and acts upon it, letting the "boarder" pay the back rent and possibly interest as well. Collectibles that have been warehoused for a long time will often require astronomical prices to justify their storage bills. In general, holding too long under these circumstances makes profits only for the warehouse owners.

Certain individuals will strive mightily to form a complete collection of anything from matchbox covers to ancient Roman gold coins. Very often, this occupies them for years. When, however, the collection has been completed and the goal achieved, there is no further challenge. Boredom sets in, and they decide to sell. As always, with a collection, the question of selling in parts, or as a unit, depends on the material. Prudent sellers avoid giving up the cream, lest they be left with the skimmed, less salable part. Packaging for an advantageous sale may require the services of a skilled specialist who will charge a fee. If it is well done and can be verified from an objective quarter, it may be well worth it.

Just as it is generally agreed that the burgeoning collector needs to sample some buying situations before undertaking larger risks, so it is generally ignored that some modest selling experiments should be transacted before a private individual has to meet the challenge of selling more important possessions. Testing out the seller's skill is secondary; what the seller is testing is the market and the problems of selling. As a by-product, it has been suggested that many impetuous buyers would be curbed if they had to sell their own or others' acquisitions.

Those who thus take up practice selling will discover that the private person is even more sinned against when selling than when buying. Where the buyer is greeted with friendliness, the seller often meets coldness. Dealers who have complained they have no problems selling, but great difficulty in buying suitable merchandise, turn out to have difficulty only in willingness to pay fair prices.

Errors made in buying come home to roost when put up for sale. The damage or crack that was covered or minimized yawns as an abyss. The somewhat worn hallmark turns illegible, the clouded glass is now diagnosed as "sick." Even that which is perfect gathers flaws under the critical eye of the professional buyer. Authenticity will be challenged, age questioned, style criticized, workmanship analyzed, and material tested. All of this is, of course, preparatory to a discussion of price. Having to sell is indeed the best schooling for the buyer-collector.

~~~~~~

Chapter 4

REFERENCES REQUIRED

Stockbrokers laugh at endless versions of the tale in which a customer orders the purchase, and after a time, the sale of a certain stock. Later, the customer either boasts or admits (depending on whether the outcome showed a profit or loss) that he had no idea of what the company in question manufactures.

There are few similar situations in which it is possible to buy and sell without identifying the merchandise. When it happens in the field of collectibles, it may be a major disaster. As prices rise, the margin for error takes on the proportions of a dangerous abyss. Both buyers and sellers recognize the need to be well informed and are less willing than in the past to depend on instinct and hunches.

A growing tendency is developing to research on a pragmatic level, as dealers and collectors observe how knowledge makes for success. Avid students are not new to collecting, but as they grow in numbers, even in narrow specialties, the untutored become more vulnerable. Little old ladies can be demons at dolls, and twelve-year-old boys become numismatic *wunderkinder* to others' cost and their own profit.

Intriguing to those outside the trade is the question of how its members go about verifying the identity and authenticity of their wares.

The well-known kingpins in the world of art, coins, books, stamps, antiques, and other fields of collecting are a handful of specialists. Some of them employ researchers, full or part time; others manage with their own scholarship. They have private libraries, laboratories, and research facilities, and incredibly complete files about collectors, collections, and individual items. Price and provenance information and complete auction records for the field in question are additional aids.

Another small group, some of whom are highly respected, in an old tradition, lean largely on instinct, that compilation of their experience. Foregoing the trappings of important dealership, they prefer to keep their business operations, and their research facilities as well, under their hats.

The average run-of-the-mill dealer has a shelf of books, a strong magnifying glass, a file of restorers' addresses, some auction catalogues, and some trade journals for research facilities.

At the bottom of the ladder are those who don't know how much there is to know, for there are fools and dolts who call themselves dealers and who take in those who know even less. They alternate between making up their own "facts" and getting them from other unreliable sources, like themselves.

What, where, when, how, and by whom is information that not only interests and intrigues but adds value. Some lucky owners *know* they have a signed Tiffany lamp, a Wedgwood & Bentley basalt plaque, or a 1918 Illinois Centennial commemorative silver half dollar.

But suppose you are not all that fortunate. All *you* know about the possession you want to sell is that it is a glass bowl, a china vase, an old coin, or a silver teapot. How do you go about making an identification?

You start by taking stock of what you do know. Oral history has recently regained some standing with historians; if it isn't abused, perhaps it can overcome the outworn cliché "My grandmother had one" that has worn out two generations of dealers.

Verbal family tradition is sometimes unreliable, especially when the "hundred year old" item turns out to be post-World War II. But sometimes real clues originate by word of mouth. If those candlesticks *were* in great grandmother's dowry, and she was married in Europe, she must have brought them from the country of her migration.

Sounder than this kind of information are documents— old letters, bills, accounts, catalogues, labels, and family records can give splendid clues. And even if they don't, they may have some value in themselves and should be kept and examined with this in mind.

If you do find that you have to go it alone, without family tradition or records, your role as Sherlock Holmes may dispense with a tweed cap, but it does require a good magnifying glass. It is remarkable how often the careful examination of an object will turn up some sort of useful information.

Check especially for any kind of notation, letters, numbers, trademark, hallmark, signature, label, date, or design that might incorporate any of the above. Exactly copy such marks, either by sketching to scale, photographing, or making rubbings if the mark or design is impressed. A layer of thin paper is placed over the marks and rubbed with a soft pencil. You can then compare them with authentic examples in books or on originals or otherwise show them for expert opinion.

Don't jump to conclusions as to the meaning of your marks. Patent numbers are not dates, and registry marks are in code to be translated. A Stradivarius label is almost certain to mean that the violin is a cheap, mass-produced fiddle, made in the early part of this century in Bohemia, Germany, or France.

Nobili, the Italian expert on fakes, relates an anecdote in which a piece of pottery found near Dijon, France, carrying the letters M.J.D.D., was brought to a French scholar because it had proved puzzling to other authorities.

This erudite individual had no hesitation in deciphering the initials to represent the Latin, *"Magno Jove Deorum Deo"* —"To the great Jupiter, the god of gods." He announced the piece was a small amphora, a Roman vase.

This learned opinion was shortly thereafter exploded, when a local art dealer examined the jar and recognized it as a modern mustard pot with initials signifying, "Moutarde Jaune de Dijon," the famous yellow mustard of the region.

U.S. laws require country of origin to be shown after 1891, but the absence of such marks does not necessarily indicate an earlier date. It may have been erased in one of several ways, by bleaching, scratching, or grinding; or it may have been brought into the United States by a tourist or immigrant who purchased it in an area where the import mark was not required.

Information as to ownership, and sometimes a bearing on age, can occasionally be found on the backs or interiors of repaired furniture, silver, clocks, and musical instruments. This may be scratched, penciled, chalked, or pin-pointed, and may sometimes be written on a bit of paper that is secreted somewhere in the piece.

In his memoir, *Connoisseur*, F. S. Robinson tells of a silver-gilt chalice of unknown provenance, which required repairs when it was to be exhibited in London. The silversmith was separating the bowl from the foot, when a small piece of parchment fell out of the hollow. It was inscribed in Italian: ". . . whereas the Jews resident in Anghiari were compelled on the feast of St. Martin to furnish a prize for a foot race . . . on the tenth of August, 1572, the value of the prize was commuted into a chalice bearing the arms of the city. . . ."

It is unusual for silver not to be marked in some fashion.

Be sure to note *all* the marks; search for them with your magnifying glass. They may be separated, some on the side and some on the bottom, with others on the cover of a vessel. Many American marks can be read directly; English and Continental silver marks are in codes which must be deciphered.

Porcelain and pottery of some types may show "where, when, and of what" printed or impressed as direct information, but both old and new ceramics may also bear hieroglyphics, signatures, and countless numbers of other marks and letters which must be translated further to indicate their origins.

Old glass is less often marked, but look for signatures on handmade art glass. Information impressed in the mold of pressed glass helps to identify. Cut glass is usually recognized by quality and design of the cut decoration, as well as the shape of the piece.

The finest eighteenth-century French furniture is signed; occasionally, English and American furniture of the nineteenth century will indicate its source by labels, but this is rare. Mission oak may have some information burned into a drawer or on the back. Style and workmanship are depended on for most identification of furniture.

Quilts may be signed in ink or embroidered stitches; oriental carpets occasionally proclaim date and maker in knotted form; clocks, watches, dolls, toys, razors, and music boxes are among items that carry an imprimatur, as in their way do books, coins, medals, and stamps.

Having checked family tradition, documents, the interior and exterior for informative repair marks, thoroughly examined your property for signatures, hallmarks, trademarks, labels, and other clues, you have gone about as far as you can on your own.

Now the information gathered should be assembled, together with clear photographs or sketches and copies of the marks.

At this stage, you probably have some general categories in which to fit the subject of your inquiry.

You know or guess that it is ceramic, glass, precious or base metal, stone, marble, paper, or fabric.

You think it may be primitive, ancient, antique, old, or modern.

You suppose it is American, English, European, African, or perhaps Oriental.

You surmise it is Jacobean, Georgian, Victorian, Louis XVI, or Art Deco.

Your assumptions may be wrong, but by having them, you can verify or discard them and then move on to solid fact.

It is now time to turn to outside sources for the next stage in our identification program. A survey of dealers' stocks is a sensible start. If the immediate locality provides an inadequate selection, try adjacent or larger urban areas with greater resources.

Look around a shop and if you see the same or a similar item, you can ask to examine it, noting descriptive tags or labels. Even if you see nothing like the subject of your search, you can make an inquiry, showing a photograph, marks, a rubbing, or the item itself.

The dealer must be approached warily for any information. Some do not like to be "bothered," considering the uninformed seller to be the best source of cheap merchandise. A well-known old French antiques dealer had a stock answer when asked for an opinion about any merchandise but his own, "I am not a policeman of curios." Others express the attitude that since doctors and lawyers charge for advice, they, as dealers, need not be imposed on by the public for free advice either.

However, there are many dealers who will be helpful, especially if the query is put in a tactful fashion. It is not only poor taste, but poor judgment, to interrupt a transaction or to ask "research" questions in the presence of customers. It is a courtesy to be appreciated when information is given by a dealer to a stranger.

At this point in your campaign to identify, you do not yet know the worth of your possession, and it is inadvisable to consider selling. If, in the course of inquiry, you get an offer to buy, courteously postpone your decision.

Not only individual shops and businesses but department stores are credible sources for identification of antiques, jewelry, prints, paintings, sculpture, stamps, coins, medals, rare minerals, fossils, and shells. Many big stores now have individual shops, galleries, and departments for these collectibles; some are their own, some leased. In almost every instance this merchandise is descriptively tagged as well as clearly priced, affording a splendid source of information.

Pawnshops, second-hand stores, and flea markets are among retail outlets where merchandise can be seen and possibly identified by the owner looking for leads and clues.

Antique shows, trade shows, and conventions of special-interest hobbies also offer opportunities to see large quantities and assortments, together with people who are anxious to talk about their exhibits, to explain what they are and why they think them desirable. In weighing the pros and cons of investing in the considerable expense of going to shows and conventions, dealers consider the value of comparing goods and prices as a positive one.

At some hobby and antique shows, special appraisal booths are set up at which "any item will be identified for a dollar," the proceeds earmarked for charity.

Question-and-answer columns on antiques and other collectibles are featured in some newspapers as a service to the general reader with a specific problem. Clear photographs and facsimiles of marks are more likely to produce replies. Art, antique, homefurnishings, and hobby periodicals often include such question-and-answer columns, in addition to special articles on featured subjects. These publications carry advertisements which are either clearly illustrated or carry such clear descriptions as to afford an education in themselves.

Dealers read trade journals with especial interest in news and advertisements regarding reproductions. A single issue of an antiques trade periodical included offerings of reproduction cast-iron banks, sleigh bells, samovars, quilts, barn thermometers, and dolls at special quantity prices. By being aware of their existence and alert to the circulation of potential fakes, readers of these ads are less likely to mistake them for the real thing.

Newspapers vary in the amount of display advertising of interest to collectors, but most of them include "Buy" and "Sell" classified columns watched by dealers. A few metropolitan newspapers feature special pages and sometimes whole sections devoted to art, antiques, stamps, and coins; some others throughout the country carry syndicated columns on these subjects.

Although recognizing a certain éclat attached to attending auction sales in fashionable salesrooms, few members of the general public are aware of the willingness of the specialists, cataloguers, and other members of the staff to discuss, compare, and otherwise diagnose and identify material that is offered to the auctioneer for him to sell. Dealers, who find they still have a problem unsolved after consultation with cronies and competitors, will often consult the knowledgeable auction specialist. Among them are highly trained researchers of awesome scholarship. Since dealers are usually good customers on both sides of an auction, they may count on aid and comfort here.

Even auctioneers on a more pedestrian level develop much insight over years of handling a great variety of goods and are good consultants to dealers in professionally appropriate circumstances.

The exhibition preceding an auction sale is arranged to

give prospective buyers an opportunity to examine and evaluate the merchandise, so that bids can be formulated in advance of the actual sale. Prospective sellers can use these previews to look for lots that are the same or similar to their own property.

Private buyers and sellers can also use the auction room as a training ground where they can flex their learning muscles by physically handling the lots to be sold. In attending the sale previews, dealers make every effort to touch, feel, observe, measure, and compare; they note variations, differences, and similarities. Often this is only for the purpose of comparing their own merchandise to enlarge the range of experience, not because they intend to buy.

Less important auctions are not catalogued. Some auctioneers run regular sales without any catalogues at all. Prestige firms publish them for every sale. For great sales, involving important collections or items, the fine catalogues become collectors' pieces in themselves. Dealers study them intensively, filing them after filling in the prices realized.

Even run-of-the-mill catalogues reward the inquiring reader with useful information. Each lot is numbered and described, usually in clear and understandable language. If a special vocabulary is used, it is usually made clear by the context. If the questioner should be ignorant of the meaning of "foxed," for example, as it refers to the condition of a book or manuscript, an attendant will not only explain, but point out the discoloration in question.

The auction catalogue description of each numbered lot, paired with a careful examination of the actual item, can help the amateur to become knowledgeable, if not expert. However, if the auctioneer does not guarantee the information there is a small print caveat to be observed.

Until some years ago, it was customary for museums to set aside certain days and hours during which the public could bring in objects for the curatorial staff to identify, date, and authenticate. Although no price would be suggested, the owner could draw certain conclusions about the value of the possession.

Now it would be difficult to find museums that follows such a practice. Other tasks consume the precious time of busy museum staffers, already limited in number by tightened budgets. An even stronger inhibition is the threat of lawsuits claiming damages because the owner was given a wrong attribution or identification and, therefore, sold the property for a smaller sum than it should have fetched. Variations of this type of claim are called "defamation of property," and even dealers are leery of being sued under these circumstances. Unless you are a generous donor to a museum, it is unlikely that an exception will be made for you. Yet you might try, and be successful in a quest for aid, especially if your inquiry is a challenging one.

Important dealers, who exchange expertise with big museums, occasionally make gifts to the collections. As it is tax deductible, such a gift has direct financial advantages and, in addition, gives the dealer the standing of a donor, one who will probably find the research facilities of the museum even more available than before. It is not unusual for the dealers who make gifts to museums to either *have* sold to them or to *hope* to sell to them. Lesser figures develop contacts of this nature with smaller museums.

The principal service of the museum to the layman in search of an object's identity is in clearly attributed exhibits, as well as catalogues, slides, and publications. Museum bulletins are outstanding sources for illustrated information on special subjects of great range and variety. These are indexed in the museum's library and available in its files, whether or not they are still in print and on sale.

Museum libraries may be consulted if the searcher can indicate a bona fide interest to the authorities. Here catalogues from other museums, slides, books, and articles relating to the museum's exhibits, plus many related periodicals can be found. In addition to exhibits, libraries, and publications, museums offer lectures of a high caliber to help the layman increase both pleasure and knowledge. Though the staff members of the museum may not directly identify your possessions, they may guide you to do so yourself.

If it is not geographically convenient to visit the museum you believe could be of assistance, you can write, enclosing a good photograph of the subject of your inquiry, asking if the museum has a similar item in its exhibits or storerooms.

Museum bookshops, designed to satisfy and assist the visitor who wants to carry home a tangible store of information on topics related to the exhibits, are additional sources providing guidance to the neophyte.

Whether you are interested in "antique" aeroplanes or left-handed zithers, someone probably has written a book, article, pamphlet, or bulletin on the subject. A seemingly endless stream of material is produced in marvelous assortment. Some is offered by commercial publishers, much by university presses, museums, foundations, societies, and even government bureaus. Quite a few publications intended for collectors are privately printed and sold by the authors; others of this kind are distributed through specialist booksellers, directly advertised, and sold by mail.

Book titles ranging from *American Axes* to *Weathervanes and Whirligigs* can be found in public libraries, especially where local branches can implement their shelves with material from central main sources. Those who can visit the libraries in metropolitan centers may be overwhelmed by the riches in the index of special reference departments. Librarians are skillful in helping the neophyte find the books relevant to a special quest. Records are among the treasures of music libraries, and those interested in them can find catalogues and guides to rare and desirable discs.

Booksellers have access to books both in and out of print. Specialist booksellers advertise in related periodicals and will send lists of their stocks. Out of print books can be had from "book hunters" and second-hand bookshops. Remainder dealers are glad to mail lists of their closeout stocks on request.

Some years ago, the archives of Wildenstein, the international art dealer, were said to contain 100,000 photographs, 300,000 books, and more than 100,000 auction catalogues. Such private libraries are rare, but the value of reference material is obviously important at every level of collecting, buying, and selling. It is easier, too, to look through books than to travel through countless shops, auctions, shows, and museum galleries.

With the exception of perverse types who acquire only to secretly enjoy hidden treasures, most collectors are happy to show their possessions and share their knowledge with others who are interested. They can be reached through directories, through introduction by dealers and museum curators, and also through clubs and societies of collectors. Some are local and some are regional and national groups.

Buttons, firearms, Wedgwood, Staffordshire, music boxes, comic books, flasks, bottles, stamps, coins, circus, and fire-fighting memorabilia are among the interests uniting collectors into clubs for further inquiry and study. Look for members of historical societies whose expertise of certain places and periods may include data you require to identify some product of a local terrain. Most often you will find them happy to share information with you.

An old brass cash register, a vintage pinball machine, jazz records, movie posters, and countless merchandise catalogues and comic magazines seem unusual exhibits in a scholastic environment, but they are only part of a vast collection of similar "nostalgia" material in the "Center for the Study of Popular Culture," at Bowling Green University in Ohio. This institution, which studies the artifacts of our society in relation to its way of life, is an avant-garde example, but other universities have more traditionally oriented museums, equally useful for those searching for information on collectibles.

The Garvan collection of Early American silver at Yale, Harvard's exquisite botanical glass flowers, and Princeton's splendid collection of oriental art are outstanding examples, and there are many others, used by dealers and collectors alike for study and comparison.

College faculty members and graduate students in departments related to a specific field of collecting may also prove knowledgeable and forthcoming. Someone in the music department may be able to identify and date an unusual instrument or music box. The art department may furnish a scholar who can authenticate a print, painting, or sketch. An old Indian basket may signal clearly to a member of the anthropology department. Here, again, it is best to tread gently in making requests for assistance, but your diplomacy may be well rewarded.

For those with neither the time, patience nor interest to do their own research and identification, professional appraisal is the easiest, quickest way, although not always the least expensive.

Professional appraisers advertise in the trade press of a particular field of collecting as well as in telephone directories and newspapers. They can also be located through trust departments of banks and lawyers.

In certain fields, the individual who wishes to become a member of the association must have technical training. In others, experience plus some sort of examination by a group of peers will qualify the individual as a member. Despite the general impression, there is no such figure as a "licensed" appraiser.

Appraisals for insurance and estate tax purposes can include jewelry, machinery, and real estate. Auctioneers and dealers are often appraisers, and like others in the business, charge a fee which is usually a percentage of the total value of the material appraised. For this fee, usually ranging from ½ per cent to 1½ per cent (often there is a minimum amount), the client is entitled to a standard form, usually in triplicate, describing the items and showing the current replacement value at either retail or wholesale, or both if required.

Common sense dictates that the client be assured the appraiser is expert in the kind of material under consideration. A silver expert may not know values in pewter or jewelry, and a specialist in ancient coins may not be up on nineteenth-century silver dollars. Sometimes you can find an expert who wrote a book on a particular subject, or otherwise has credentials in a special field. Customs appraisers are a good choice.

When dealers appraise, it is wise to make sure they are not downgrading in order to buy cheaply for themselves. Experience dictates that it is better to have the appraisal made "for insurance purposes," and with the information obtained, to sell elsewhere.

Although the highest hopes of the possessor may not be realized by the actual identification, "second best" may be quite good. Don't be too discouraged if told that the "diamonds" are not real. They may be what is called "strass" the original false diamonds made of paste, invented in the eighteenth century, and not at all worthless.

Gold jewelry, rejected as not being ancient Etruscan, of 400 B.C. might be by the Roman jeweler, Pio Fortunato Castellani, who together with his skillful sons, exquisitely imitated ancient, medieval, and Renaissance works in gold and precious stones in the nineteenth century. This was done at a high level of art, without intent to deceive, and his jewelry is much appreciated by connoisseurs who pay well for it.

Certain early nineteenth-century American silversmiths, wishing to give the impression that their silver had been made in England, marked them with what are known as pseudo-marks. These are quite properly listed in complete books of marks under the names of their makers and without any detriment to their goodly value.

A "stretched" brass bed, with some modern parts added to

the original to make it queen or king size, is worth more than an untouched brass frame of less desirable proportions. Early soft-paste porcelain made in Europe and England in the sixteenth through eighteenth centuries is actually an imitation of true hard-paste porcelain. Yet it is highly prized and astronomically priced and although, in a certain sense, it is not true porcelain, a small bowl fetched $180,000 in 1973.

Knowing what it isn't is only part of knowing what an antique or collectible is.

Insiders' Sources of Reference Information

TO FIND	THEY CONSULT
Patent Records	The Official Gazette of the United States Patent Office
Trademarks	The Trademark Register of the United States
Dealers and their specialties	Mastai's Classified Directory United States and Canada
	International Directory of Arts (Published in Berlin)
	Classified telephone directories: under art, autographs, stamps, coins, books, antiques, etc.
U. S. Museum Collections	Official Museum Directory of American Association of Museums
Private, Corporate, and International Museum Collections	International Directory of Arts
Appraisers	American Appraisers Association, New York
	U.S. Appraisers Society, Washington, D.C.
	Art and Antiques Dealers Association, New York City

TO FIND	THEY CONSULT
Experts	Who Knows—And What
	Directory of American Scholars
	International Directory of Arts
Restorers	Museum Conservators
	Directory of Art and Antique Restorers by Porter
	International Directory of Arts
	Classified telephone directory
Firms now out of business, to identify and date products	City, state, and regional directories—back into nineteenth-century
	Guide to American Directories
Historical Societies	Directory of Historical Societies and Agencies in the United States and Canada
Libraries	Directory of Special Libraries and Information Centers
	Subject Collections (Guide to special book collections and subject emphasis)
Collectors' Clubs and Associations	Encyclopedia of Associations
	Listings in Specialized Trade Publications
Book and Price guides	Books in Print
	Paperbound Books in Print
	Private Press Books
	Guide to Reference Books
	Guide to Art Reference Books
	Booksellers catalogues
	Advertisements in trade press

TO FIND	THEY CONSULT
Periodicals, trade and collectors' newspapers, magazines, and club publications	Ayers Directory Ulrich's Periodical Directory
Special articles	Readers' Guide to Periodical Articles Art Index Quarterly Standard Periodical Directory
Biographies and dates of craftsmen and artists	New Century Cyclopedia of Names
Auction prices of antiques, art, collectibles	Art Price Annual International Art Market Art at Auction The Connoisseur Sales Annual Auction catalogues with prices realized for individual sales from the auction firm, by subscription, or on receipt of price with request.
Courses on collecting or about collectibles	World of Learning School catalogues
Reference Books as a guide to choosing books to be consulted	Reference Books: A Brief Guide for Students and Other Users of the Library, by Barton and Bell Guide to Reference Books, by Winchell, critically evaluates them. The American Reference Books Annual, by Wynar, also appraises annual output.

Chapter 5

BUYING DEFENSIVELY

Money is to collecting, what sex is to marriage. Intermingled, intertwined, and totally involved with any and every kind of collecting is the matter of price. No matter how dedicated to the subject, how rich, or far from rich, how aesthetic, scholarly, naïve, or unworldly, everyone with an interest in collecting must be aware of price.

It may be true that for some it is of less importance than for others. But no one avoids it, and few want to. The fact is that for almost everyone it is part of the fascination, the excitement, the risk and essential gamble that makes collecting such a thrilling activity.

Just as in business, the scornful jibe, "He never had to meet a payroll," is reserved for those who offer opinions without the experience to back them up, so, in collecting, students who know a great deal in theory, but have no money involved, may be considered uncertain guides by those who are risking their own. They may well be consulted to determine values, but when it comes to price, then the specific judgment will be made by the one who pays. Some believe that no true connoisseur can be formed without trial by money—that, at any level, it is only the test of price decision that makes a seasoned collector. It has also been observed that some of the inept bargaining by museum officials can be traced to the fact that they are dispensing institutional funds rather than their own money.

Even for those who consider price to be extraneous, and who wish to rise above material and mundane considerations, there are two instances when it dominates. Once, when an item is bought; again, when it is sold. Although so often expressed in tandem, an enormous gulf divides the two, and they are best so separated to facilitate threading the price labyrinth from the inside out.

A special situation prevails in the field of collecting because of the absence of a manufacturing cost figure as the foundation for a wholesale and, thereafter, retail price. The original cost of antiques, art, and most other collectibles is meaningless. The two-cent stamp, the ten-cent pamphlet, the dollar bottle may be priced in the hundreds or even thousands of dollars. And when, as has recently happened, articles are manufactured especially for the collector's market, the usual commercial markup goes by the board for a much larger profit margin.

How then, with no substantial foundation, can there be a price "structure" at all? Because, although many items are unique, most are not; and even the former can be put into some sort of category. It is the "staple" collectible that composes the basic stock of most dealers, priced according to certain more or less flexible elements.

The actual cost to the dealer, overhead calculated to a percentage of cost, known or guessed replacement cost, the rarity or scarcity factor, plus the dealer's instinct about the item's salability are combined to give the price at retail. Even dealers with a largely wholesale business establish a retail price and then compute the discount "to the trade." Those whose business is largely retail must also price with the dealer discount in mind, should another dealer wish to buy.

In addition, there is the matter of style, or personal temperament and approach to business. Some dealers consider a satis-

⇒ factory markup to be doubling the cost price; others settle for ⌝
a bit less; others for much more. There are no stockholders, ⌟
boards of directors, or other outsiders to be accounted to. Most
business in this field is privately owned and run by the owner.

An internationally known antiquities "operator" handles few
sales a year, but each one this dealer is involved with brings
him a fivefold to tenfold profit in multiples of tens of thousands.
Another dealer, better established and with his expertise in a
similar field of art and antiquities, will sell an object that cost
him $10,000 for $13,000 or $14,000, in order to place it with
its peers in a museum collection, and considers doubling the
cost an excellent profit. However, this dealer has a business
establishment and an inventory and is constantly selling.

A nineteenth-century squeaking toy cat of plaster and papier-
mâché was sold for $90 at an elegant antiques show preview to
a dealer who resold it to another for $185. This latter dealer
promptly priced it at $240—all within an hour!

An old-timer, reminiscing about the "pioneer" days of Carni-
val-glass trading in 1965, mentions a transaction in which a
compote bought by a wholesaler for $11 was marked at $100
at retail and sold to a dealer for $80, after the regular 20 per
cent discount.

A leading dealer in Americana relates picking up an eighteenth-century American wall cupboard from another dealer for
$30. It is now in his personal collection and not for sale. He men-
tions $8,000 or $10,000 as the possible price range, were he ever
to sell it.

Although dealers trade lies like fishermen, occasional glimpses
like those above do disclose some startling figures. Obviously,
such deals are not an everyday occurrence, but they are not
without parallel in the secretive annals of profits in collectibles.
All other factors aside, price based on what the market can bear
is intrinsic to the structure of collecting.

Veteran dealers in a specialty, always the elite of the collecting trade, generally determine their asking prices on the

same basis as do lesser dealers, but they more often handle those items of "star quality" that permit of high prices and great profits. The astronomical prices that make headlines are always a result of it. Just as in the theater, the right actor has found the right part in the right play, so, in collecting, it means a confluence of many fortuitous circumstances. One of them is the buyer with enough money, another is the seller with enough chutzpah.

The controversial economic theory that prosperity starts at the top and trickles down seems operative in collectors' markets. Price trends are made at the top, not the bottom of the ladder, as star-quality radiance is shed on lesser examples of each category.

When a Meissen coffeepot fetched $94,000, a Chinese porcelain jar $573,000, a bottle of French wine $9,600, and a Louis XV writing table $410,000, all dealers who had Meissen or Chinese porcelains, French wines and fine French furniture found additional selling power. It was said that most dealers hastened to their shops to raise their prices on learning of these sales; however, this was perhaps an exaggeration. However, although Victorian furniture in the French style is a very poor relation of the signed, superbly crafted, exquisitely proportioned masterpieces in rare and exotic woods that brought over $400,-000 each, nothing is more certain than that dealers all over the world were soon assuring customers that the newly raised prices on such Victoriana were wonderful values. "Now that French furniture is bringing fantastic figures . . ." went the sales talk referring to 1880 Rococo.

For the buyer, the best defense is offense. Ask to be shown pictures and descriptions of the items that are bringing those "fantastic figures." Observe the difference between the eighteenth-century original and the nineteenth-century copy, which may be in the relation of a piece of coal to a diamond. You may find that you are also educating a dealer when you resist nonsensical upgrading.

Overpricing is sometimes the result of ignorance on the part of the dealer. When the buyer's standard of values is equally uninformed, Ossa is piled upon Pelion to reach rarified heights. The only defense for the buyer who can't establish a price judgment for an item is to pay only what a reproduction, facsimile, or contemporary piece would be worth. With the price of manufactured goods so high, it may be that a quality item that is truly an antique, or merely old and good, could be obtained in these circumstances.

Disproportionately high prices can sometimes be accounted for by the insider who happens to know that several dealers have joined together to put up the money to buy an important item. In this way, they not only share the risk, but each is on the alert to find a customer. The jointly owned piece can be whisked from one shop, showroom, or gallery to another, as customers appear. Having so many shoulders put to the wheel puts as many hands out to share the profit, often more than would be expected in less communal circumstances.

Prices vary, but dealers' disclaimers as to high markup vary even more. Some use the poor-mouth technique, complaining that they must pay high prices which allow for little profit, although they admit the selling price is high. Others beat the drum, claiming to take much less markup than do their competitors. A most successful dealer, who for decades has supported a large family and his aged parents out of the business, invariably brings up the difficulties of making a living on a 10 per cent markup. He is right, it would be difficult indeed, but he has never tried it.

Experienced buyers recommend that no one ever be overawed by a prestigious shop, claiming that since those used to dealing in better merchandise are not easily impressed except by outstanding quality, good merchandise will be marked at moderate prices. On the other hand, those who deal in inferior material may possibly tend to overprice the same piece, seeing it as a rare opportunity to get a higher markup than usual. Elegant shops may actually offer better values than those that are purposely neglected in order to encourage buyers to believe they are discovering unknown treasure which must therefore be cheaply priced. It is just as well not to take this for granted.

Staple items, which are fairly common examples of standard types of antiques, such as Victorian whatnots, grocery cannisters, pressed glass, plated silver, brass and copper pots, fireplace equipment, and similar pieces are sold to dealers through "supermart" or warehouse wholesale operations at discount prices. Attempting this on a so-called retail-discount-store technique, with no further price allowance for dealers or decorators, a California dealer claims to sell for half the price of those in antique shops of the traditional sort. Should he be successful, others will no doubt follow.

In a generally rising market, all prices do not rise, nor do those that rise do so at the same rate. While eighteenth-century silver was making new highs, and in the same period, as reported from Paris, eighteenth-century decorative objects were selling at low prices that indicate dwindling interest. While Japanese buyers were paying record prices such as $37,000 for a Utamaro print at Sotheby Parke Bernet, with the big buyers knowing exactly what they wanted, they left many lesser items to be bought as bargains. Guided by individual taste, rather than price and investment trends, good buyers still make good buys.

In their turn, Palissy pottery, Barbizon paintings, Art Nouveau, and African art have been priced lower then than they had been before. Prices of Chilean stamps, pre-Columbian art, Carson City silver dollars, Gothic furniture, buttons, and handmade laces have had syndromes of regression at times, as have those darlings of the front page, Impressionist paintings.

The dynamism of a booming bull market, and the stampede to buy before inflation, push prices even higher with enormous momentum, but somehow, even then, there are always exceptions.

In talking with customers, dealers have added another certainty to death and taxes—rising prices of all antiques, art, and other collectibles. In conversation with one another, however, they also consider negative possibilities and try to sell the doubtful material as quickly as possible. Thus the dealer who pushes or pressures you to buy may know something that you haven't yet heard. Even in an inflationary economy, a prosperous economy, and a "demand" market, prices are subject to vagaries of taste, chance, fashion, and manipulation. Try to be sure that your love for your acquisition will endure for worse as well as better prices.

The presumption that high prices delight all collectors is usually made by those who think in terms of selling. Although the private person whose possessions are now worth more money will gain satisfaction from that fact, as well as the endorsement of his or her taste and judgment, the immediate results are an increase in insurance premiums, more anxiety about accident and theft, and above all, a likelihood of limitations on the acquisition of additional treasures. As long as the individual is still enlarging the collection, stable prices are more advantageous. Many an "incompleat collector" is saddened by the same high prices that make others joyful. The decision to abort the collection is a solution, but hardly a happy one. If the collection is for pleasure before profit and unless the seller is skillful, it may not even be advantageous.

Zooming figures of increased values dazzle and titillate. Within one year, a complete set of 1934 National Park plate blocks of stamps rose 267 per cent in price, a Japanese print rose 58 per cent, an abstract painting 70 per cent, an 1852 gold Greek coin 350 per cent, an Indian robe over 200 per cent, and a case of 1967 Château Latour wine rose over 150 per cent. A Rembrandt print, which sold for $11,500 in 1972, fetched $48,000 in 1973.

Such figures must attract speculators as flies to honey; in fact, some might well be the result of speculative activity, having been previously developed by an interest in rising prices. Artificially controlling the supply, creating a phony demand by use of public relations tactics, buying-in at auctions at preset prices, and advertising to buy at inflated prices are some of the questionable but successful means by which prices can be and are sometimes pushed up.

It has been said that the antiques, art, and collectibles market is subject to similar pressures and manipulations as the stock market. Rumor and gossip are used to make certain wares popular, prices are pushed up, then those who planned it all sell their holdings, leaving the suckers to hold the bag. The truth is that all of these techniques originated in the collecting field, many in ancient times, and the probability is that the stock market tricksters learned from collecting tradition. Some of the tactics used today are modern, but the basic strategy goes back to antiquity.

When stock market analysts discovered, in the 1960s, that certain art works, antiques, and other collectibles had far outdistanced the average securities portfolio in profit performance, some tried to cash in by organizing investment services along these lines. Others tried to launch price-guide publications, so that market prices for collectibles could be followed like stock market prices.

The "big board" still consists of stock listings, but books on investment in collectibles and price guides seem to be here to stay; however, their connection with Wall Street has become tenuous indeed.

Price guides have emerged as publications which claim to list the average selling prices of antiques, art, and collectibles. Some are small volumes, covering narrow categories, such as political buttons, razors, marbles, steins, fruit jars, glass insulators, and bottles. Others undertake to list tens of thousands of prices, under such broad titles as *Collectors' Price Annual* or *Annual Antique Prices.*

Since dealers are usually closemouthed and notoriously untruthful in reporting the price received for a particular item, most price guides gather their information from published advertisements of offering prices, public auction sales at which .they happen to have reporters, priced auction catalogues (when available), prices marked in shops and at shows (sans discount, and usually high), and dealers' lists also showing prices offered. Whether or not they are fed into a computer is of consequence only to the convenience of the compiler; it adds nothing to the accuracy of the material fed in.

The preface to an updated edition of one of the longer established price guides credits the revisions to information from knowledgeable dealers and collectors, correlated with current sale and auction records. Since there is no such thing as an "official" price, the logical conclusion would be that price guides offer more or less educated opinions as to the so-called average current retail price on the subject in hand.

An example given of the problems inherent in these listings tells of a particular drugstore-window bottle that sold for over $500 in a private transaction. A similar bottle of equal merit sold in another place, and with other parties involved, for $120. The price guide listed $240 as the price for such a bottle!

It is apparent that the disclaimer carefully made in every price guide, to the effect that "every effort has been made to be accurate, but the compilers and publishers cannot be responsible for any errors or losses incurred by those who use this list," is well advised.

Among the situations that throw off the averages in price guides are those in which dealers make good buys at very low prices. Often this is properly entered in the record as: Purchase . . . $40. If the books showed that this item was sold for $400, the profits of the business would be that much higher and taxed accordingly. Therefore, for the record, the item is "sold" for $75 or $80. The dealer has, however, in reality sold the item to himself, paying for it with money out of his pocket. The object is taken out of stock for a time, and reappears at some future date, possibly to be sold to another dealer "off the record."

The very real market, based on the prices that dealers pay one another, does not show at all in price manuals; the all-important matter of condition is usually covered by the statement that the prices quoted are for "mint" pieces only. No account is made for repair and restoration which can lower prices by 50 per cent or more, nor for discoloration, chips, stains, scratches, or other imperfections which normally are reflected in prices.

On the other hand, price guides are useful in helping to establish the relative values of objects. Desirability of color, shape, size, maker, and origin as reflected in the marketplace will show up in some degree of price relationship, offering guidance to both buyer and seller. If one bottle, differing only in color, shows a price double of one in another color, that message needs little interpretation and the guide may have paid for itself. In general, however, price guides serve the seller better than they do the buyer.

At first, dealers were generally averse to the idea that private sellers as well as buyers would have access to price guides, and thus could learn the value of their possessions. On the other hand, dealers could see the advantages of being able to point to a high retail price as the "market" price when selling, and in general, most dealers have accepted the price guide as a permanent aspect of the business, both to be coped with and to be exploited.

The well-known "halo" effect, which confers distinction and value on items exhibited in museums and galleries and pictured in books, also occurs when high prices are listed in price guides and can be manipulated to those ends. Insiders make sure they know the origin of a price guide. Many are privately printed by dealers and collectors and those with no inhibitions against creating high fictitious prices do so, to personal advantage. Printed price listings are a great aid to sharp traders whose customers are impressed with such "proof positive."

Price guides have contributed to making prices higher; buyers should use them warily, remembering they are usually high retails, include no discount, and basically are what someone asked and did not necessarily receive for an object.

Misunderstood by many as authoritative and infallible, price guide listings are *not* quotations of the prices for which private individuals can sell their possessions. Unlike daily final stock market figures, they do *not* inform of the price for which the item could have been sold nationally the day before, thus giving an idea, within fractions, of how it will open on the market the following day.

A form of masochism that even the most normal collector cannot always resist is reading the prices in old catalogues, advertisements, listings, and annuals of price reportage services. Although the "old" prices of presently high-priced possessions give comfort and pleasure to those who made their acquisitions in whatever "good old days" preceded the ones that followed, this is never compensated for by the frustration attendant on studying those that got away. The fact that, in most cases, the purchases now lusted after were never even contemplated does not assuage. The retrospective of those very low prices is painful.

However, those who live in the past do not function well in the present. In almost every generation of collectors, there are those who miss the boat, passing up desirable material in the vain hope of finding better buys, more in line with the prices they used to pay. Those whose ideas are frozen into past pre-inflation prices become paralyzed and cannot buy at all in an inflationary period when prices rise rapidly.

Young people, whose memory banks do not include recollection of bargain prices, are the customers who venture most and who sustain a booming market. Unaware that a brass bed could be bought for under $25 before World War I, they pay $400 to $500, reckoning that the price is in proportion to other furnishings available.

Keeping a balanced perspective on values and prices is difficult for dealers as well as collectors. At certain times it seems that those who block out experience and prudence are the most successful, but then sometimes price fluctuations reinstate the proper proportions of courage and fear that make for good balance.

Constant comparison shopping is the buyer's best guide. It gives confidence as well as experience and the accrued knowledge always gives the signal when the item and the price are both "right." Knowing when not to buy is only half the struggle; knowing how to recognize a good buy is the other half.

﹀﹀﹀﹀﹀﹀﹀﹀﹀﹀﹀﹀﹀﹀﹀﹀﹀﹀﹀﹀﹀﹀﹀﹀﹀﹀﹀﹀﹀﹀﹀﹀

Chapter 6

PRICE YOURSELF INTO THE MARKET

You may have heard the story of the dealer who, offered a treasure for such a small fraction of what it was worth, insisted on paying the owner a little more. It is undoubtedly a fable, because when dealers in real life are offered bargains, they usually counter with an offer for less.

They explain that they have to do this because experience indicates that when they agree to pay the price that is asked, the seller often panics and refuses to sell at all, reckoning that it must be worth much more.

Perhaps the greatest disadvantage the private individual encounters in selling antiques, art, or collectibles is the customary unwillingness of dealers to make an offer of the prices they will pay. As a rule, the seller is required to name the price expected. The buyer hopes that ignorance of the true value of an object will be reflected in a low figure asked. Should the price asked be too high, the buyer can always attempt to lower it by bargaining, and failure to achieve this, can always be followed by refusal to buy. However, if the price is less than the dealer expected to pay, a more or less reluctant acceptance can follow the attempt to get it for even less. The name of this game is "Heads I win, tails you lose."

Obviously, under this system, the seller cannot readily go to several dealers to learn which one will pay the most, and then sell it to the highest bidder.

When questioned as to the fairness of this maneuver, dealers practicing it claim that if they made the first offer, it would be misconstrued as an effort to "steal" the items for too little. Others say they do not want to be used to bid up the price. A few dealers bluntly admit that this technique is a time-tested formula for an occasional "sleeper" (the term for underpriced merchandise) to find its way to a wide-awake merchant.

This is not to imply that dealers do not ever pay fair prices. They must pay market prices for most of their wares, to have stock to sell. However, a certain percentage of this stock comes from unwary sellers who do not know the value of their possessions. Your interest as a seller is to avoid contributing to this percentage. You *can* get a fair price, but this takes some doing.

As a private buyer, you buy at retail. As a private seller, you sell at wholesale. Between these two figures, the dealer functions to make his profit—a profit a dealer must make to cover the cost of doing business. Obviously the dealer must pay less than what the item can be sold for in the retail market and, in addition, must allow for a discount should he sell it to a dealer.

Antiques, art, and collectibles have cost and retail prices not unlike commercial merchandise. The difference between the cost and selling price is also called the markup, not all of which is profit.

The cost of doing business, which includes rent, light, telephone, advertising, and similar expenses, will vary according to the type of operation and location, as well as the volume of business. The markup also varies, and when it can be checked, which is infrequently, it is on individual items, not on average. Thus a $20 price tag on an item that cost a dealer $10 might be reckoned as typical, but $300 retail for a $200 cost could be equally acceptable to the same dealer. However, an item that cost $10 might be priced at $100 if the dealer had made an outstanding buy.

A newspaper article reporting the return of a stolen pair of silver antique English candlesticks valued at $10,000 noted that a dealer (who bought them and on learning they had been stolen called in the police) had paid $450 to the "private seller," in this case the thief. Unfortunately the story does not include the retail price the dealer had intended to mark them.

Trade discounts from the retail price are a sort of professional courtesy between dealers. They may be given on an over-all basis of as high as 30 per cent or as low as 10 per cent for any quantity purchased. It is also not unusual for discounts to be graded according to the amount of the sale, like 10 per cent for up to $100, 20 per cent to $250, and 30 per cent for more than $500. Most dealers also give some discount to their regular retail customers, and many will give a discount from the ticketed price to almost any buyer.

Discounts ←—

Although there are no records to check, dealers admit that private individuals selling most kinds of antiques and collectibles can hope to receive 50 per cent to 70 per cent of the retail price only when they sell very desirable items. Run-of-the-mill merchandise will bring 35 per cent, or less, of the expected resale price. Since the dealer's type of trade, current inventory, amount of money on hand to buy, and general business condition govern the "desirability" factor, the private vendor's chance of getting the high percentage is most uncertain.

Private inds. Resale to ←— *Dealers* ←—

In the rare book trade, a third to half of the expected retail price is obtainable if the dealer has an immediate prospect for selling the merchandise, and 20 per cent to 30 per cent is considered good on books bought for stock.

books

Should the private seller not be aware of the list price, the chances of getting even less than the quoted percentages become greater. The primary protection against selling for too low a figure is at least to know the approximate list or retail price the dealer can expect to get. With this information, you have at least a fighting chance to get a fair price.

How then to search out the "listed price" which will indicate the amount you can realistically ask? If you have access to shops, galleries, shows and various "markets," you can look at the price tags and tickets on items that are the same as, or similar to, yours. In art galleries each work is numbered and can be priced by asking an attendant, or some other person attached to the firm, to look up the price in a discreetly placed catalogue.

Price tags and labels vary in the way the information is indicated. Some show the list or retail price in clear figures and indicate the actual amount or percentage of discount in code. If the cost price of the merchandise is shown, that is in code. In some instances, the entire information shown on the price tag is in code.

The use of code for the list price clearly indicates that the dealer expects to haggle with retail customers. A coded discount price or percentage presage the same thing on the wholesale level. The use of code for stock cost is self-explanatory.

You don't have to be a cryptographer to break most price codes. The majority can be cracked with a little guessing. At worst they can't withstand the pricing of many items by the customer.

These codes are based on ten-letter words. Some dealers substitute Z for the last letter of the code word, so that Z equals zero. If the dealer's name consists of ten letters, that is often used. Antique dealers often use their initials prefacing the word "antique."

Some coded labels (example A) indicate the percentage of discount (preceded by the letter D) to be expected by dealers, with the retail price plain.

Others (B) indicate the exact trade or discount price in coded dollars (preceded by the letter D) and the retail plain.

Another method (C) shows both retail price and cost in code without indication of discount.

Still a different variation (D) shows no retail price, just a stock number. This last refers to the stock book, where it appears against three columns: Cost   Trade Price   Retail.

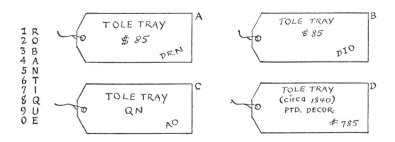

Although ethical dealers frown on the practice, and many customers will not buy from them, there are still dealers who do not show any prices on their wares, quoting verbally when asked. If you are "price shopping," you can count on such gentry being alert to the possibility and resentful in response. Their quotations will usually tend to the high side, since they don't expect to sell to you. On the other hand, such dealers have been known to quote exceptionally low prices on the whim of the moment, almost daring the customer to buy. Veteran buyers observe the absence of marked prices as an indication that they can be considered flexible and will not be firm until some bargaining has been done. The seller who is scouting for list prices is advised not to take first quotations from verbal sources too seriously.

Prices advertised in metropolitan, suburban, and country newspapers should be examined by the prospective seller looking for the retail market price. Trade and special-interest periodicals will also offer clues.

A veritable deluge of price lists can be elicited by responding to the thousands of advertisements that appear every day, week, and month in general and trade advertising columns.

Some are typed, some mimeographed and otherwise duplicated, some are printed. They vary from "absolutely free" to "send SASE," referring to a self-addressed stamped envelope.

If they are priced, they vary from ten cents to one or two dollars, and many are obtained for the cost of postage only.

The following is from one display advertisement in a collectors' magazine. The private seller, looking for retail prices, could do worse than invest in lists of this kind.

"Send 15 cents for each of the following lists of items for sale: Banks—Bells—Blue Willow—Calendar Plates—Carnival Glass—Copper, Brass, and Pewter items—Cruets and Syrups—Cut Glass—Flow Blue—Haviland—Jewelry, also Fans, Combs, Shoe Buckles, etc.—Lamps—Majolica—Milk and Opaque Glass—Musical and Related Items—Nautical and Related Items—Penny Glass Containers—Perfume Bottles—Pin Cushions—Samplers and Needle Work Mottoes—Shaving Mugs—Steins—Silverware—Paper Items—Toothpick and Match Holders—Toys and Games—White Ironstone."

Auction prices are too often quoted and too seldom analyzed to warrant the weight they carry in controlling the market for antiques, art, and collectibles. Consideration of the special circumstances of each transaction would be too much to ask of the most inveterate market watchers. Whether it was a sentimental response on the part of the winning bidder which drove the price to an all time high, a duel between determined enemies, or a genuine reflection of demand seldom goes on any record.

Yet the auction catalogue with the prices realized noted next to the lot number and description does become the statistic that is quoted.

As a rule the collector-buyer will be informed by the dealer-seller of higher auction prices as they influence the price in the shop. Many dealers subscribe to the "prices realized" catalogue services which the more important auction firms offer. It is not necessary to subscribe in order to see such prices, or to sit for hours marking catalogues during a sale. The private vendor who is interested in knowing what a limited number of items have brought at auctions may visit the offices and inquire, referring to date of sale.

If you know of sales which included lots similar to items you wish to sell, you too can quote them to get better prices when confronted with a hard-to-convince buyer.

Whether prices are gathered verbally, through plain or coded price tags, through advertising, dealers' and collectors' price lists, price guides, investment literature, or auctions and price-realized catalogues, they must all be interpreted, to be practical and useful to the seller.

Awareness of the fact that quoted prices can be, and often are, manipulated is as important for the seller seeking price information, as for the buyer in any area of the art and hobby market.

Stock market manipulators can artificially (and illegally) create a public record of high prices by a spiral of "inside" sales. This can be done more easily (and legally) by speculator-swindlers in the field of collecting.

There is nothing actually illegal about advertising collectibles to sell at a high price; if it is done cleverly, it gives the impression that the goods in question really sell at that figure.

It isn't considered ethical to advertise to buy at high prices, and then always find reasons why what is offered isn't "exactly" what is wanted. However, this too is often accomplished.

It is not only legal, but accepted practice to protect one's goods from being sold at auction for much less than its worth. But when items are put into an auction for the purpose of being "bought in" by the owner at a high figure, to create a public record that a certain artist's work, or type of antique or book, medal or stamp is now very valuable and desirable, it too becomes a technique to create phony, falsely padded "list prices."

You may accidentally profit from riding on the coattails of such questionable tactics by shrewd operators if you happen to already own what they are promoting. If, however, you are buying from them with the intention of reselling and profiting by the investment, then buyer-seller, beware!

As we have noted, price guides are most useful to the seller in establishing a list price against which to project the price he hopes to receive for the item or collection. Since guides are quickly dated, it is wise to use a current one when selling. If possible, imitate dealers and compare several, indicating the highest price shown as your potential list price as you approach your customer.

Parallel with this price-guide activity, there has been a spate of investment literature, much of it in handsome, finely illustrated books. Antiques, art, furniture, and silver have been among the subjects viewed and analyzed in terms of speculative profit, and prices are quoted in past, present, and future tense, to indicate what the writers believe to be the profitable trends.

Almost all of this material, on whatever level of sophistication it is written and on whatever plane of quality it deals, emphasizes the *buying* rather than the *selling* aspect of investing. There is almost always a tendency to quote high prices in newspaper headline terms, to marvel at how they have risen, but there is an absence of information on how the private individual can actually get such prices when selling.

‸‸

Chapter 7

TRADING WITH "THE TRADE"

Splendid establishments on such streets as Madison Avenue, Bond Street, and the Faubourg St. Honoré, selling art, antiques, rare books, coins, manuscripts, and other costly and choice collectors' delights, may seem to have little in common with thousands of less distinguished and often unimposing, even mediocre and shabby, antique, curio, coin, stamp, secondhand, and resale shops, but they are related in a way that transcends their differences of quality, prosperity, and style. It takes all of them together to make up "the trade," that totality of the collecting organism.

At each level of the business, there are ties meshing above, below, and often sideways as well. Intertwined they form a seemingly unregimented, individualistic, egocentrically run, highly personalized, disorganized organization. Few transactions are exactly alike, so an essential flexibility is inherent. Although it is ridden with gossip and backbiting, co-operation in the trade is not uncommon, especially when former opponents see some possibility of joint benefit. It is a form of business that includes many who are rapacious, along with finer spirits as well. For some members of the trade it is an addiction, for others merely a mundane form of livelihood. For outsiders it is a mystery, but as insiders, we can see that its workings have a certain logical structure. Cynics call it buying cheap and sell-

ing dear. In kinder terms it might be called finding the right
wares at the right price and finding the right buyer at the
right price.

The hierarchy of dealers starts at the bottom with pickers,
who are also known as scouts, knockers, and runners. These
individuals need no shop and are constantly on the move,
ranging through homes, thrift shops, flea markets, shows, auctions, and shops, always on the lookout for choice and desirable
material with a ready market at higher prices. They search for
bargains of any sort and also to fill special requests from dealers.
Many are specialists and collectors themselves and enjoy scouting as a profitable hobby.

Some pickers are employed by individual dealers who take
whatever they buy for them. The dealer advances the money
and pays a fixed percentage (20 per cent is usual) over the
cost. In other cases, pickers work for several dealers, bringing to
each some specialty of particular interest; this may also be on
the same fixed-percentage basis.

Independent pickers use their own funds to buy, offering
their purchases to dealers on a highest bid basis. The relationship between regular pickers and dealer outlets are such that
sometimes the dealer cannot profitably use what the picker
brings, but accepts it rather than refuse and risk the picker's bypassing the shop in the future.

Pickers cover country auctions on which more important
dealers could not afford to spend the time. They also travel
from shop to shop, often seeing in one what another requires,
arranging the transaction. Pickers travel from one city to another,
from city to country and vice versa, constantly on the alert for
good buys. There are some who hold regular auction sales, for
dealers only, with the pickings of these trips. Another type of
scout covers a particular area, localizing the effort, but preferring
to work in depth and thoroughly. Retired schoolteachers,

artists, and librarians are among those who supplement income in this way, in some cases working as pickers for top dealers and galleries.

Aggressively oriented pickers who travel will place advertisements to buy locally. If called in, they are not inhibited by the responsibilities that might suppress the sharper practices of a local dealer who has a shop and a repeat following to keep him in line. Such pickers are on the lookout for victims.

Although dealers at every level have their tributary scouts, they also have allied dealers with whom they enjoy especially good and easy relationships. As we shall see, they form combinations with them to buy together as a "ring" at auctions and also, as opportunity warrants, join with one or more individuals to make a joint purchase when a large monetary outlay is required.

Like any businessman, the dealer has a given capital which must be turned at a profit to pay taxes, the costs of doing business, and include a living for himself, plus a further accumulation of capital for growth and expansion, so that more merchandise can be bought.

Unlike other businesses, the collecting trades cannot expect a regular seasonal turn, marking down those items which did not sell, until the entire stock renews itself. By the very nature of collectibles, they often increase in value as they are held. Thus the dealer needs a proportionately larger capital investment than do most other retailers, since he holds onto his slow-moving stock. As a matter of fact, in a rising inflationary market, dealers commonly raise the prices of items they have held for a long time.

Occasionally, anxious to make advantageous current purchases, dealers will expedite the movement of older merchandise by putting it into auctions, selling it to other dealers at special discounts, or even, as a last resort, offering especially good buys to their retail customers. Cash on hand to buy at any time is a basic need for those who deal in antiques, art, and collectibles, since windfall purchases, made when the occasion arises, are the mainstays of a profitable business.

At any given time the stock of a single dealer may, and probably will, include remnants of a personal collection, individual purchases from private sellers, scouts, auctions, other dealers, warehouse disposals, house sales, complete collections purchased from collectors, results of trades or exchanges, items imported from abroad, estate or trust liquidations and consignments, as well as merchandise re-purchased from old clients years after the original sale.

In addition to their regular channels inside the trade, through which they acquire merchandise, dealers have others as well. Outside sources for information leading to purchases may come from funeral directors, real estate dealers, appraisers, auctioneers, lawyers, judges, and banks, as well as employees of storage warehouses and movers. As dealers learn of estates and collections to be sold, they can maneuver for position. Having the right connections often means the opportunity to buy a household, or the contents of a vault, trunk, or strongbox, to good advantage.

In some social circles, well-connected people can earn a commission by telling a dealer that Madame A recently said at bridge that she was thinking of selling her rubies or that Mr. Z's collection of coins is beginning to bore him. The dealer who reads the obituary columns, and himself discovers that one of his collector-customers is now deceased, pays only for the newspaper. The dealer who learns from a cook that a couple is on the verge of a divorce, which will mean a collection must be sold to pay for the settlement, pays gladly and proportionately for the information.

Sometimes dealers watch and wait for years, hoping that a

particular item or collection, very much wanted by a client, will become available. Some have files, showing where particularly desirable rarities are privately held, in the hope that the information will be required.

When bankers and lawyers have to liquidate estates which include antiques, art, or collectibles, they usually call in well-established appraisers and dealers because they want to deal with reputable individuals or firms. They may be held accountable for the disposition and want to be beyond suspicion of collusion. However, very often this is done without competitive bidding, and therefore that dealer who gets the opportunity usually finds it lucrative.

Dealers use their connections to sell, as well. A lawyer or banker may have a client who is looking for an investment in art or antiques and will introduce him to a dealer with whom he has had a satisfactory selling transaction.

Every dealer dreams of cornering the market in some desirable specialty, but few except art dealers get the opportunity. Art dealers who control the output of an artist under contract, or the estate of a deceased artist, can manipulate the prices by controlling the supply. However, there is nothing to keep any dealer from becoming a specialist in a certain ware, a certain period, or a specific maker. If the dealer is important enough and can invest enough, he may become a controlling figure. Even if the scale is smaller, a turn in collecting fashion, or a historical accident, can create this importance. Any who dealt in antique or semiantique oriental wares, albeit in a modest way, had an opportunity to profit when collectors reslanted their interests after the reopening of Chinese-U.S. relations in 1972. Since the Chinese government siphoned only run-of-the-mill nineteenth-century antiques to the few buyers who could enter China to buy, the dealers over the world who had fine oriental antiques moved into a very desirable position. Added to this, an influx of Japanese dealers invaded world markets, searching for rare and choice Chinese and Japanese antiques and art.

Foreign dealers come to the United States market both to buy and to sell. Regularly calling on private collectors in the antiques sector are English dealers and firms, employing the same elegant manners as do the English custom tailors who travel a select American circuit in search of business from their established clienteles. One London antiques dealer visits New York every autumn, for eight weeks, with the contents of several large crates which she displays in a hotel room to a steady stream of society women, decorators, and antiques dealers. For the first two weeks a percentage of the proceeds is donated to a charity that is assisted by many prominent society people. This dealer brings furniture, glass, porcelains, tea caddies, lamp bases, clocks, and similar decorative antiques. When she returns to London, she has a notebook full of orders to fill, for which she will send photographs for advance approval before shipment.

Another firm of London dealers sends photographs, with exact and carefully detailed descriptions and measurements of choice and costly furniture and accessories, to past and potential customers. These are followed up with personal visits by salesmen with ambassadorial manners who "discuss" the client's needs.

Book, coin, autograph, and stamp dealers also tend private and trade contacts throughout the world. A Roman dealer in antique gold coins had both a Hungarian and a Brazilian client in town on the same day and found it difficult only because he couldn't lunch with them both at the same time. Certain items bring better prices in different markets, developing a traffic pattern which tends to move each to the place where it is most valued.

Many services abroad cater to American dealers of antiques and curios, who prefer to stay home while stocking their shops. A British firm advertises a record of twenty years of shipping container loads to the United States. A "container catalogue" is available free to dealers, as are "stock lists." These latter include clocks, pattern glass, art glass, cut glass, china, metal, pewter, oriental items, dolls, steins, and many more items, all priced in dollars. Orders of over $500 are given a 20 per cent discount, and money back is guaranteed if the merchandise is not as prepresented.

French and Belgian firms also advertise, and many dealers have private arrangements for merchandise to be shipped to them. Austria and Spain are also sources for such wholesale lots. A decline of the dollar's buying power in Europe is reflected in higher prices for the staple items which appear in such shipments.

Another aspect of the geographical collecting equation is the city-country antiques cycle which no longer reflects the old city-country relationship. Years ago, folk art, country artifacts, farm implements, and other forms of the pioneer-agricultural life style were bought in the country and brought to the city. Nowadays, the so-called country buyer gets container loads from abroad and buys in metropolitan centers, supplementing this with what is obtainable locally, for the country-located shop or barn.

In the United States there are still some national and regional stylistic preferences, such as a bias in the Northeast for New England Colonial and in the Southwest for Spanish Mission and Indian decoration. Florid Victorian flourishes in the Southeast, and the Midwest hankers for Eastlake in furniture styles.

Almost all collectibles move in an orbit to their natural retail-sales level within the trade, going from scout to dealer, from wholesaler to subdealer, or from dealer to dealer. When arrived at the market strata where the retail price is consistent with other comparable material, it will be offered to the collector at going market rates. Possibly the buyer's best hope for achieving good value for the money spent for antiques, art, and collectibles is to intercept this progress, buying at the lowest trade level whenever possible.

Variations in Antiques, Art, and Collectibles Trading
Channels

Private Seller	Manufacturer of Reproduction	
Picker	Wholesaler	
Small Dealer	Jobber	Museum
Larger Dealer	Dealer	Auction
Specialist	Private Buyer	Collector
Collector		
Auction	Manufacturer	Thrift Shop
Dealer	Corporate Dealer	Picker
	Subscriber	Dealer
Private Seller		Collector
Dealer	Manufacturer	
Collector	Corporate Dealer	Flea Market
Auction	Wholesaler	Collector
Dealer	Jobber	
	Retailer	Garage Sale
Faker	Private Customer	Dealer
Dealer		Auction
Collector	Collector	Dealer
Auction	Dealer	
	Collector	Private Seller
Private Seller		Auction
Picker	Secondhand Dealer	Dealer
Importer	Picker	Museum
Wholesaler	Dealer	Dealer
Dealer	Auction	
	Collector	

These lists indicate the movement of some collectibles as they flow through the market's trading channels in which they circulate. This is a continuous process, bringing them into the hands of private owners and back into the trade again. Even museums may sell and thus recirculate material.

Chapter 8

THE CYNIC LOOKS AT DEALERS

Years ago, the comic stereotype of the collector was either an eccentric old oddball or a foolish, middle-aged clubwoman. Dealers in collectibles were cast as slightly fey, unworldly characters, except when they were visualized as suave and polished gentry, who just might be swindlers. As in all caricature, there might once have been some trace of truth, but even in the past it was minimal. Today, both collectors and dealers defy these and any other efforts to type them according to age, sex, life style, or class distinctions.

There is, however, one characteristic common to those who become dealers in antiques, art, autographs, books, coins, stamps, and other collectabilia; they are likely to be individualistic personalities, somewhat more resistant to being clamped into the patterns of an industrial-technological society than most. Hardly to be described as free souls, they might better be called free-style entrepreneurs, and it as such that the buyer must come to grips with most of them. With the exception of a new and different species, the mass promotional corporative collecting merchandiser, elsewhere noted, most dealers, large or small, run personality-oriented operations which reflect the style of the proprietor.

It is hardly surprising that dealers are often somewhat thorny when they buy. What amazes is how unfriendly and crotchety they can be when customers come into their shops. Run-of-the-mill antiques shops and second-hand dealers are reputed to be the worst offenders, but dealers who sell books, coins, and stamps do not always greet the public with enthusiasm either. The attitudes in the more elegant galleries and shops may be reserved, but are at least polite; mere politeness would be considered overexuberant cordiality in those establishments where the visitor is eyed as an invader.

This often grim approach to the public reflects no deep-seated misanthropy, but results largely from the fact that such shops are considered open territory for an hour's diversion after lunch for otherwise aimless persons. When they are accompanied by racketing children, when they handle fragile wares carelessly, disparage the merchandise, and then rarely buy, it is easy to understand why there is a movement among antiques dealers to charge admission. Add to this the growing losses to shoplifters, the need for constant surveillance, precautionary mirrors, locked cases, constant counting and checking of merchandise, and a general note of suspicion seems credible enough.

However, the first sign of intelligent interest by a potential customer will dispel incivility and frost, to replace them with courtesy, if not outright affability.

Just as the dealer is suspicious of the unknown customer, so the customer returns the mistrust, worrying about being cheated by offerings of reproductions, fakes, imperfect, stolen, or over-priced items. While some buyers, in hunting for the item that will increase in value far beyond the normally expected increment, hope to outwit the dealers, most merely want to hold their own, making a fair exchange of money for merchandise.

Rising prices bring out reproductions; even dealers can be fooled by them. However, since they differ from outright fakes, in being made for a popular commercial market, they can usually be traced to their manufacturing or wholesale sources and their characteristics noted and thus avoided. Museums, for example, sell reproductions which are marked in a way that alerts to their representation of original source pieces. Gift shops, department stores, specialty shops, decorator showrooms, and importers are marketing outlets for imported and domestic wares that challenge authentic originals. Collectors of glass, pottery, porcelain, pewter, and prints—items all especially liable to reproduction—often keep watch to become experts on what in the way of copies is being marketed in their fields. Advertisements in trade journals, including antiques trade publications repay careful attention; they are addressed to dealers, offering reproductions. Many reproductions have trademarks, slight differences in design or pattern, variations in color, size, proportion, material, or workmanship that, once observed, forever proclaim them as different and unauthentic. Even those that seem to have no giveaway sign of their dubious background will be exactly alike, and so both old and new become tainted in the eyes of those aware of the problem.

The problem is compounded as time passes, and in a generation clever reproductions become absorbed. However, the problem is at its worst when an item first appears on the market. Dealers who would not knowingly buy them are not yet alert. The others dole them out, one by one, to postpone recognition by quantity.

The best protection is the signed statement under the dealer's letterhead on the bill. The dealer who might be making a mistake will allow you to return the item if it turns out to be a reproduction sold as an original. The other, who knows what it is, will probably be leery of signing, and you can then draw your own conclusions.

An entirely different situation prevails when fakes are involved. These are made with the sole purpose of fraud and therefore the stakes are much higher. Antiques, art, autographs, books, coins, and stamps with high monetary potential make up the targets; this is not the area for small-time operators.

In most cases, the first tipoff to a fake will be the price. As a come-on, it will usually be a comparative bargain, as against the market price of the real thing. The anxiety on the part of the buyer to make that substantial saving, to snatch it away before the seller recognizes its true value, will often tip the scales in favor of the purchase of the fake. Eager buyers don't want to be confused by the facts.

The nineteenth-century French autograph collector who bought the letters of Cleopatra, written in French, will not easily be topped for succumbing to self-persuasion, but others do pretty well. Knowledge of many fakes is kept out of the public domain by embarrassment on the part of the victim. Few print collectors haven't taken a chance on one that looked very good through low-priced glasses, only to discover they had oversold themselves.

Dealers who have been fooled, like best to pass on their mistakes to other dealers. This rehabilitates the ego of the one who has been "taken," by proving that other professionals also can succumb to that same mistake. Unfortunately, the fake eventually ends up in the hands of a dealer whose ego is not so sensitive, or who just doesn't recognize the fake, and so it gets out into the open market.

It has been claimed that fakes cannot enter the market without the connivance of at least the first dealer, the one who launches it and who may even have commissioned its creation. This is questionable territory, where gossip far outstrips confirmed facts. Those who know, don't tell; those who tell may know, or they may fabricate. The painting copied while it was being cleaned and restored; the highboy, in the cabinetmaker's shop for a minor repair, that had an exact twin within a few months; the chair made as a copy which could not then be told from the original are tales still being told in a generation when good craftsmen grow scarce and can make a fortune at simpler tasks.

It is known that dealers both here and abroad were involved in such enterprises in the earlier decades of the twentieth century. Indications are that most of their well-faked creations are safely in famous collections and museums. Unless the collector is buying material in the costly upper strata, the problem is not likely to arise. At that level, all of the batteries to test authenticity, provenance, and pedigree are, or should be, massed.

In any case, dealers themselves are not likely to be those who do the faking, but rather artists, artisans, craftsmen, and restorers. They are the primary sources to be watched and cultivated for news and information as to fakes. They know the secrets, perhaps more certainly than the experts who guess, and it is they who can tell "where the bodies are." For buyers who want an education in recognition of fakes, no school will excel the workshop.

Insiders who keep abreast of what's old and new in fakery always have good contacts with those who actually handle restoration and repair. They try to spend time in studios and laboratories, cultivating friendship, while chatting and watching the work. The dealer who has his own workroom has a great advantage, but misses out on the visits to those working for the trade in general. Although each dealer wants his own secrets kept, sometimes asking that the work he brings in be kept out of view, he will always be alert to see what is in progress or needed in that of others, and what has been completed. Filed in a dealer's memory, this kind of information may turn out to be profitable at some future date.

In no other area but collecting, do so many former amateurs and hobbyists move to the other side of the counter, to become professional dealers. It is a natural and often fortunate transition, bringing much talent and dedication to the trade. However, not all collectors who want to become dealers grasp the many aspects of business that are involved in a profitable operation. Those who have a natural flair, or who learn quickly by experience, develop a going operation, while plenty of others are unsuccessful for a variety of reasons.

Some sell their original stock, the result of years of collecting, at prices which are higher than what they paid, but below replacement costs. They are soon picked clean of these bargains and, having made inadequate or no provision for prudent restocking, are forced to panic buying, the results of which prove difficult to sell at a profit. There are many other pitfalls for novice dealers, eventually causing the retreat of those who are dependent on its success for a living.

Thousands of dealers never meet the moment of truth, because, having other sources of income, they never do more than play at running a real business. Some remain on the fringes of the trade for years, buying and selling from their homes or low-rent shops. Since they do not meet the hard test of competition or survival, their prices may be giveaway or absurdly high. Many are not well informed and glibly pass on nonsense as fact and serve as conduits for reproductions and fakes into the market. The naïve and beginning buyer is much safer in the hands of a profit-minded professional than a romantic trifler, no matter how convincingly the latter may assay the role of dealer.

Standards for evaluating dealers are about the same as for plumbers or doctors. The probity of the individual governs the fairness of prices quoted, the candor with which information is given, general ethical standards, and responsibility. Skills and knowledge are a matter of experience and background. Finding reputable dealers is largely a matter of checking their reputation for these qualities with collectors and other dealers.

Whenever possible, the buyer will prefer to trade with honest and responsible individuals and firms. However, antiques, art, and collectibles must be followed where they can be found, and all too often, the desired object is in the hands of an unknown and untried dealer whose bona fides are not easily established. In such cases, the item sought must be checked most stringently to verify value and authenticity.

Because the buyer may discover an unhappy truth about the purchase of a collectible only many years later, when offering it for sale, one veteran collector suggests a short cut for inexperienced beginners. Advising that such a purchase be immediately taken to another dealer and offered for resale, it is suggested that the "critique" of the merchandise that will be given by the potential buyer will offer a salutary evaluation of the original transaction, with perhaps a chance to make an adjustment, or return, should it prove at fault.

Observers such as Pliny, Martial, and Juvenal, in describing the art and antiques sales quarter of Imperial Rome, mention dealers' techniques for selling and idiosyncrasies of collectors that might well be commentaries on twentieth-century collecting. Until that period, when growing middle classes in industrial countries began tentatively to buy and collect, dealers merely honed, refined, and revised the basic skills that had made for success in the trade for over 2,000 years.

Then, after World War II, although the accumulation of classic treasures by the wealthy and powerful continued, a new factor entered collecting. Literally, masses of people found they had the means to acquire collectibles. In part, it expressed the drive for a higher standard of living and snobbish emulation of the life style of the upper-economic groups. Another force was the natural yearning inherent in people to enjoy the ownership of rare, curious, interesting, unusual, or beautiful objects. The discovery that it no longer required the money of a Croesus or capitalist tycoon to be a collector was still another factor. At first, except for its expansion to include many more dealers, there was no change in the basic buying and selling expertise that had become traditional.

However, lured by the potential of a mass market, interested businessmen began to examine the possibilities of modern merchandising methods applied to collecting. What developed in the mid-sixties was a new industry, launched with the discovery that it is not only possible to manufacture collectibles, but also to manufacture collectors!

Suggesting and insinuating, if not promising, that profits can be made by investing in so-called limited edition items, promoters have launched hundreds of thousands, perhaps millions, of people into new roles as subscribers and collectors.

Commemorative medals, medallions, and plates were the first items these new corporate dealers promoted; many have since been added. The advertising and promotion techniques have been so successful that multimillion-dollar corporations have been formed, conglomerates organized, and their securities traded on the stock exchange. Individual companies have had sales of sixty and eighty million dollars annually as new profit dimensions have been brought into the field of dealing in collectibles.

The basic ploy, the essential original concept that distinguished this program from any other previous approach to selling collectibles, was the mass offer of privately issued items, often in series, made in editions limited by a subscription *deadline*. Some of these manufacturer-dealers arranged for subscribers to a limited edition to pay in advance; in this fashion there was never any bothersome inventory on hand. Series were usually produced over a period of time. One firm which specialized in articles made of silver received a total of almost 10,000 subscriptions for 36 plates in a series. Each plate was priced at $150.

Sometimes a contract called for subscribers to have the privilege of canceling after buying an individual piece; others obligated the subscriber to complete the contract. Advertising stressed the deadline, indicating that it would be the last chance to buy before the item became a "rarity." Apparently this appeal, automatically making the purchaser into a collector, found half a million subscriber-collector targets for one firm in an eight-year period. Many of the new collectors had never before collected anything but empty bottles for the two-cent refund.

The "limited edition" collectible might be a silver ingot, issued at less than $10; enamel boxes in series of six at $100 each; glass, pottery, porcelain, copper, brass, pewter, and silver plates, from $10 to $500 each; china birds and figures, from hundreds to thousands of dollars. Some were sold only to charter subscribers, others also went into department stores, gift shops, jewelry shops, antique shops, and any sort of retailer who would buy them for resale.

Christmas and commemorative plates, which had hitherto had a modest to substantial collectors' market over many years, were also swept into the boom of limited editions promotion. They were advertised by direct mail, in newspaper and national magazine ads in seemingly limitless assortments and series, and inevitably heralded as "investments." Certain items which had been made in limited quantities of dozens or hundreds, due to the difficulties of manufacture, and in some cases, small demand, as were the Dorothy Doughty bird groups and the Boehm bird figures, and had appreciated greatly in price over a period of years, were quoted as positive proof that all limited editions would do the same. "Limited editions" of 20,000 and more scandalized serious collectors, but left others, hopeful of profit, undaunted.

The advertising income from the so-called "antiques of the future" created a novel prosperity for some publications. One issue of an antiques trade publication carried ten individual and separate advertisements for a certain "limited edition" glass plate of unknown quantities. In that single issue of the paper, prices for this plate varied in each advertisement. Starting at $275, it was offered at $285, $300, $325, $350, $450, $500, and $550. Cynics suggested that the higher prices were inserted only as lures, to convince naïve buyers that the investment was already profitable. How such a price range impressed collectors may be wondered at. Possibly many did rush to buy at the lower price as a "bargain."

Some dealers compared this boom with seventeenth-century tulipomania and predicted that it would also burst, leaving hapless investors. But others maintained that the nature of the mass collectors' market may have its own logic, and they quoted Barnum and population growth for an optimistic forecast.

Suggesting both outrage and amusement at the lengths to which the boom had gone, Tiffany & Company ran the following tongue-in-cheek advertisement in the New York *Times* November 17, 1972.

"LIMITED EDITIONS"

This season seems to be replete with offers of so-called collector's items issued in "Limited Editions," often represented as Great Art, but too often of questionable artistic merit. Some of them are huckstered with sophisticated 20th Century versions of the snake-oil technique of the 19th Century calculated to appeal to the greed of the customer with implied promises of increased future value, as well as with attempts to scare the customer into a quick purchase or else this "priceless golden opportunity" will be gone forever.

So, to top all Limited Editions once and for all, we offer the celebrated 128 carat Tiffany Diamond, the largest and finest Canary Diamond in the world, in a Limited Edition of "one" for the sum of $5,000,000. What's more, in our judgement, past history and everything else considered, it will easily be worth $10,000,000 one hundred years from now.

Mail orders will not be accepted if postmarked after November 17, 1972. First come, first served, of course.

TIFFANY & CO.
New York

~~~~~~

Chapter 9

HEADS THEY WIN, TAILS YOU LOSE

A hardware or clothing "merchant," but an antiques, art, book, coin, or stamp "dealer"? There seems to be something about collecting that suggests more negotiating and trading than obtains in other business fields. And for a good reason. It is true; there *is* something.

Without disparaging those whose interest in rare, curious, beautiful, or old objects has taken them into a very difficult kind of business, it is a fact that the fluctuation of values and prices, the dependence on quick judgments, the need for decisions that involve financial risk so sharpen the dealer that he is more than a match for the private person who approaches with possessions to sell.

Therefore, granting that most dealers are honest, reliable gentlefolk of the highest integrity, the seller must watch out for those pitfalls which await, and which are, because of the inherent nature of the transaction involved, mostly slanted in favor of the dealer. However, despite these disadvantages, you can sell your possessions at a fair price by understanding the problems and refusing to become a victim.

Private sellers who hear dealers constantly complain that it is easy to sell, but hard to buy, are surprised to discover that it's not so easy to sell to these same dealers. They haven't properly translated the dealer's meaning, namely, that it is difficult for dealers to find what they want at the prices they want to pay. What they want to buy is merchandise that will sell quickly at a substantial profit. This means further that it must be bought at a price which is low and sold at one substantially higher.

But why should seller David approach dealer Goliath at all? For the very good reason that dealers have access to many customers. They know what those customers want and might buy. They require stock for their shops and galleries. They try to have cash on hand to make desirable purchases quickly, thus providing the seller with desirable money.

Despite the headlines proclaiming record prices for certain art treasures, antiques, and other collectibles, the recipients of these high prices are not always the original sellers. In many cases, at least one dealer, and often several, plus an auctioneer have been the intermediaries before the completion of such a transaction. If the private seller makes the mistake of starting at too low a level in disposing of the goods, then the passage to the higher-quality plane where it can fetch a high price will occur without a fair share of that price accruing to the original owner.

We have credited pickers, scouts, and runners with unsavory tactics, but established dealers are not strangers to many of the tricks by which people are parted from their property for a fraction of what it should bring.

One veteran dealer, candidly sharing his system for buying antiques from private individuals, suggests asking the seller to identify the most valuable piece. The dealer finds it is usually of little consequence, certainly never the best piece. He then offers a lump sum, less than the seller has asked, but excludes the "choice" item to show his honesty and respect for the seller's sentiment which he prefers not to pay for anyway. If, in addition, he should assure the seller of the "priceless" nature of the unsold piece, he may well be satisfied with himself.

Testimony from a European witness tells how dealers abroad sometimes treat themselves to private jokes. Such a one, retreating from an unsuccessful foray, having failed to buy privately at a satisfactory price, may "nail down" the item forever, in a spirit of nastiness. He does this by "admitting" the true worth of the piece is much greater than he can afford to pay, naming it as a huge and ridiculous figure. This leaves the owner forever unable to achieve the price, forever unhappy, and presumably leaves the dealer forever laughing.

Above all, those who advertise "We buy contents," offering to pay a sum for the entire lot, want to avoid alerting the private seller as to the value of individual items. Experience has taught that the now-educated seller will then offer the valuable units to others, more willing to pay higher prices. Rather than point out the desirable material, the dealer will buy the household as a lot and then sell what he does not want to other dealers or, possibly, the junkman.

When a prospective buyer offers to send in an "appraiser" or to take an item to be appraised, one would think that an alarm might sound in the seller's mind. Apparently it did not when an English country home was visited by a dealer who had advertised that he wanted to buy paintings, and on being told that the owner thought his was by a famous artist, suggested it be sent to London to be checked by "an expert." The buyer reported back that it was not authentic, buying it from the disappointed owner for about $500. A national scandal was caused when, within a few weeks, the original owner read in a London newspaper that his picture had been sold at auction for over forty times the price he received, and properly attributed as he had thought. The buyer was able to prove that he had been swindled, but if he had not happened to see the news item of the sale, he would never even have known about it.

There is a long tradition of "psyching" the seller to feel uncomfortable and inadequate and to indicate that the antiques, art, or collectibles he or she is offering represent inferior wares and therefore must be sold at a "reasonable" figure. Since the average private person is an inexperienced and often inept seller, many succumb and accept too little for their treasures.

Keeping the seller waiting for a long time in an uncomfortable situation; brusquely inquiring for the asking price; smiling sardonically at the price mentioned; and making a low counteroffer, good "only for today," are some of these techniques.

Private individuals who are tentative or diffident can easily be thrown off balance, especially if faced by the "partner" act. In this situation, the dealer readily agrees to a fair price, but before closing the deal, must show the purchase to his partner who either has the cash or will write the check in payment. The partner appears and acts appalled at the price to be paid, noting all sorts of flaws in the purchase, mentioning a much smaller sum as a practical price. The original "buyer" defends his judgment, but becomes convinced of his error. However, he battles in defense of the seller to get the hard-headed partner to pay a fraction more. By this time the "lucky" victim may have been mesmerized into accepting it.

A very old and still-successful technique for buying cheaply from a naïve seller is that of picking out some few ordinary items and offering a ridiculously high price for them, while lumping what is rare and valuable with "uninteresting stuff" at a small fraction of its worth. The seller is so excited at being offered $30 for what is obviously not worth anything that in haste to get the $30, he literally gives away hundreds.

Another variation of this is to pick out what is valuable and rare at low prices, while falsely praising what is left behind as "too rich for my blood."

Items are never bought or priced individually, but in groups, so that the seller cannot determine what units in a lot are of especial value.

It usually turns out in these situations that the cream has been skimmed off the top, leaving what is now unsalable, because it could only be sold in conjunction with the better material as a "tie-in."

Since the picker is at the bottom rung of the merchandising-collecting market, it is obvious that the prices paid on this level are the lowest. If possible, the private person should avoid selling to pickers, although they are not always readily recognizable.

The unabashed "Second Hand Store," which once supplied the needy and frugal with the castoffs of the well off and frugal, has gone the way of "Second Hand Rose." It has been replaced by the socially acceptable Thrift and Resale shops.

By an inverted snobbism, the purchase of thrift-shop clothing and homefurnishings has become a special status symbol. Whatever the psychological or sociological overtones, it has breathed new life into the old second-hand operation, which has in this new respectable guise become an important way station in merchandising collectibles.

The charity thrift shop is in a special category to be examined later. The commercial thrift shop or resale shop, which advertises "will clean out entire house," buys its merchandise outright. If you want to sell quickly, you can call in your old second-hand dealer, now to be found under "Thrift—Used—Resale" headings. You have asked to be "picked." The hazards are the same as they always were. In exchange for speed and convenience, you get low prices and the possible disposal of a valuable treasure for little or nothing.

There are some pointers on how to avoid being "picked":

If you have a collection to sell, go to a well-known dealer in that specialty.

Don't answer advertisements to buy which do not have traceable sources.

Find out the name of the person with whom you are doing business. Check the address, and if the sums warrant it, bank references.

If the amounts offered are less than half of "list prices" you have checked, refuse them and bargain for more.

If you are selling part of, or an entire household, make up lists of the property and check them in advance.

Find a dealer whose stock is about on the quality level of what you have to sell. If your merchandise is inferior, he won't be interested. If your merchandise is superior to his, he won't have the trade to buy it directly from him, but will have to resell it to another dealer. The dealer who has a ready market can pay you the best price and resell it directly at retail.

Farsighted dealers, who sell particularly good merchandise, record the transaction with the name of the buyer for two purposes. One is a matter of current bookkeeping. The other is for future buying.

When it is hard to find merchandise on the market and an opportunity arises to sell the very items that were so much cheaper when sold a decade before, some dealers turn to contacting their old customers and offer to pay as much as "double what you paid me." Alluring as that might sound, it is not always a good transaction for the old client who may not be aware that scarcity and inflation have skyrocketed some prices by ten and twenty times, if not more.

If a dealer should call you to suggest that you take a profit by reselling back to him, check the current market price for that item, and then ask 70 per cent of that. It is likely that a quick sale is in the offing for him, and you will probably get your price if you persist.

Do not hesitate to write to dealers in other localities if you think you have something to sell of special interest to them. A local dealer not trading in the item may be unable as well as unwilling to pay a fair price, having perhaps to sell it to another dealer to realize any profit.

Dealers travel and will call on you if your wares seem of interest. Photographs and facsimiles of rubbings serve well in these situations. Books, autographs, and other material safe for mailing can be sent first-class-registered mail to the dealer who can reply with an offer by mail or telephone.

No scientist peering through his microscope is more exacting in that scrutiny than a dealer examining a potential purchase. It is educational to watch those in the trade during the presale exhibition of an auction. With or without the aid of spectacles, a jeweler's loupe, or magnifying glass, you may be sure that few imperfections, repairs, or restorations go unnoticed by observant eyes.

Since they are establishing the value and thus the price to be bid, this is understandable and in fact should be emulated by all. However, when you call in or call on a dealer for the purpose of selling your property, you must be prepared for a similarly thorough third degree of your wares.

Beware, however, of the dealer who finds serious flaws and then still negotiates to buy. By putting you on the defensive, implying or saying that your wares are undesirable, you are made to feel that you are lucky to get anything at all for them.

If you find the price offered too low and the criticism of the merchandise disproportionately great, express your conviction that a reversal would be in order and try another dealer or a different type of market outlet for a better price.

"Downgrading" is a technique developed to discourage you from insisting on a fair price. Such an instance would be a lithograph which appeared in a limited edition of 150. When you bought it with the number 147/150, you observed that it was a very high number and almost the last of the run. The dealer no doubt told you that it made no difference to its value and that obviously the print was a splendid and outstanding example.

When you decide to sell it, you may find that although the dealer (possibly the same one) will agree with you that the first number is unimportant, he will regretfully advise you that the fact it is so high makes it harder for him to sell and "therefore . . ."

Now is the time for you to hold fast, because in fact he either wants to buy it or doesn't, and the high number has become an excuse to downgrade it and get it from you for less.

Coins bought as mint have been graded to uncirculated when offered for resale. Silver, sold for its fine patina, the result of minute signs of wear, is often downgraded as scratched. If you think your possessions are unfairly judged, resist and try another outlet.

The list of reasons why a dealer does not want to pay the price you ask is very long. "Not the right color . . . too small . . . too large . . . out of fashion . . . funny signature . . . poor condition . . . repaired . . ." A good rule is to get another opinion rather than to accept the first criticism and a lower price than you expected.

Sometimes a dealer just doesn't want to say he isn't buying simply because he has too much money tied up in stock, possibly has similar items, or is overstocked on other wares. Don't be discouraged, try another.

Even when the dealer has sold you the item with fulsome praise in much detail, he will examine it suspiciously when asked to buy it back. One reason, the valid one, is to observe that it hasn't been broken, bent, torn, or repaired. An oriental rug that has lasted a hundred years may be damaged in a day. A very well-known and reputable dealer in silver tells of buying back a pair of antique candlesticks and discovering that only one was the original of the pair he had sold; the other was a copy.

Such things may happen and it is natural that dealers are wary in the repurchase of items. However, be sure that the dealer is not trying to avoid buying back something he overpraised and overpriced when it was sold to you.

It is not unusual for a dealer who refuses to buy from a private seller to offer to take the same goods on consignment.

This means that they will be left in the shop at an agreed on price, in the hope that they will be sold. Payment is to be made after the sale.

Generally speaking, this is not advantageous for the seller. The dealer's lack of investment in the item means there is less incentive to sell it in comparison with regular stock which has been paid for. When interest is expressed by a customer, dealers often say that the items are on consignment, leading to offers of lower prices than asked.

Although a commission of 20 per cent is considered ample on consigned goods, the owner has no way of knowing that more hasn't been taken. When the offer to buy for less is transmitted, the owner can't tell if the dealer is sharing fairly. After the merchandise has been on consignment for a while, the tendency is to accept a low price, out of discouragement.

If you ever do leave items on consignment, be sure to get a written memorandum describing the item, noting responsibility for breakage or loss, the cost price to the dealer, and a date limiting the period it is to be held for sale. If the merchandise is of considerable value, it might be best to have the document attested by a notary public.

"Sell in haste and repent at leisure" is the sad refrain following many a selling transaction. Newly bereaved widows have hastily accepted offers they should have postponed considering. The news of the death of a famous musician had barely been announced before his widow received cabled offers for his cello, a notable instrument. In this case, outraged sensitivity on the part of the family dictated that when the instrument would eventually be sold, it would not be to the impatient authors of the premature offers.

Pressure to conclude transactions hastily is not a tactic of dealers known for integrity. When it is observed, it is a signal you may be doing business with the wrong party. You might consider starting over again with someone else.

~~~~~~

Chapter 10

VERY PRIVATE ENTERPRISE

Bypassing the dealer, to buy directly from the private seller, is advocated by collectors whose experience in buying more cheaply in this fashion has been good. Others find that there are drawbacks which exceed the advantages.

The principal advantage, to avoid contributing to the profits which make for high prices, presumes that the private collector is a skillful buyer and would pay a price lower than whatever retail a dealer would charge for a given item. That depends on many circumstances and cannot be taken for granted.

Private buying is an aspect of collecting with special facets. Various types of collectors' clubs encourage it by lower advertising rates in their publications and through special meetings, fairs, and conventions, organized for the purpose of in-group transactions.

National stamp-collector organizations have developed an admirable standard procedure called a sales circuit. The priced stamps belonging to members wishing to sell are entered in booklets which circulate among members in rotation.

As members wishing to buy receive the books, they remove the stamps they want, mail the price to the organization, and send the books with the remaining stamps to the next person on the list. After the original owner of the stamp receives his share of the money, the club commission is used to defray the cost of operation, and any surplus goes into the treasury.

New members of any sort of collecting club are warned of one unsavory aspect of club transactions. Dealer-collectors and others on the fringe of the trade may join clubs, pretending to be private collectors. In this guise, they trade with new members, taking advantage of their inexperience to buy, sell, or barter unfairly.

Predictably, in certain so-called collectors' clubs, which are really dealer organized and dominated, there is a tendency to downgrade co-operative buying and selling activity. On the other hand, straightforward dealers often encourage it. They find it relieves them of antagonizing customers by refusal, when the latter offer to sell them unattractive or unprofitable goods. Some antiques dealers will sometimes encourage customers to organize tag or garage sales and even help them price the merchandise. This assures the dealer of good will, and nothing is lost in the way of profitable business by dealers who carry better-quality antiques.

Among problem situations, which some have experienced in private buying, are included unrealistically high prices asked, questionable legal ownership or right to sell, stolen goods, wrong attributions, outright fakes, poor restoration and repair, and, finally, lack of recourse. Although not every dealer is above reproach or will return money to dissatisfied customers, the mere fact of dealing with an established place of business gives confidence to many buyers.

In a classic swindle, individual buyers have been set up for what is supposed to be a genuine private sale, but is actually a sales trap. Such a one is a bogus "house sale" for which one or several dealers will arrange to stock a house or apartment with merchandise, then advertise, "moving out of town, must sell homefurnishings and antiques." Furs and jewelry supposedly offered by private individuals are also advertised by retail or wholesale dealers of dishonest leanings under a similar setup.

Obviously, experienced dealers would not be taken in by such tactics, nor would alert and sophisticated private collectors. It has been noted that such ads sometimes include the phrase, "no dealers," creating amusement in the trade. Dealers claim that this usually indicates that dealers have refused to buy, or that the price wanted is absurdly high, or something is being sold that has flaws a dealer would spot. In any case, dealers need only claim to be private persons and could buy if they wished. Old-time European dealers were noted for taking the refusal to allow them in as a challenge, disguising themselves, if necessary, to pass as strangers in a town where they would be known and recognized.

Having observed that there are several approaches to the question of buying directly, it is worth noting the situation of the private person, who, after exploring the angles of selling through dealers, decides to explore the possibilities of becoming an individual direct selling agent, on his or her own behalf.

The buyer's age-old dream of eliminating the middleman prevails in reverse, as the private seller of antiques, art, and collectibles considers the possibilities of reaching the ultimate buyer directly.

All the various channels for such a private "private enterprise" require an outlay of time and energy and, in some cases, even a little money. All of them have certain problems which we shall try to anticipate and thus bypass. They do have advantages which appeal to certain individuals and meet certain types of situations.

Getting the best and highest purchase price and keeping it all is the ideal goal. Handling the transaction from start to finish gives the trader-collector an opportunity to learn more about a special field and to make further contacts. For adventuresome souls it offers a challenge; or it may be the only system by which to dispose of everything you wish to sell, since dealers and auctioneers and sometimes even charities may not be interested in all you have, at any price, or under any conditions.

Before extending your horizon to farther markets, look for a buyer among your friends and acquaintances. Perhaps the very objects you want to sell have been coveted as well as admired within your own circle.

Unless there is some need for privacy in the matter, when you announce your intention to sell, ask your friends to mention it to others. Business contacts and tradespeople are also likely prospects.

If a friend is interested in buying, describe how you identified the item, established the value, and arrived at the retail list price. Indicate price guides, price tags, or auction prices as your source for the latter.

Candidly explain how much you could expect to get from a dealer, or at auction less the commission, then give your friend a slightly lower price which includes a personal discount. The time, trouble, and possible expense you save by selling directly warrants it, even from a business viewpoint. If your friend buys, ask to be paid at once, or make detailed arrangements for payment in writing. The delicate line between business and friendship seldom can sustain dunning for debt. If you are lucky, you will have made a sale and *kept* a friend.

Flea markets provide another kind of direct selling effort. These informal markets, which are organized for both private and professional traders at rental fees that start as low as $5.00, have been springing up like mushrooms after rain.

Whether in the city, suburbs, or country the flea market is largely a weekend and holiday event. Some are sporadic, others scheduled regularly, after the pattern of their European prototypes. Usually an organization or private entrepreneur rents or arranges for a suitable area and advertises the event. Some are free to the public; some charge an entrance fee.

The seller may show from a car or station wagon, or set up tables, screens, boards, or whatever seems feasible for display. Only ingenuity limits variety and style of presentation.

The reputation and style of a flea market depend on its sponsors and those who frequent it. Some emphasize arts and crafts; others are limited to antiques; still others are generalized second-hand and junk markets. Many are combinations of all of these.

If you have more material than you care to or can carry to such a market, it is advisable to bring a rounded sample selection of what you want to sell. An interested buyer will ask about this, and you can exchange names and addresses for future contact and transactions.

Price plainly. Be prepared to give a discount for special reasons. Watch your merchandise carefully since light fingers sometimes make salables into disappearables.

The fee for a stall or booth or room space at almost any established antiques, coin, stamp, or similar show is quite steep, even without considering transportation and extras. It takes a going business to sustain these expenses, and many experienced dealers complain that they sometimes do not make any money at a show. However, the contact with customers, opportunity to buy, and good will generated may in the long run be worth while, and most return hopefully to the next show or exhibition. For the one-time effort of a private seller, the low-cost flea market is feasible, but the professional show is off-limits as too costly, even if the amateur were accepted by the management, a doubtful possibility.

Decorators and interior designers are potential customers if you have art, art objects, or fine homefurnishings to sell. Although they can, and do, buy these wares from showrooms, galleries, and dealers at discounts, these discounts are within fixed limits, and usually the client knows what they are, so the fee is controlled. Almost all decorators are interested in occasional opportunities to buy decorative wares at lower prices than they can buy through dealers. If they buy for their own accounts and stock these things until a client can use them, they are entitled to the larger profit.

Advertise suitable material for decorators in their journals, and post notices on bulletin boards of decorators' societies. Send lists of your items to their offices.

Another way to sell through decorators was suggested by a lady who refurnishes often and whose redecorating plans, as submitted by her interior designer, usually include getting rid of decorative material. This client, who once had to quickly and disadvantageously dispose of some fine furnishings and antiques to make room for her new decorative scheme, since has always asked her decorator to take over the resale operation. As a commission fee, she pays him one third of what he gets for her. She is a good, constant, profitable client, so it may not work for all as well as it does for her.

Selling directly to collectors has drawbacks for the poor bargainer. Some collectors are such shrewd buyers that even dealers count their fingers after shaking hands with them. If you don't know the value of what you are selling, don't try to cope with private collectors in the hope of getting fair treatment.

On the other hand, there are collectors who buy only through dealers whom they trust. Even when buying at auction, they prefer to pay a dealer commission for advice, consultation, and bidding, in order to have the assurance that the purchase is a sound one. Other collectors have enough faith in their own judgment to assume the risk of buying unadvised. These latter are always interested in buying privately. In these dealings, proofs of ownership, authenticity, pedigree, and value will help you get your price more readily.

While many large corporations are well known for their art collections, the field of corporate collecting includes companies of all sizes, with many interests besides those of fine art. Here is another market for the private seller.

Traveling collections of photographs, graphics, painting, and sculpture have achieved the widest publicity. But these expressions of art also adorn corporate halls and walls. Some of this is purely decorative; some seriously surveying a field of art. Much of it is in executive offices and board rooms, more telling than the thickness of the carpet in terms of standing and power.

The commercial and industrial background of a company may dictate its form of collecting. A large soup company has a collection of tureens. Banks own coin and paper money collections as well as mechanical and toy banks. Silver manufacturers have antique silver collections; and one of the finest glass collections in the world, the Corning Museum of Glass, belongs to the Corning Glass Works in Corning, New York.

If you want to sell some item of interest to a corporation, perhaps even its own old or antique products, containers or advertisements, write to the company and ask for its policy in reference to buying such materials. Since some companies sponsor collections, with no relation to their products, you might check into what they do collect.

It can be more profitable to give than to sell your possessions, if the recipient is a tax-deductible beneficiary. This form of private enterprise, encouraged by the federal government, solves many a problem for collectors and private individuals wishing to dispose of antiques, art, or collectibles.

Not only museums but religious, educational, charitable, scientific, and literary organizations are included as qualified recipients. By shopping in reverse, the donor who would prefer the deduction to cash will try to match the beneficiary to the gift.

Compared to the more arduous task of finding a buyer, finding a taker has considerable appeal. As a rule, letters inquiring whether institutions would be interested in gifts bring replies by return mail. For material too modest for a great museum, small museums will prove hospitable. If no strings are attached as to right of resale, no problems as to beneficiaries will arise either. Questions relating to the value of the gift, hence the amount of the tax deduction, can be negotiated with the recipient, the Internal Revenue Service concurring, as we shall see later.

Thrift shops and charity rummage sales also offer tax-deductible arrangements of advantage when possessions are slated for disposal. Some charities employ appraisers who fill out the amount at "fair market value" of the objects donated. For others, the donor may fill in the figure, to be calculated in the same manner, as specified by the Internal Revenue Service. Since the original cost of the item is not a consideration, but rather its value at the time of the gift, antiques, art, and collectibles are especially rewarding for both the giver and the recipient cause. An object that cost the donor very little may with inflation, along with other factors that have enhanced the value, bring much more monetary satisfaction as a tax-deductible gift than in any other form of disposal.

The generosity of thrift shops and charities in these matters is conditioned by competition among them for the merchandise, so the donation is more often overvalued than the opposite. However, not all who price the merchandise are experienced appraisers, and sometimes they do not spot the truly valuable material, so that neither the charity nor the donor profits. Sometimes the picker and dealer are the beneficiaries of the greatest amount. If there is any doubt about the value of a possibly important gift, it is advisable to check with an outside opinion.

The ritual of the tag or garage sale is characteristic of the American cycle of obsolescence. After a number of years, most families seem to accumulate a quantity of still useful, but undesired, possessions in addition to a cache of valuable heirlooms, gifts, and decorations that are more of a burden than a treasure.

As they multiply and engage valuable space, some enterprising member eventually decides that a housecleaning is in order. Moving day is another occasion for such a house sale, but the project may come about in these other ways as well:

If you are offered too little for the possessions you want to sell, and think you could get more by selling them yourself . . .

If an antiques, book, or some-other-specialist dealer, whose customer you are, can't buy your material, but suggests helping you put together a tag, garage or house sale . . .

If no one wants to be your middleman, and you have a houseful for disposal. . . .

Detailed manuals on how to run private second-hand sales have been published and may aid those who are unacquainted with the methods employed by successful householders. Most bona fide sales of this kind are successful, bringing in several hundred dollars over a weekend if well advertised and well run.

Before undertaking a garage sale, check with local regulations. Laws limit advertising, the number of sales you can hold in a given period, and set requirements for licenses and proof of sales tax payments. This has been the backlash of success.

In addition to the proliferating bona fide garage sale, enterprising operators have developed a technique which they bring to commercially organized second-hand sales, falsely presented as private sales, under the name of garage, tag, lawn, barn, rummage, and estate sale.

Some antiques and second-hand dealers, together with sellers of other collectibles, noting the vast number of such sales and reckoning the volume in millions of dollars, which they consider are siphoned from their established businesses, have made a concerted drive to hinder garage-type sales by pushing local ordinances to restrict them.

However, the garage sale is established as an American institution and will hardly disappear, even if it is somewhat restricted.

Local laws permitting, advertise in the local newspaper. Post signs in your supermart, laundromat, club, church, office, public library, and on any bulletin board you can find. If possible, organize such a sale with one or more neighbors, then there is always someone to watch the store, watch the customers, sell the goods, and take the money.

Before you price your wares, check flea markets, second-hand stores, antique shops, or other sources of comparable items, then set your price at just a bit less.

It is inadvisable to include any items if you aren't sure of their value. Delegate a family member to list and check on old phonograph records, books, magazines, comics, bottles, and similar promising new collectibles.

Call it trade, exchange, barter, or swap, this most primitive of all private-enterprise systems has its advantages and defects. There are many satisfied veterans of the trade-exchange experience, but many others shun it, firmly convinced that they have always had the worst of any bargain of this kind. Those who are successful have the instincts of an old-fashioned horse trader. They know how to glamorize their possessions so the other party avidly desires them. The wily trader keeps cool and assesses values coldly.

The *cause célèbre* at the Metropolitan Museum of Art, during the Hoving administration, in which it appeared to many experts that great art was exchanged for lesser art and valuable pieces replaced by less valuable ones, to the museum's loss, indicates that experienced professionals in the art world may be no better at the complexities of trading with canny dealers than the average layman.

There is never any reason for a dealer to make a truly even exchange, nor any kind but that in which your item is taken at a wholesale price, and you get his at regular retail or higher. The dealer is in the transaction only to make a profit; you want to make an exchange for what you think is preferable material. The fact is, he really doesn't need your property, but you think you need his.

You are at a better advantage trading with another private person, except if the other party is an experienced trader and you are an amateur. Try to make the best deal as objectively as possible. It is harder to press for a fair exchange when you are overanxious to have the other's item and are dissatisfied with your own. Too often, the one who wants to dispose of an item sees it as something which has lost its bloom and mentally discounts it as worth less, if not worthless.

Veteran collectors advise selling at the best possible price and buying in the free market in a separate transaction. On the other hand, if you have something you really don't want and nobody will buy from you, you can always try to exchange it for something that is more appealing or useful.

^^

Chapter 11

AUCTION ACQUISITION

The auction sale is in a very old tradition. The idea of selling to the highest bidder goes back many thousands of years. It has been traced to the dispersal of the spoils of war to the highest bidder on the battlefield and was already highly developed by the time it flourished in ancient Rome. The classic description of the Emperor Caligula as auctioneer of the furnishings of his own palace, practically decreeing what his subjects should bid, has probably made auctioneers envious from that day to this.

Nowadays such duress is permissible only at charity auctions; otherwise auctioneers must employ the tricks of their craft to cajole bids. They have many, all designed to bring good prices for the lots they cry. However, some are legitimate techniques, while others range from shady to outright fraudulent. The buyer at auction must recognize, distinguish between them, and cope, in order to enjoy the advantages of buying by bidding.

Never, in all its history, has the auction been more popular than today. Autographs, antiques, art, books, coins, stamps, oriental rugs, homefurnishings, and jewelry auctions are frequent events in metropolitan centers. In the country, farm, household, barn, estate, general, and specialized antiques auctions are plentiful, with additional dealers' and wholesalers' "truck auctions," in which merchandise from the city often makes a round trip in a single day.

Having partially replaced movies and picnics as a source of diversion, and presently gaining on spectator sports as a form of recreation, auction sales are considered free and cheap entertainment by increasing numbers of people, many under thirty, who thrill to the excitement of the descending gavel. "Let's see what's doing at the auction" sets off numerous, aimless excursions that often end in determined bidding and buying.

Crowds of thousands at tent and outdoor auctions generate their own festive auction fever, and as commercial success begets growth, this type of operation is becoming an important sales outlet in direct competition with retail stores. Often auction sales will bring higher prices for the identical items that are plainly tagged in stores, which lack the dramatic showmanship and carnival atmosphere of an auction to generate demand.

Masses of merchandise, some antique, some in the category of modern collectibles (some merely second hand), much in the way of reproductions (falsely termed antique), and some new goods (especially chosen for flashy appearance), make up the "lots" of the professional merchant-auctioneers whose need for merchandise to sell in volume at regular intervals makes them less than discriminating.

In every field there are auctioneers of questionable standing, known by reputation for the extent to which they stray from acceptable ethical practices. In those regions where every auctioneer must have a license to conduct a sale, they too have licenses, so "licensed auctioneer" is not a phrase that impresses insiders. Auctioneering is a business of selling for commission to the highest bidder. With every deviation from neutrality on the part of the auctioneer, either the buyer or owner of the goods stands to lose. At its best, integrity is established by the objectivity with which a sale is conducted by an auctioneer who is impartially disposed to both parties.

Certain auctions are out-and-out swindles, where nothing is ever offered that is not covered by a "shill" or house employee who bids only to push up the price against private bidders, all merchandise having been especially purchased to offer at such phony sales. These are often found in resorts, although there are other permanent and gypsy auctioneers who work in the same manner. No catalogues are offered for this, the lowest level of the auction business. The auctioneers are more like side-show pitchmen, strong on entertainment and florid descriptions. Experienced observers, recognizing such auctions, find it amazing that a sufficient turnover of sheep continues to make fleecing them a full-time profitable occupation. Unconscionable prices are the goal, as machine-woven carpets are sold as rare hand-woven orientals, gimcrack pottery as choice porcelain, and cheap, showy jewelry passed off as rare and precious.

There are many gradations of auction operations, from cheap side shows to elegant and quality establishments where bona fide sales of choice and museum-quality lots are commonplace events, although they are not above having public relations departments to promote them.

The majority of established auctions are somewhere in the middle. Although not beyond reproach, they are not beyond the pale of respectability either. The cynicism of insiders is expressed by their efforts to start at least one step ahead of the game, by knowing the source of the merchandise to be auctioned and of circumstances pertinent to its value. Auctioneers publicize the ownership of the lots they offer whenever that information will add luster to the sale, but in many cases it does not, and then they fudge the facts or speciously misinform.

When auctioneers arrange with importers to sell regular stock on a split-profit basis, when professional restorers offer the results of a year's "improvements," even neophytes would avoid bidding if they knew the truth.

"Various owners" and "other owners" may provide some anonymity, but gossip and the grapevine play their parts in providing information regarding the owners of the lots to be auctioned. Sometimes a dealer will recognize items by virtue of having originally sold them, or a generous tip to an auction employee will clarify a question of ownership. For important sales, records as well as memory are consulted. Who restored a piece, and how well, may become an important factor. What an item sold for in a previous transaction and rumors about its provenance may concern another prospective bidder.

Having verified in advance that certain lots in the sale aren't really from a famous expert's collection, or that the best part of it was withheld, or that a much-publicized piece has been more than half-restored, the astute insider examines the lots, catalogue in hand, with a proper poker face.

Prudent buyers visit the public exhibition as well in advance of the sale as expedient, in case of need to research or check, rather than wait for the last minute to view. The three rules for buying successfully at auction have been cited as "inspect, inspect, and inspect." Veteran bidders deliberately examine every aspect of interesting lots, taking detailed notes in the catalogue. They never seem to be looking *at* an object, but for something *about* it. Attendants will open locked cases or otherwise expedite the handling of fragile or precious items. Regulars tip them from time to time for these and for other courtesies.

Though estimated prices expected are printed in some auction catalogues, or will be furnished on request, insiders do not put too much stock in them, preferring to make their own decisions as to market values, investment potential, and their own intended bids.

Carrying magnifying glass, jeweler's loupe, tape-measure, notebook, a small magnet to spot metal repairs and fake bronzes, the well-equipped bidder is ready for anything and often gets it. Buyers who are insecure, or who prefer confirmation, may at this point confer with a trusted dealer, and having decided to buy, ask him to bid at an agreed upon price, for an agreed upon commission, usually 10 per cent of the winning bid.

Most conditions of sale, as posted or read in the salesroom or shown in the catalogue, include arrangements for payment, deadline for removal of purchases, methods of running the sale, and similar notice of responsibilities of buyer and auctioneer. None of these ever comes as a surprise to an experienced auction buyer, who makes it a point to know the terms of each auction sale, reading the fine print, most of which protects the auctioneer.

For untold years, it was always stipulated that neither auctioneer or consignor assumed any risk in relation to condition or authenticity of any lot. However, precedent has been created by Sotheby Parke Bernet in its Madison Avenue gallery, with a five-year guarantee of authenticity of the authorship of certain lots of art and other objects, as described in bold type in its catalogues. Despite certain exclusions for findings that may be developed from yet unknown scientific techniques, and limitations on works created before 1870, this is an important step advancing the prestige of this auction house as a market for antiques, art, and other collectibles.

One subject not mentioned in any conditions of sale is the touchy one, never acknowledged by an auction firm, but very much in the insider's calculations, of the "ring." Unlike the Emperor's clothing, it is there, but everyone pretends not to see it.

Although the seller at an auction in which a ring is involved may have more at stake than the buyer, the latter also comes within its orbit. Having decided that it is better business to bid as a unit, than competitively against one another at public auction, a group of dealers will form a ring for that purpose. The members decide on the top price to be paid by the ring, and one member is appointed as bidder. It may be a permanent group, or one acting together only for a specific sale. If they secure the item within the price, as planned, a second, private auction is held. Now each dealer bids individually and the winner pays the treasurer, splitting the difference between the public and private sale price among the members of the group. The real loser is the seller. The auctioneer's commission is less than it might otherwise be, but the ring is countenanced in every auction house in the world, simply because there doesn't seem to be any way to stop it.

Classic protection for the seller is the reserve price, the lowest price the seller will accept. At one time, some first-rate auction houses would not accept a reserve price, claiming that this proved they were impartial. Owners who knew that the ring could "steal" their property would have to go to the trouble of themselves bidding to the lowest acceptable price, or having someone do it for them. Eventually, most auction firms accepted a reasonable reserve price. If a lot does not fetch this price, it is returned to the owner at a fee lower than the regular commission would be, were it sold.

The ring doesn't win every lot it marks as a target, and doesn't expect to. With few exceptions, dealers have no interest in paying prices that do not allow for a satisfactory profit, and if another buyer bids past that price, the ring bidder will stop. On occasion, the ring pays even more than an item is worth, in order to discourage further forays against it. Usually, in this situation, the effort is to make the opposition overbid and end up with the lot. This does not always work, and the ring may become the winning bidder at an inflated price. In that case, the private sale bidding may be less than the price paid. An occasional loss comes to little enough when it is shared and considered a business expense.

An individual dealer may also decide to teach one of his customers a lesson, bidding an item up to a ridiculous price to keep the customer from buying elsewhere than the dealer's shop in the future. In such cases, the dealer will try to preserve anonymity.

A well-known English dealer who is opposed to the ring system says that successful bidders against the ring have complained that mysterious scratches, dents, tears, or breaks have appeared on the lots won away from the ring. On the other hand, some collectors tell of bidding against the ring and still getting bargains. Still another point of view is expressed by collectors who prefer to ask one of the principal dealers, with whom they trade, to make their auction purchases for them. They pay 10 per cent of the price for this service and find it a bargain. Not only will the dealer advise as to the desirability of the lot, but if a member of the ring, he may gain exemption for the item from group bidding.

Other presale business on insiders' agendas may be concerned with a system of signaling the auctioneer. Certain collectors and dealers are almost eccentric in their anxiety to buy in perfect secrecy. They arrange with the auctioneer for signals of varying complexity to indicate their intentions. This is usually in the conviction that their bids will cause competition to bid even higher, if the source is recognized. They touch their noses, ears, or buttonholes, twist their pencils or catalogues, happily incognito.

On the day of the auction sale, lots are seldom available for last-minute viewing. Final decisions as to price limits on lots of interest having been duly made and noted in advance, buyers can concentrate on choosing a vantage point. Many prefer to sit toward the back of the salesroom, wishing to observe the action. In addition to trying to spot secret signals, note who is bidding for the ring, and observe the general bidding, suspicious souls check on the auctioneer who may take bids where there are none, and see if any "shills" are working for the house.

Others, aware of the rule that the bidder nearest the auctioneer is the winner in case of a tie, prefer to be as close as possible. Still others choose the area where the lots will be shown during the bidding. Coin, stamps, and jewelry items are among those so small that the last minute glance is meaningless. Some auction veterans prefer not to be too close to the item being bid on lest it encourage auction fever.

This auction fever, the runaway urge to possess at any price, is often responsible for wild and costly bidding that throws the averages and price guides out of line. It refers to what seems to be an uncontrolled compulsion on the part of bidders to top the bid before. Sometimes it is merely based on the fact that each thinks it must be worth having if the other wants it. This is the ideal situation for the auctioneer who develops the competition should it wane. Insiders are not troubled by auction fever. They don't pay $200 for an item they had previously noted to be worth $40 at best. Usually the irrational contest is the result of a clash of wills between two individuals who are personal rivals, or when a rare item is wanted by several collectors to fill in a series. Dealers only get involved when they are bidding at the behest of clients, or want to create a run on something which will make their own stocks more valuable. That isn't auction fever.

Cajolery, humor, competitive envy, and panic at the loss of a prize are among the battery of inducements to bid that are employed by skillful auctioneers. Professionals are impervious to them all, coolly keeping within the limits set by their presale decision.

Artful bidders often let the action get started without them, moving in to bid while the price is still well below their intended top, hoping it will slacken to a close. They do not jump in at an early stage to activate the bidding. They usually stay with the auctioneer's normal rise, seldom making extra jumps except to impose a change of pace to shake out the competition, a delicate maneuver.

The ploy of the candid auctioneer, who points out, "You are bidding against yourself, sir," is expressed when there is an authentic underbidder. When an auctioneer purposefully has you bidding against yourself, he never tells you. Mail and telephone bids, as well as presale bids left with the auction firm, are ethically executed by ethical auctioneers, but may be manipulated by those less trustworthy. Book, coin, stamp, and autograph auctions are often conducted largely by mail bids;

those in the field learn which firms conduct their sales most ethically. Recommendation and experience are required before important purchases are made in absentia.

Headlines proclaim new auction highs as they occur in inflationary and booming markets for many collectibles. Museum directors spend huge sums that literally belong to no *one*, certainly not to the bidders. International industrialists, whose billions make their hundred-thousand and million-dollar bids seem casual figures, push prices to astronomical heights. Even on more pedestrian levels, high prices spearhead interest in new areas hitherto unexplored and presage upward movement in old, as dealers and collectors accept auction prices as signals for ascending market directions.

This also works in reverse, as low winning bids at important sales deflate price structures. Every auction is a gamble, and dealers and collectors observe the action for its effect on their values, adding tension to the scene. Astute traders are aware that although the auction sale is an exciting stage, presenting dramatic roles to certain lots and their buyers, this doesn't always carry over. What seems glamorous with a lot number attached, in the spotlight, under split-second competitive bidding, may become just another slow-selling item in the shop.

On the whole, new highs and dramatic situations aside, dealers and collectors buy carefully at auction. They buy there because that is where merchandise is available, and on the average, sells for somewhat less than retail, if somewhat more than wholesale. However, it is not the rule, but the exception, that brings the bidders back for the hoped-for bonanza bargain that seldom but sometimes occurs.

Even before the auction is over, veteran auction goers pick up their goods as soon as possible. This lessens the possibility of error or breakage. Lots left after a stipulated period are warehoused, and according to conditions of sale, assessed with special charges. At certain types of large sales, deposits and bidding numbers safeguard both the auctioneer and the underbidder who might have won the prize.

Rueful but anxious underbidders have been known to waylay the winner, offering a quick profit. If the figure offered approaches the price a dealer had intended to ask, the transaction may be quickly completed. Collectors usually clutch the treasure more closely as they refuse, enjoying the sensation of victory.

There are more, but the ten most important commandments for buying at auction are as follows:

Never bid on uninspected items, no matter how alluring they seem in that spotlight.

Repairs always cost more than you expect, so don't scant them in reckoning the highest price you can pay.

Never change your mind about the price you decided to pay when you inspected the item. Keep your notes handy, so you can refer to them during the sale.

Be sure you know the multiples in which you are bidding. Is it per pair or per piece? Per piece or per dozen? This can hurt if you get it wrong.

Note conditions of sale, including terms of payment and whether checks are accepted.

If you must give a deposit before obtaining a bidding number, get a receipt. Secure clear receipts for all payments.

Note the exact amount of your winning bid. Keep control of your bidding number at all times.

Do not take it for granted that the opening price asked is the reserve price. Some auctioneers accept more, others less, to open bidding.

If you change the size of the increment, signal clearly. Don't try to be a big shot at auction, it makes you look like a big spender and that's what you are trying to avoid.

If you know that you have been taken advantage of because you were foolish or greedy, grin and bear it. If you have been cheated by having prices changed or lots switched, threaten, scream, and carry on. It might help.

ww

AUCTION DISPERSAL

Although the buyer wants to pay as little as possible and the seller to get as much as possible, a view of the auction from the seller's angle is more complex than a mere reversal of roles. The private seller has a unique set of problems, casting auction advantages and disadvantages in a special light.

On the positive side, an auction attracts customers with money to spend, and the sale will be for cash. The time lapse between the arrangement and the sale might be a few months; often it is less. If there is a catalogue, the mailing list may go beyond any local scene to a world market. Special circumstances or auction fever may drive the price well beyond its market value, as hitherto expressed. The risk of too low a final bid can be hedged by a reserve price.

These, in brief, are the advantages of an auction and apply generally to simple country auctions, estate sales, stamp, book, or coin auctions, or an international art sale with closed-circuit-TV bidding hooked on to overseas telephone cables.

Although a cat may look at a queen, and the person of modest means is welcome to offer items to a Bond Street or Madison Avenue auction firm, things have a way of being sorted out. Some important houses have organized subsidiary showrooms for lesser lots; they also recommend regional auctioneers if they deem the situation to be appropriate. On the other hand, and possibly in return, local auctioneers will steer important sales to their metropolitan contacts.

While the huge sums fetched at auction achieve headline prominence, even such a great and glamorous international auction firm as Sotheby Parke Bernet reports a majority of unit sales in its Madison Avenue gallery at under $500. Both its more modest Eighty-fourth Street New York branch and its Los Angeles salesrooms sell a majority of lots well under this figure.

An auction firm contracts with an owner to sell certain property to the highest bidder for a percentage of the price fetched as commission. This percentage usually runs from 15 to 25 per cent, depending on the firm and the amounts involved. If great sums are in question, as for masterpiece paintings, or multimillion-dollar estates, it is understood that better terms can be arranged.

When auction firms compete for sales in the million-dollar category, they actually bid against each other, by offering the estate or owner more advantageous terms. If a sale is expected to bring millions of dollars, the usual commission may be shaved to very low unpublicized percentages.

The procedures which initiate any auction transaction start when an appointment is made with a representative of a large auction firm, or the auctioneer himself, if it is a smaller one.

Depending on whether the items to be sold are small and portable or large and bulky, the meeting will take place in the auctioneer's offices, the vault or warehouse, or wherever the goods may be seen, but most usually on the seller's premises.

The auctioneer, on agreeing to sell the goods, will give an opinion as to the prices they are expected to fetch.

If he doubts that his clientele is the best possible market (or that the commission earned will be worth his while), he may suggest another auctioneer, a suitable dealer, or some other means of disposal, such as a house sale, with marked prices.

Presuming that he does agree to auction your property, you can usually rely on an experienced auctioneer to closely estimate the prices you can expect. You do risk an overanxious auctioneer making too high an estimate if business has been poor or if the auctioneer wants to fill in a quiet period. Reliable auctioneers pride themselves on the closeness with which they hit the mark in these estimates.

Having decided on the reserve price, the terms and commissions must be settled. A number of questions arise to be answered.

Will the percentage of commission be figured on each lot or the gross?

What is the insurance cost? Who pays it?

Are delivery charges involved? How much? Who pays?

When will the sale take place?

Will there be a catalogue? Illustrated?

Who pays for the photographs? What will they cost?

What is the size of the mailing list?

Which auctioneer will sell your goods? Is he experienced?

Need any items be repaired or cleaned? What is the charge?

What other goods or collections will be auctioned with yours?

How will the sale be publicized? Who pays for advertising?

What is the duration of the presale exhibition?

Is there provision for locking small items in cases?

Who will be in attendance to answer questions, show lots, and give price estimates to viewers?

All of this is the auctioneer's responsibility to arrange, and he knows better than you how to achieve a successful sale. However, unless all these factors are clear to you, you may be unpleasantly surprised by the outcome.

Of all the arrangements and decisions to be made between the consignor and the auctioneer, the most important is the agreement on the reserve price. This is the base below which the item cannot be sold. It is the seller's best and only protection against the ring, and the only safety net for getting a fair price. If the auctioneer insists that the sale be unrestricted, without a reserve, you are headed for trouble, should you go ahead on that basis.

The reserve price is the lowest price you will accept as a bid. If you set this price, the auctioneer agrees to let you buy back or "buy in" your own possession. If the bidding does not reach your price, the item will be returned to you, as noted before, for a fee less than the commission would have been on a sale. It has usually been quoted in the neighborhood of 8 to 10 per cent.

You should be aware, that you, as a private seller, are a very important but individually small part of the auctioneer's business. Even though there are many private sellers, they are seldom regular clients in the same way as are dealers, who constantly buy and sell at auction. It is important to insure that your interests are not sacrificed for the benefit of regular clients of the auction, with whom the auctioneer might want to maintain a good relationship at your expense. With a reserve, or upset price, your interests have at least minimum protection.

An attempt to further consolidate the position of auction over dealer, guaranteeing a price in advance of the auction, was made by Sotheby Parke Bernet when it broke new ground, guaranteeing an agreed price to the owners of important estates and works of art, for a fee of 7½ per cent of the guaranteed figure. This would be added to the regular commission, up to the prearranged amount. Thus, even if the property did not sell for that sum, the owner would be assured of receiving no less than the gross guaranteed amount, less applicable commission. Any proceeds in excess of the guaranteed price would require repayment of the standard commission only. Exception, single objects and large estates are eligible for this form of "insurance" which does not apply to all property accepted for auction. In effect, this makes it possible to hedge, without "buying in" at the reserve price.

Experienced old-timers tell of a specialized parasite of the auction room, who might be called an auction tout. This person would hang around the presale exhibition, and depending on who paid him, would either praise or denigrate certain lots. By pretending to be a knowledgeable critic, the tout would hint at inside information, speaking within earshot of potential buyers. Whether or not this is still practiced today would be hard to prove. Almost anyone who has attended an auction preview has observed certain individuals who loudly comment on the character and value of a lot. Insiders know that important dealers and collectors are very secretive about their buying intentions, so such a person would be suspected of something, if only pretentiousness.

Another auction trick is a staple one, often used on behalf of the seller, usually a dealer. In this case, the owner of the lot makes an arrangement with a friend or colleague to bid the price to a predetermined high figure. Then, if no one else has been persuaded to bid, the owner "buys in" his own goods for the purpose of making a new high.

Any type of collectible can be handled this way. It is often done when a dealer has a large stock of the work of an artist and wants to point to a market price authenticated by an auction catalogue. This system has been a good trend starter in the past and will undoubtedly be used again and again. Dealers throughout the world sometimes raise their prices because someone has successfully pulled off such a coup.

There are other tricks of the trade to the seller's advantage and the buyer's disadvantage. A classic is known as "salting." This kind of sale will be held in an old house, and as noted before, unscrupulous auctioneers try to give the impression that the merchandise, brought in from elsewhere, originally furnished the house.

Human nature being what it is, an auction of the property of notorious, famous, or very rich people will attract a larger crowd and bring higher prices than will the lots of ordinary folk. Therefore auctioneers publicize whatever possibilities come under the hammer. Run-of-the-mill lots are "sweetened" by mixing them with romantically ascribed items and with better-quality goods. This is fine if *your* ordinary wares are brought into better selling company, but may not be quite so fine in the reverse if *your* better goods are used to trade up somebody else's junk.

It is also wise to be aware of the rhythm of an auction sale. The less important lots go first, then there is a buildup to the more important, followed by a crescendo of the best, then a downturn of importance, which is punctuated by occasional interesting lots, to keep the audience attentive and bidding to the end.

There isn't much chance of an unwary seller's blundering into a completely phony auction, because these consist entirely of lots which have been bought by the auctioneer or confederate and assembled for the purpose of fooling the public into the belief that it is a valid sale of privately owned lots. However, there are shady sales which include some bona fide private lots along with the setups, to give the latter an aura of respectability. In these cases, the honest seller becomes an unpaid front man, hardly a desirable role.

If you have goods to sell at auction, take the following precautions:

Check the firm's reputation with collectors and dealers. Be sure you understand the terms of the transaction. Double-check the details surrounding the sale of your lots. Furnish the cataloguer with all pertinent information. Aim for a minimum of about 75 per cent of the price fetched. Try to be present at the sale of your property. SET A RESERVE PRICE.

Check the dates for auctioneers' standard sales for different specialties. Get in well before that date, so the sale can be well balanced to your advantage.

~~~~~~

Chapter 13

CREATIVE COLLECTING

Not all private buyers are victims or schlemiels, menaced and manipulated by dealers and promoters. The trade expression, "advanced collector," indicates this person has background in a well-defined field, is keen to learn more, is interested in further acquisitions, and has a degree of experience in collecting. Although not entirely free of the hindrances of being on their side of the counter, advanced collectors surmount many of them by collecting and buying defensively, avoiding snares and hazards through recognition and awareness.

Deciding what to collect, whether to opt for a well-established subject that has been thoroughly defined or one relatively unexplored, requiring research and offering greater possibilities of price appreciation, is an important step. A creative collector may spark a revival in a neglected subject, perhaps an unknown Barbizon painter, or, as some did in the 1960s, pioneer in fields hitherto disregarded, such as glass insulators or barbed-wire fence.

Before getting into series items such as coins, stamps, or any sort of limited editions, defensive-minded buyers survey the possibilities in terms of the mathematical odds for appreciation, as well as acquisition. Sniffing out trends and avant-garde movements occupies investment-minded collectors. Others, unafraid of already high-priced and popular materials, prefer the security of involvement in already established fields.

Having chosen a specialty, the clever collector next defines the scope, direction, and meaning of the enterprise. Accident, sentiment, or personal style notwithstanding, interesting collections are planned with certain criteria in mind. What will distinguish this from other collections in the field? What will it illustrate about its subject? Who will it interest besides its originator? A buttonhook collection is as valid, if not as valuable, as one of ancient gold coins; both must make some kind of statement to be respected.

Money remains indispensable to successful collecting, but canny buyers can make a little of it go far, often by pyramiding, exchanging, bargaining, or otherwise expanding from a small base. It has been pointed out that it is better to cut the shape of the collection to the size of the budget, than to constantly suffer temptation and disappointment for lack of funds to implement overambitious projects.

Prudent collectors set up their budgets in terms of what is affordable on a weekly, monthly, or annual basis. Wealthy individuals are likely to estimate what percentage of their capital they choose to invest in collectibles. In any case, it is better to be in financial control of the collection, rather than to allow the collection to control one's finances.

Concentration distinguishes advanced collectors. They set boundaries on the scope of their projects and stay within these limits. Collectors of pennies ignore dimes, and Bible collectors disregard lives of saints. A noted collector, who centers his interest on a few postimpressionist artists, flies from New York to Tokyo or Brisbane on the slightest rumor that a great painting in his field may be available. Yet this "art lover" has been in Florence many times without once visiting the Uffizi or Pitti museums because they don't include "his" artists in their collections.

Similar concentration, energetically applied by activist collectors, goes into every aspect of locating pertinent material. Bottle collectors dig in garbage dumps, toy collectors rummage in cellars of old candy stores, barbed-wire collectors search the range; early radios are sought in what are now television repair shops. Each field has its territorial possibilities which compulsive collectors comb in competition with dealers. Wholesale outlets, supposedly out of bounds to private buyers, are invaded by the advanced collector who may offer to buy "for cash" and is willing to dispense with a bill, thus giving the dealer an opportunity to pocket the price, rather than show the sale on the account books where it is taxable.

Collectors jockey for position to get first choice of desirable items as the dealer brings them in. They periodically drop in to see new items and chat about exhibitions or auctions. They bring newspaper clippings, articles, and books of interest. Cultivating dealers stands high on the priorities of advanced collectors. It is desirable to be considered a regular customer, with the advantage of a better discount and the hope of getting in on a grapevine that may sometimes offer precious inside information.

Some will ask that dealers keep track of their wants and notify them when objects of interest appear. They may identify themselves, "I'm the hairpin lady. Please don't forget I'm looking for anything unusual. Here's a self-addressed postcard. I'll come at once in response." A majority of dealers go through the motions of assent, without any intention of ever making an effort. A few are candid enough to refuse, wishing to avoid charges of favoritism, suggesting that the first who comes will be offered first choice. Others will oblige and help in the formation of collections, and it is this that the advanced collector hopes for.

Many a "new collectible" or "modern nostalgia antique" started out as the project of an innovative collector who nursed it through shaky beginnings to profitable maturity. In searching for a potential investment subject of this kind, an aggressive collector or dealer seeks material currently available at low prices in considerable quantity. If it is too scarce, it won't have the momentum for popularity. There has to be enough snow to keep it snowballing.

Nostalgic appeal, either camp or romantic, is a requirement. It can be promoted if it is not obvious. Thus dubbing pressed glass of the 1930s as "Depression Glass" gave it new facets and aided its successful exploitation. On the other hand, early movie material generates its own appeal without further blowup.

Series or set possibilities enlarge the collectible's potential in several ways. People whose imaginations are inadequate to pioneer a collection on their own will eagerly grasp for one which is charted by the development of a series. Many collections are programmed from old catalogues which form a structure for them.

Research requires some investment in money and much in time and energy. Outlining the scope of the collection and locating the material may require travel as well as reading, and perhaps literally, digging. Old catalogues, factory records, and advertisements have taken on new importance in relation to the new collectibles and are much in demand by the advanced collector.

Advertising placed in suitable periodicals, direct mail, and personal contacts will be meshed with a network of scouts and dealers to form a supply conduit as the pioneer builds inventory and connections. Value and price relationships take shape as availability and scarcity begin their traditional balancing act.

New clubs and budding study groups reflect the talent and energy of the promoter-collector, now perhaps collector-dealer, who starts them on a regional level before going on to forming a national association. Trading having begun, a market now exists, and more or less quickly, becomes part of the collecting scene. Special listings in the "offered" and "wanted" columns appear regularly; more dealers buy and sell the new collectible, some even join the originator in specializing in the item or field.

At this stage, a publication generally emerges, probably sporadic at first, but, if successful, becomes a regularly issued and often properly printed and edited journal. A book by the collector-originator then takes its place in the cycle of events heralding the establishment of a new collectible. A price guide is seldom far behind, this may be produced by an established publishing firm, although self-published material of this kind has been profitable for many.

Entire shows dedicated to the material are possible if successful promotion has taken root in fertile ground. Pioneers become authorities, and material is brought to them for confirmation of authenticity. Some lecture and write without becoming dealers; in other instances they go into business, often with great financial success.

The techniques of bargaining for price are developed by experience, putting the private occasional buyer at a permanent disadvantage. "How much is that little old broken thing?" is hardly a subtle ploy likely to lead to the buy of the century. However, veteran collectors do have techniques they find useful in buying.

They suggest one should always assume there is a discount, and one should inquire only as to its size. You are to agree, when told that the object of your interest is the finest widget ever to appear on the market, but you are to note regretfully that the hairline crack in it is that much more a tragedy and makes it almost worthless. Never accept the first price asked, as it will drive some sellers crazy; thinking they might have asked for more, they sometimes rescind the offer. Never haggle over any price until you are absolutely sure you know how much it is worth to you. You may get it for less, and you don't want it for more. Don't discuss price discounts until you are ready to buy.

∿∿∿∿∿∿∿∿∿∿∿∿∿∿∿∿∿∿∿∿∿∿∿∿∿∿∿

Chapter 14

SELLING POSSESSIONS SUCCESSFULLY

Adapting Big Business Know-how

"Creative selling," that finely honed craft of the business world, means much more than finding someone who wants to buy what you have to sell. It means making someone want what you have decided to sell.

The odds for selling antiques, art, or collectibles, as we have seen, are not in the private vendor's favor, so it requires a plan, plus the energetic execution of it, to beat the system. The plan that works best is an adaptation of the classic commercial sales campaign, revised and scaled to the needs of the private seller. The trick is to harness the basic selling program of big business to private needs.

Although originally developed to move mountains of soap powder, millions of candy bars, and countless carloads of furniture, the technique is easily and profitably applicable to a non-business as small as that of the private vendor selling a single item, a collection, a household, or an estate.

All you need to start your own custom-made sales campaign is a sharp pencil and a large sheet of paper.

The Product

First, check off what makes your merchandise or "product" valuable.

Age	Pedigree
Attribution	Period and style
Beauty	Quality
Collectibility	Quantity
Color	Rarity
Condition	Size
Fashion	Source and origin
Historical interest	Subject
Marks	Utility
Material	Workmanship

Next, list how these value appeals make your goods desirable for a particular kind of buyer.

Relevance to certain collections?
Interest to educational institutions?
Museum quality?
Pertains to anniversary or commemoration?
Suitable for home decor?
Appropriate for business or industry?
Useful for art or profession?
Associated with glamorous personality?
Future worth to investor?
Unusual scientific specimen?
Ethnic or religious connection?
Fashion revival?

The Market

Now you form a list of potential customers and pinpoint your prospects under whichever type of outlet is most suitable for your merchandise.

DEALERS

Exclusively specialists in field
Wide range of inventory
Country barns
High-priced, top-quality stock
Neighborhood contact
Internationally known gallery
Department-store boutique.
Dealer group in one location
Resale shop

AUCTIONS

Prestigious high-quality art/antiques/furs/jewelry, etc.
Specialist as books, coins, rugs, etc.
General all-purpose city auction
Sell-everything country auction
Mail-bids-only auction
Antiques auction
Household auction
Storage-company auction
Jewelry auction
International auction
House auction

SELL IT YOURSELF

Friends and acquaintances
Flea market on your own
Established shows and exhibitions
Decorators
Private collectors
Corporate collections
Museums and similar institutions
Tag or garage sale
Swap—trade—exchange
Thrift Shop or Charity donation

ORGANIZE TERRITORY

Divide prospects into personal calls and mail solicitations
Schedule personal visits
Address mailing list; include SASE
When possible, use telephone

Price Structure

Price realistically on data, not fantasy
Price competitively, use price guides, advertised prices, price tags,
    codes, auction prices
Price according to your market
Set reserve price for auction
Retail "list" for flea markets, shows, tag sales
Use retail "list" for flea markets, shows, tag sales
Use wholesale discount for dealers, decorators
Retail "list" for thrift, charity donations
Ten per cent discount from retail "list" to institutions

Budget

List the expense you incur while selling.

Postage	Advertising
Stationery	Insurance
Telephone calls	Selling-space rental
Photographs	Price guides
Carfare or gas	Packing materials
Auction commissions	

Hold these to a reasonable sum in relation to your expected sales receipts.

Promotion

Free publicity is the best kind. If you have an interesting story to tell about a collection, or you can somehow romanticize the sale of an entire household, you can phone your story, or write it up for your local newspaper, television or radio station. If the object was a gift from royalty, was brought from China fifty years ago, or if it is the only, largest, last, or most of anything, try to make a story of your selling it.

Your local librarian may be interested in forming an exhibition of your collection, or items from it. This may then receive helpful publicity for later selling.

Every available bulletin board offers you promotional possibilities for notice of your selling activities.

Advertising

You may not have to advertise at all as both dealers and private collectors are constantly offering to buy in both general and special interest publications. However, if you embark on a more aggressive campaign, there are helpful guidelines.

Descriptions in classified advertising columns must be precise, detailed, and clear.

Mold Blown Daum Nancy French Cameo Scenic Vase 10″ t., 5″ diam., shown in Blount's French cameo book. Mottled orange background with mottled dark green trees in relief.
Box 436

The price may be given, or bids may be requested, as for a mail auction. If no price is given, the intention is to trigger a correspondence.

My entire private collection of quality Indian artifacts consisting of authentic old leather pouches, bone, stone, flint and clay relics. Many unusual items seen only in state museums. Sold as a collection only. Member of State Archaeological Society.

Fairly reasonable rates for classified advertisements in nationally circulated weekly and monthly periodicals give the private seller an opportunity to reach the same audience as the dealer.

If the potential sale warrants it, a more costly presentation, a display ad which stands apart from the classified listings, may be required. A photograph or drawing may be used to illustrate, if desirable to show an outstanding object.

DIRECT MAIL

Direct mail advertising, in which you send either printed, mimeographed, or otherwise reproduced material to your chosen targets, is often the least expensive and most successful. The limitations of space are not as stringent, but the necessity for precise descriptions equally important. Here, too, the series or page number of an item located in an illustrated catalogue or book should be used whenever possible.

A personal letter, whether typewritten or handwritten, is

also a form of direct mail advertising. If the mailing list is small, you may find this the most satisfactory way of making your sales.

PHOTOGRAPHS

Although it is a temptation to crowd several items into one photograph, one item to a frame is best for selling purposes. Head on or straight down with minimum space distortion, plus inclusion of a ruler to show size in inches will aid in clarity. Black backgrounds are best for clear glass, otherwise use contrasting backgrounds. If the color photographed is not absolutely true, black and white might be superior, with added description. Glass frames and covers distort the light and should be moved whenever possible before the picture is made.

ADVERTISING COPY

Try to start your ad with an arresting phrase. It might be something like "Comics for Serious Collectors," "Prize Primitives," or "Special, just found in an old candy store." If you can't think of an appropriate one, mention your merchandise at the very beginning. "Early Teddy Bears," "Old Hatpins," or "Grandfather Clock" will do if they describe your wares.

Don't overpraise; precision counts more than glowing adjectives and will sell better. Mention the outstanding virtue-values. Be exact and honest about condition. Give all the pertinent measurements, marks, and such data. Describe with reference numbers referring to books and catalogues whenever possible.

If your selection or collection is too large to detail in an advertisement, advertise your list as free. Ask for a self-addressed stamped envelope (SASE), if you wish. Some advertisers do; others do not.

Direct mail and bulletin board announcements will also be more successful if they emphasize "what, where, when, and how" before embarking on flowery phrasing.

When tag sales are organized by professionals, they circulate, post, and mail notices like this:

TAG SALE

Wednesday   August 15   1–8 P.M.

16 River St.

Upper River, N.Y.

Complete contents of old Upper River home: Fine Empire library table—velvet wing chair—marble-top coffee table—oriental and other rugs—desk secretary—double bed—refrigerator (This listing covers an entire page. . . .)

A GOOD SALE, MANY COLLECTIBLES AND ANTIQUES! DON'T MISS IT!

Sale by XXXX Associates   Phone Number

Sales Training

The craft of salesmanship has been perfected so that almost any man or woman can be taught to be successful. Here is a short course tailored to the needs of the private vendor.

Introduce yourself at once when calling on a dealer, collector, or auctioneer. Never put yourself in the position of being turned down because you came in "off the street." Some in the trade will not buy from unknown persons, fearing the goods are stolen. Give your bona fides. Telephone or write in advance for appointments.

Always be assured in your manner. No matter how urgent your need for money may be, don't indicate this. Hard-luck stories are not only a waste of time and energy, but actually tend to depress the price, convincing the buyer that you have to sell at any price.

State your price clearly and firmly. Hesitation indicates that you are unsure of yourself.

Salesmanship is a matter of persistence. Don't be discouraged easily. If you make enough calls, the percentage will work in your favor.

Never Apologetic

Avoid being embarrassed because you are selling. Never allow yourself to be put on the defensive. If you indicate to a dealer that you are a potential customer who happens to be selling certain unwanted items, but may make purchases later, you may feel more confident in the more cordial atmosphere.

It won't hurt to imply that you have more and better where this came from. Mention of friends who also have fine possessions to sell may also help to inspire a more satisfactory transaction in your favor.

Looking Prosperous

There is an intangible negative tone that emanates from dealers when poor or shabbily dressed persons approach to offer merchandise for sale. It is better to dress up, than down, when going on a selling expedition.

Setting the Price

Try to get the dealer to make the first offer. Some won't, insisting that the seller make the first move, so that it can be countered by a lower one. If you must state your figure first, make it higher than the actual price you will accept, but not ridiculously so. Be prepared to trade, to split the difference when an impasse seems unavoidable and the price is fair.

Be a name-dropper, especially if your story is true. An element of snobbery in people responds with better prices when the item once belonged to someone rich, famous, or notorious.

Assemble a little portfolio or folder of your backup material. Auction catalogues showing the same or similar items, newspaper clippings, photographs, bills, and price guides may give credibility to your claims.

Timing

Time your sales approach. Dealers buy before shows and exhibitions. If they have had successful markets they are "open to buy" on their return. Buying is done well before the Christmas season, not in December. Dealers in resorts want to buy at the beginning of a selling season. Auction houses run regularly scheduled events, so present your goods in time to have them offered under the most suitable circumstances.

Short Cuts in Clusters

Look for short cuts and timesavers in selling. There are many permanent marts, markets, and fairs in which dealers, catering to a field of collecting, join under one roof for lower rents, joint advertising, and shared-customer traffic. These clusters of dealers are composed for the purpose of fostering one-stop shopping. They also serve for one-stop selling. The private vendor can see many prospects under one roof.

Prudence and Safety

If you have precious jewelry or other material of great value, it may be wiser to show these things in your bank vault, by appointment, rather than carry them about. Security also advises that box numbers are more advisable than names and addresses for purposes of advertising.

There is a famous old maxim in the art market. "Never buy the original of a copy that is in the Louvre." It is equally good advice to "never sell the original of a copy in the Louvre."

Chapter 15

^^^

DON'T TAKE WOODEN NICKELS

Since no one ever collects anything expecting to lose money, all collectors might be considered to be investors of a sort. Aside from the pleasures of ownership, they hope for an eventual increase in value, to be realized when the possession or collection is liquidated. This is in the traditional approach, with long-term appreciation expected to bridge the gap between the retail price at time of acquisition and wholesale price at time of disposal.

However, at certain periods of inflation, devaluation, or re-valuation of currencies, a flight from paper investments attracts many as a value hedge. A sort of panic buying of antiques, art, and collectibles, including gems and jewelry, takes place, usually without reference to the appeal to the buyer except for its potential value. At these times, there is a proliferation of buyers whose sole purpose is eventual resale at a profit. The market in general responds to these superficial as well as to intrinsic factors, and, as boom prices are reported, attracts even more speculative buyers.

Many of these eventually find they can lose money in collectibles as well as in other speculations. Not only skillful buying and selling, but deft maneuvering through the purely financial aspects of the antiques, art, and collectibles market are necessary to survival and success.

Having chosen to gamble in any field of collecting, the speculator would be well advised to make advance preparation by considering the following questions:

How much can I afford to invest?
Is this a short- or a long-term speculation?
If I don't make a short-term profit, can I afford to convert to a long-term investment?
What is the risk on the down side? How much can I afford to lose?
What is the intrinsic value of the item?
Am I paying a low, medium, or high price?
Has the price been artificially stimulated?
How much profit do I expect? In what length of time?
Is the item fragile? Can I insure it?
How will I know when to sell?
Where can I expect to sell? To what sort of buyer?
Is there a continuous market for the item?
What are the costs of selling?—auctioning?
How much can I borrow against this possession?

Those who want to play with big chips should know the possible combinations of the game in which they are getting involved.

Caught up in the belief that there is room for little fish in the collection-speculation pond, many small investors, disillusioned with their experience in the stock market, succumbed to the lure of a mass-market collecting formula promoted as a limited-editions bonanza. It is indeed a formula for getting rich; however, those who do are the manufacturers not the collectors.

Medals, plates, spoons, ingots, paperweights, figurines, and even jewelry advertised as limited editions have been made in quantities as high as 30,000 and 40,000, even 100,000. What is limited is the time period in which some are offered for sale, rather then the number made. Many, authentically limited in number, are sold at what seem to be unlimited high prices. Cautious promoters carefully abstain from promise of higher future prices; others are uninhibited in this matter.

A single company manufactured over 400 different medals in 32 different series in one year, recording sales of over $80 million. A "society of collectors" organized by such a promoter totaled over 125,000 members, indicating they were past or current buyers.

A few limited-edition promotional items that were selling for more than the still available issue price were constantly publicized and advertised, leading to the suspicion that this might be a come-on. Most had no market at all, some could be sold for less than original retail price, according to private advertisements.

According to veteran collectors and dealers, the more profits commercial limited editions created for their promoters, the more problems would be ultimately created for their subscribers when they became sellers. Experienced and successful speculators deny that there is a single formula, but it would seem that those who buy with the intention of reselling at a profit might benefit from the following consensus of experts' suggestions.

Informed appreciation of the commodity or art form is the safest basis for investment.

Buy at a price that allows for a foreseeable profit.

Calculate the odds for rarity or at least scarcity.

Know your sales outlet before you buy for resale.

If a market collapses, cut your losses; sell. The first markdown is the cheapest, unless you are prepared to wait for an unlimited period.

It is axiomatic among collectors that those who buy for investment are usually disappointed, and those who buy for enjoyment find that time enhances sound values. If something is promoted for investment value, it is no longer likely to be a good investment by that time.

Not only the speculator, but every seller who knows the cost, can readily measure the success (or failure) of a sale by using the following conservative calculation as a model.

A clock was purchased for $100. After five years, it was sold for $200 upon being advertised.

> Selling price $200
> Cost   100
>
> Compound interest on $100 at ?% for
> 5 years ....
> Inflation at annual rate of ?% for
> 5 years ....
> Cleaning and repair of clock ....
> Pro-rated cost of insuring clock as part
> of household insurance policy ....
> Cost of price guide to establish value ....
> Cost of newspaper ad ....
> Cost of packing, mailing, and insurance ....
>
>   Total Expenses......

When these expenses have been deducted from the $100 "profit" on the sale of the clock, it will be much reduced if there is any at all.

If there is no record of the cost, if memory does not furnish it, and if the clock was acquired as a gift or bequest, the seller may tend to consider the cost as zero and the selling price as profit. By this naïve calculation, many objects are sold for much less than current market value, much to the satisfaction of the buyers.

Surely if a hundred-dollar bill were received as a gift, or even found, it would seem the height of foolishness to exchange it for less than its face value. So with a possession; if it is sold for less than its wholesale value, part of it has been given away gratis.

The speculator, the investor, and the average person who sells personal possessions will find it prudent to keep records in reference to costs of accumulating, keeping, and selling.

BUYING

Price paid
Sales tax
Appraisal fee
Research costs
Travel to purchase
Cartage and packing
Commission fees

OWNERSHIP

Insurance
Cleaning and repair
Research, such as book and periodical purchases
Membership in collectors' clubs, etc.
Storage in vault or warehouse
Educational costs (courses, etc.)
Travel and convention costs related to hobby
Interest loss on money invested

SELLING

Advertisements
Photographs
Price guides
Auction catalogues
Appraisal fees
Telephone and postage costs

Travel costs to sell
Cartage and packing
Books and periodicals to identify
Repair or refinishing to improve sales appeal

Whether or not these figures will ever be needed by an accountant to process a financial or tax statement, they are of importance to the seller in analyzing a true position in reference to the sale.

The liquidation of any collection worth more than a few hundred dollars should be planned by its owner while it is still being accumulated. In the event of death, or some other traumatic circumstance, the widow, heirs, executors, or other responsible persons should have an available program to protect its value in dispersal.

Lack of knowledge about the collection on the part of the persons charged with its sale cannot be compensated for by any degree of honesty. Dealers are always alert for the opportunity to buy estates or parts of them through banks and lawyers for this reason. It takes more than cut-and-dried legality to sell to best advantage.

In forming the plan, the collector's own experience should be the basis for recommendations as to selling channels. Choice of individual dealers or auction firms can be made, with some flexibility allowed for changing circumstances.

A record of the original costs, updated appraisals, description of the scale and purpose of the collection are important levers for the realization of full-value potential.

Whenever a gift of a valuable object is made, it is sound practice to attach a description so the recipient appreciates the value and identity of the new possession. Although it might be in poor taste to attach a dollar value to a gift, there are situations when it would be desirable. A gift unidentified may be a gift undervalued and wasted. In any case, a description helping to identify a possession might well be considered as an enrichment of it.

Although headlines publicize large and dramatic gifts to institutions with tax-deductible appeal, there is a steady stream of modest gifts of personal possessions to various philanthropic organizations which also boast these attractions. The ubiquitous thrift shop, which recycles almost any object with a claim to utility, has become an American institution. Social critics claim that the well-to-do, who may otherwise not be careful shoppers, have been known to shop around and frugally compare tax deductions offered by various charities before making their closet-clearing contributions.

There is no single overriding formula to determine the dollar tax advantages of this kind of giving rather than selling. However, even on an average income, the permissible deductions can be of some consequence and are worth investigating. The Internal Revenue Service offers information detailing the necessary procedures, and it may be prudent to check this carefully before making a gift with a tax deduction as its ultimate purpose. Accountants, tax specialists, and lawyers who are expert in these matters offer the best guidance.

Both government and private advisers recommend securing and saving acknowledgments, vouchers, and appraisals in support of gift claims, these to be attached to the donor's own detailed lists. Since some organizations are not as prompt and efficient as others in furnishing receipts for such tax-deductible gifts, it is a good idea to make a calendar note of the date of the gift so that, if it becomes necessary, a follow-up request for an acknowledgment can be made.

In recognition of the value to the nation of gifts to religious, educational, charitable, scientific, and literary organizations, the federal government encourages them by tax laws which allow deduction on income tax returns. These apply to antiques, art, and collectibles as well as to cash and other property donated to properly qualified groups. The economics of this is a matter

of each individual's financial situation and a common consideration for those of substantial means.

Wealthy owners of art and other costly possessions often find
it saves them money to make tax-deductible gifts to museums or
similar government-approved institutions. Although there is a
ceiling on the proportion of income which may be so deducted,
large sums can be saved by those in the higher tax brackets
through this arrangement. Estate taxes can also be reduced
by tax-deductible bequests, often leaving the heirs with more
than if they had inherited the whole estate plus the burden of
the resulting taxes.

Within a single decade, almost ten-million-dollars worth of
fine antiques, paintings, and rugs have been acquired for the
White House and State Department as tax-deductible gifts.
An official in charge of these acquisitions allows that national
and family pride play some part in this patriotic generosity,
but he notes that the "overiding thing is the tax deduction."

The Internal Revenue Service stresses that the "fair market
value" is the starting point and the essential aspect of the
allowable contribution deduction, indicating in its publications
that valuation is often a bone of contention between the donor
taxpayer and the Department of the Treasury.

For the individual who decides to donate and wants to
determine "fair market value," the government defines it as
"the price at which the property would change hands between
a willing buyer and a willing seller, neither being under any
compulsion to buy or sell and both having reasonable knowledge
of the relevant facts."

Appraisals are not always necessary for minor items of property or where the value of the property can be easily determined by other methods, but it is required that appraisals
for property over $200 in value contain at least the following
information:

A summary of the appraiser's qualifications.
A statement of the value, and the appraiser's definition of the value
he has obtained.

A full and complete description of the article to be valued.

The basis upon which the appraisal was made, including any restrictions, understandings, or covenants limiting the use of disposition of the property.

The date the property was valued.

The signature of the appraiser and the date the appraisal was made.

In addition, for art objects, the kind of data that is required should include:

A complete description of the object, including the size, the subject matter, the medium, the name of the artist, approximate date created, the interest (reversionary interest) transferred, etc.

A history of the item including proof of authenticity, such as a certificate of authenticity and a table showing succession of ownership.

A photograph of a size and quality fully identifying the art object, preferably a 10×12″ or larger print.

A statement of the factors upon which the appraisal was based, such as:

Sales of other works by the same artist, particularly on or around the valuation date.

Quoted prices in dealer's catalogues or the artist's works or works of other artists of comparable stature.

The economic state of the art market at or around the time of the valuations, particularly with respect to the specific property.

A record of any exhibitions at which the particular art object had been displayed.

A statement as to the standing of the artist in his profession and in the particular school or time period.

Although an appraisal report meets these requirements, the Internal Revenue Service maintains the responsibility of reviewing the appraisal.

(This is a splendid model for a buyer's basis for making an important purchase and well worth the investment in research required, which unfortunately, is too seldom employed in a private situation.)

An interesting indication of the pitfalls that endanger governments as well as private citizens involved in valuation of collectibles is further stated by the Internal Revenue Service. "While not the situation in most cases, appraisers who are associated—other than for making the instant appraisal—with either of the parties to the contribution have rendered appraisals that were essentially nothing more than shams devised to give color or legitimacy to grossly inflated valuation figures. The opinion of an 'expert' is not binding on the Internal Revenue Service; moreover, all the facts associated with the donation may be considered."

Having found a "significant number" of cases in which it appears that taxpayers have worked together with so-called experts, to arrange for the purchase, overappraisal, and donation of an article, the Internal Revenue Service has announced that it will give special scrutiny to deductions involving art objects and collectibles. Obviously if Caesar must caveat, lesser men need also beware when they buy and sell.

A qualified appraiser must also describe and value the goods involved in the settlement of an estate large enough to require the payment of death taxes. On the surface, it would appear that the beneficiary should desire as low an appraisal as possible, so that the estate tax would be minimized. However, if there is any intention to quickly sell the inherited goods, this would boomerang. The profit on the sale would be subject to a short-term capital gains tax if sold within a six-month period. After that time, the profit resulting from the sale would be taxed at a lower rate, but it might still add up to more than if foresight had been exercised at the time of the appraisal.

An appraisal is not an exact or inflexible formula, it is a judgment; and even qualified professionals take a degree of guidance from the client and the situation. Appraisals for insurance purposes are usually at replacement value. Appraisals can vary with the individual appraiser's experience, with regional, economic, or market trends. They can be made at retail or wholesale levels, or somewhere in between. Inflationary forces may quickly outdate an appraisal, as will special situations arising unannounced.

Experts predicted that a certain double-gourd porcelain Ming vase would sell at auction for about $4,000. A duel between bidders at Sotheby Parke Bernet in New York, rocketed the price to $85,000. It can be imagined that for some time thereafter, appraisers had difficulty in valuing similar vases in that particular and unusual combination of underglaze blue and underglaze red on a yellow background! It could be surely predicted that the market would rise, but by how much? A single pair of competing bidders might never again create a similar situation. On the other hand, the owner of a similar vase would want to increase his fine-arts insurance in anticipation of a much-multiplied price.

In most cases, professional appraisers charge from ½ to 1½ per cent of the amount of the total appraisal, with a minimum for either a single item or a complete household. These fees bring out the instinct for thrift in many people, who look about for free or cheap appraisals, usually from dealers of their acquaintance.

Thus the unwary set a trap for themselves, as appraisals made in these circumstances may be at a very low figure in the hope that the merchandise can be bought at the undervalued price. Even at best, the appraisal can be off by a large percentage if the appraiser is not an expert in that particular field. Another disadvantage of the "free" appraisal is the obligation the seller may feel to offer the merchandise to the appraising dealer, thus inhibiting opportunity for comparison.

In general, it is best to pay for a professional disinterested appraisal, clearly specifying that the material is not being offered to the appraiser for sale. Items brought to an auctioneer with the intention of learning what they will bring at auction are not being appraised in the technical sense, but the result is an indication of value to the owner. As we have seen, even the most responsible auctioneer is only hazarding an educated guess.

It is usually close to what the item will fetch at auction, but special situations can never be entirely ruled out.

The fact that an individual advertises an appraisal service does not necessarily mean you are dealing with a qualified appraiser. Since appraisers are not usually licensed, you would be well advised to choose from those belonging to groups or associations which have standards to maintain and which require that their members pass the muster of their peers. Inquiries as to reputation and experience in specialized fields are never amiss.

Leaving your goods to be sold on consignment is seldom desirable, but there are times when it may seem to be a resort worth trying. In that case, the so-called "memo" or memorandum, which is used between dealers who have occasion to borrow merchandise from one another, is less than adequate. It is merely a receipt, not an agreement. When a private seller leaves valuable property to be sold, and paid for only after it has been sold, it is preferable to spell out the arrangement in advance.

The retail price of the consigned items will be decided by the dealer, not the owner of the goods, and in any case could not be controlled by the latter. Any decision as to the amount of commission to be kept by the dealer is equally futile. The only protection for the owner of the merchandise is to agree with the dealer on the sum to be paid in lieu of the return of the goods. The following form to be signed by both parties in duplicate, and notarized, will avoid problems, discussions, and difficulties later.

1. Detailed description of the merchandise consigned, including size, color, shape, marks, age, and condition.
2. Sum the owner will receive if the item is not returned intact as described.
3. Allocation of responsibility for loss, breakage, insurance, cost of transport, packing.

4. Date agreement commences.
5. Date of termination of consignment agreement and return of either money or merchandise.

No matter how friendly the relationship between the consignor and the consignee, an agreement such as this is a businesslike procedure that should be welcomed by both. Unforeseen circumstances such as illness, death, burglary, bankruptcy, or fire may be unlikely, but if some such disaster should occur, a fully signed and notarized agreement would be more useful than a flimsy, inconclusive "memo" form.

Despite the protection of the consignment agreement, the owner should be sure to have adequate insurance at current replacement values on the consigned merchandise. Insurance coverage on possessions, whether they be jewelry, antiques, coins, stamps, books, autographs, pictures, musical instruments, cameras, or other valuables, is at least as essential during the period of selling effort as at any other time. If the value of the goods is of any consequence, it should be protected while it is being viewed by prospective buyers, either in the home or wherever it is offered for sale.

Along with the insurance policies, a backup file should contain copies of appraisals, original bills, and photographs, or snapshots, of the items insured. Not only will an insurance company settle more promptly with this information at hand in the event of loss, but it may also be of aid to the police in locating missing merchandise.

Even when properly insured, costly treasures should be further protected whenever possible. Sometimes museums are interested in borrowing for summer loan shows, giving the owner a worry-free vacation. They will carry additional insurance and often the value of the exhibit will be enhanced by virtue of the prestige acquired. Valuable silver and jewelry as well as art objects are additionally secure in bank or warehouse vaults and can be viewed there by prospective buyers.

It is always best to read the fine print of insurance policies at the time of their issue. Limits on paying for breakage and other calamities had better be ferreted out before, rather than after they occur.

All items, mailed or otherwise shipped to the buyer, should be securely packed, registered, and insured for full value. If there is any likelihood that they may be returned to you (approvals often are), make sure that *your* insurance covers the safe return, despite assurances from the other party who may be careless in packing or insuring properly.

Keep carbon copies of correspondence relating to the sale of personal possessions; keep your carbons and printed copies of the advertisements you originate and clippings of the ads you answer. Very often an ugly or costly discussion can be eliminated or nipped in the bud by such precautions.

In addition to husbanding all documents relative to individual items or the entire collection, illustrations of similar pieces from books, newspapers, or magazines may turn out to be of value. Auction catalogues showing the same pieces in listings or photographs also make up such dossiers indicating history, pedigree, and sources of ownership as well as price records. Proof of ownership and value may add to the value at some future date.

Under all circumstances, get descriptive receipts when you leave your valuable merchandise anywhere. This includes repair, framing, upholstering, and replating, as well as storage situations.

Auctioneers are licensed and bonded in most parts of the country. It is possible to review the fiscal responsibility of an auction firm directly through a bank. Date of settlement of accounts of your sale lots is best established in advance, as some firms are prompt in this matter, while others are not. It is disagreeable to have to ask for your money as sometimes happens.

Be sure it is understood that you will be paid directly by the auctioneer, not by the buyers of your lots.

Make sure the auctioneer has a record of the reserve price, and have your own record properly verified by the auctioneer. Agree in advance on what it will cost you to exercise the reserve, should it be necessary.

If there is any question as to the authenticity of a lot, as described in the auction catalogue, there may be a requirement that the owner must return the money. This should be questioned in advance and the responsibility understood, if there is such.

It is customary for dealers to wait until a check has cleared before mailing or shipping merchandise. This seems to be a good rule for private sellers as well and can easily be enforced when a transaction requires mailing or shipping. However, face-to-face situations may put the seller in the embarrassing position of refusing to accept a check. Unless the buyer is personally known to the seller, the preference for cash had best be explicitly adhered to, and without exception. If the buyer insists on paying by check, the transaction could be handled in the seller's bank under the direction of a bank officer before the merchandise is handed over.

If the seller should be persuaded to accept installment payments, these should be secured by notes which had best be processed through a lawyer and a bank.

There are those numismatists who knowingly collect wooden nickels for fun and profit. But there is neither fun nor profit for those who unwittingly get a poor substitute for cash when they sell their possessions.

Any procedure for recourse made by private buyers, who believe they have been victims in a fraudulent transaction involving antiques, art, or other collectibles, is best initiated *before* anything goes wrong. As a matter of fact, it can be anticipated and possibly avoided by getting a proper bill.

A receipted bill on the letterhead of the dealer, or firm, making the sale will show the date, price, description, terms, and guarantees in detail. Penny-wise buyers who forego this to avoid paying sales taxes will wish they hadn't, should there be any problem later. It is this document upon which any complaint must be based, so it had better be carefully drawn and thoroughly checked before money changes hands, with both parties agreeing to its meaning.

Agreement to accept the return of an object and to refund the price is usually subject to its being in the same condition as when purchased. Make sure the description mentions all flaws, blemishes, and repairs. An exchange of photographs of the item, to be initialed by both parties, is a useful precaution in tricky circumstances.

If an item is guaranteed to be by a certain maker, be sure the name is spelled correctly. Don't be embarrassed to make these demands. Indications that they are unwelcome is a warning to be noted and calls for alertness.

The credit rating of the seller is a critical factor if the transaction involves a large sum which might have to be refunded under the guarantee. This too must be checked in advance.

In many cases, no more than mention of dissatisfaction with a purchase is required for a willing response from the seller. In every instance, the first step in a complaint is a request or a suggestion, rather than a demand. However, if no interest is shown by the vendor toward making an adjustment, the next move on the buyer's part is gathering firm evidence that the item is not as was represented. This should be of a positive nature, not a hunch or guess. It might be explained, but if an exact duplicate, down to the mark or signature, were purchased in a department store which had dozens more, it would be an understandable challenge of an item purchased as an antique original at a high price.

Disagreements between various dealers and their customers may be submitted to arbitration under the law in some states, if both sides agree the verdict will be binding on them. This would seem to provide a sensible solution to many disputes. However, it is not always possible to arrange this.

If the seller insists that you are wrong, suggest calling in any third party who is an authority to judge. Should this be refused, make a formal complaint to a local collectors' or dealers' association. Meeting a negative response to consider the case, take your problem to a small claims court, if its monetary range encompasses the cost of your purchase.

As a last resort, you may have to find a lawyer and possibly go into a court of law in a civil action, or make your complaint as a criminal action to the proper authorities. However, the threat of publicity attendant upon either course may press your opponent to arrange a settlement you will find acceptable.

Part II

AMERICAN INDIAN CRAFTS

Department stores decorated as Indian trading posts reflect the boom in Indian artifacts that is part appreciation, part fad or fashion, and largely profit oriented. North American Indian art, new and old, achieved commercial recognition when the great nineteenth-century collection formed by Colonel George Green before his death in 1925, and increased by his heirs, was sold at auction in New York in 1971.

Prices such as $4,600 for a buckskin robe and thousands of dollars for baskets, blankets, and rugs brought an avalanche of tomahawks, wampum belts, and other artifacts spilling out of attics and closets, to be sold in a wide range of outlets.

Pre-1940 Navajo rugs which sold for a few hundred dollars at best, a decade before, were soon bringing over $1,000, while prices of $2,500 and more for contemporary Navajo rugs were not unusual. Silver and turquoise jewelry, formerly of principal interest to arty bohemian ladies, became indispensable accessories for internationally famous fashion figures. Bracelets, finely crafted in silver and turquoise, now sold for hundreds of dollars, and an elaborate "squash blossom" necklace might go for several thousand.

Ability to discern between commercial souvenirs, trinkets, and finely crafted art became a necessary skill, as junk was priced high to further the confusion. Souvenir shops, department stores, art galleries, craft shops, flea markets, antique shops, auctions, and non-profit outlets for Indian crafts are among the sources which offer all qualities and varieties, requiring the wise buyer to trade warily.

Whether Eskimo sculpture is in fact art, artifact, or merely curiosity, whether it fits in as ethnic, primitive, or Indian craft, it is undoubtedly gaining in popularity, price, and appeal to investors.

Simple subjects of animal and Eskimo life, carved in rounded static forms, originally were anonymously made, but, recently, many are signed and the works of some artists are singled out as more valuable. The most common material is gray soapstone; ivory and whalebone pieces are more rare and more costly. Prices in the past ten years have doubled, and while many small pieces are still comparatively low in price, the larger works by name artists are merchandised as art and priced accordingly.

INSIDERS ADVISE

"Indian Made" is not "Indian Handmade." The first may come from a factory with one Indian employee.

Taiwan, Hong Kong, and Japan are sources for so-called Indian crafts. Look for signs of missing labels.

Japanese collectors are among those foreigners who appreciate and buy American Indian handicrafts.

Indian silver jewelry is sometimes "restrung," with some original material mixed in with other stuff, so a single necklace, or pair of earrings, produces several units.

Handmade Indian rugs often show a missed thread where the colors change. No two are ever exactly alike.

Machine-made Navajo rugs are imported from Mexico and Guatemala.

Non-profit organizations which sponsor Indian crafts offer some of the finest merchandise and best values.

If you learn to know baskets, you can make wonderful finds, as few are expert in differentiating the various kinds.

Antique baskets of the Southwest Indians are most valuable.

African, Philippine, Chinese, and even European baskets can be, and often are, confused with American Indian examples. They are collectible and desirable, but should be much less costly.

Fine baskets by Northeast tribes, such as the Iroquois, Ojibwa, and Micmas, are available, less expensive, and good for beginning collectors to start with.

Rare old baskets are seldom reproduced, as the labor required is hardly available nor could it be paid for fairly. It takes 14 months to make a feathered basket which could bring $850.

Eskimo sculpture has been selling for about 10 per cent less in Canada than in the United States.

Some Eskimo artists are carving abstract works. This new departure has not yet developed an established value.

Price of Eskimo sculpture is determined by size, quality, carving material, and the reputation of the artist.

Each Eskimo carving should have a number and identification tag from the governmental control unit.

North American Indian Arts, by Andrew H. Whiteford, and *Indian and Eskimo Artifacts in North America,* by Charles Miles, are recommended reading, as well as George Swinton's *Sculpture of the Eskimo,* and Frederick J. Dockstader's *Indian Arts in America.*

ANCIENT AND ANTIQUE GLASS

While glass is fragile, it is also durable, and under certain fortuitous circumstances, can last for thousands of years. Not only fragments, but complete ancient vessels continue to be found, particularly in the Near East where glass is thought to have originated.

Important pieces are snatched up by museums and collectors, however, less significant but plentiful specimens can be readily bought for minimal sums of less than $25. Only a few years ago, a typical sale at Sotheby's in London brought prices of between $25 and $150 for Egyptian, Roman, and Syrian glass of the early Christian Era.

Islamic glass is more coveted, and even lesser items bring hundreds of dollars. Medieval glass is of considerable rarity, and an early German drinking glass of handsome design will fetch figures in the high hundreds at important auctions.

Renaissance glass of every country is most precious within its own borders and is usually anxiously competed for. Venetian glass is of universal interest for its mastery of style and technique and is as costly as it is precious.

English and Continental glass of the seventeenth and eighteenth centuries is bought, as much by general antique collectors as by specialists, to round out period collections. Prized are Irish Waterford and Bohemian carved and engraved glass, as well as the enameled glass of Germany, France, Spain, Portugal, and Switzerland that influenced Early American output.

INSIDERS ADVISE

Glass is the most difficult of all collectibles to identify and authenticate, the easiest to fake.

Even experts insist on comparing an item with a proven piece before making a difficult judgment.

Pumice and sandpaper are used to create false signs of wear on glass, to indicate age.

Every authentic glass has its "right" weight and sound; sometimes this is a better proof than appearance alone.

Glass flaws can be covered by ornamentation, such as painting, etching, and metal holders.

A coin enclosed in glass shows the age of the coin, not the age of the glass, which may be much later.

Pontil marks indicate that the glass may have been made any time from A.D. 100 to the present date.

Impressed trademarks can be ground off and the scar described as a pontil mark.

Consider collecting ancient glass; values are still good as the competition is not great.

Plain old glass is sometimes later enameled or engraved, to make it more valuable as a collectible.

Imitation of iridescence, due to long burial in the earth, can be achieved by use of chemicals.

If you dig for old glass, be sure to label your finds with information about location.

Old glass that is damaged may be cut down to a new form. This lessens the value, so is often disguised.

Experts grind nicks and chips and can even graze off scratches, in addition to concealing major blemishes and cracks.

Avoid buying "sick glass." It can be disguised briefly with a light coat of mineral oil, but may be permanently fogged.

Most successful efforts to cure "sick glass" are made by half-filling the container with denatured alcohol or water and adding a cupful of fine, clean sand, then swirling.

Ventilate cabinets where glass is stored. Don't wrap in tissue paper for long-term storage. Dust and grime are deteriorating agents, as is dampness.

Never use a combination of bleach and acid (vinegar) to clean glass; it releases chlorine which injures the glass.

Avoid using ammonia for cleaning glass.

Use oil to release stoppers or tightly wedged units of glass.

Don't soak decorated glass. Never use hot water to wash glass. Wash at least once a year in gentle soap flakes.

A World History of Glass, by Kampfer and Beyer, *The Book of Glass,* by Gustav Weiss, and *Glass Through the Ages,* by E. B. Haney, present background material. Countless books cover individual periods and types of glass.

Although great museums the world over have collections of antique glass that range from fine to superb, the Corning Museum of Glass, in Corning, New York, is outstanding. Its exhibits cover every aspect of the history of glass from 1500 B.C. to the present.

ANTIQUITIES AND ETHNIC ART

Ancient and primitive materials have moved into the salons of the trend setters. Their decorators literally spotlight Roman marble torsos, Egyptian bronze falcons, Sassanian silver dishes, pre-Columbian sculpture, African fetishes, or New Guinea hook figures.

The canny owner of a fine and famous collection of Impressionist and School of Paris paintings, who had shrewdly accumulated it before prices went too high, has switched to buying only ancient and primitive art. Announcing "It's the next big thing," she seemed to be wearing some of her new collection when seen on Madison Avenue with an Etruscan necklace over her sweater.

Headlines confirm her hunch. Figures of hundreds of thousands, even millions of dollars are mentioned as prices for carved Mayan stelae, stolen out of jungles, and Greek pottery of debatable provenance. An aroused community of scholars and historians is fighting to preserve remaining archaeological sites and treasures from the depredations of looters, dealers, collectors, and even museums, greedy for the pillaged art. Huge sums are involved, hair-raising tales of piracy and adventure are told, and the modest collector of Colima or Nayarit Mexican terra cotta, or Etruscan black pottery, is torn between pleasure and guilt at being even peripherally involved in such thrilling goings-on.

Although it is just as well that modest collectors have conscience in such matters, the truth is that they are as much sinned against as sinning. Fakes and forgeries are as common for the relatively unimportant items that scholars overlook, as for the important and costly ones. Since pedigree and provenance are difficult and more often impossible to come by, because even authentic material is illegally torn from its source, the opportunities for fraud are much taken advantage of.

Ethnic materials are likewise popular targets for fakery. The market for African art has not yet recovered from being undermined by fraudulent offerings that frightened many collectors away. The ethnic arts are also prone to seasons of popularity and decline for reasons of fashion, to which they are susceptible.

Scholarly collectors are indifferent to fashion. They stay with their specialties. Dedicated collectors of Greek, Roman, Etruscan, Near Eastern, oriental, or ethnic arts ignore current fads in truly timeless interest. And that is just as well for new collectors and dealers because they need the experts when the individual periods and cultures take their turns in the marketplace.

INSIDERS ADVISE

Don't fool around in these fields unless you are prepared for serious study.

Experts disagree even more over antiquities than other art, so you will have to make judgments yourself.

Don't buy items stolen from excavations. It's not only unethical, but usually a fraud.

Clay items are the easiest to fake, and little that is profitable is overlooked.

Don't hesitate to buy what appeals to you, but don't pay more than you would if it were a comparable handicraft item, unless you are satisfied of authenticity.

When a controversy like that over the Metropolitan Museum's bronze horse arises, study the differing opinions and if possible, look at the piece for yourself. This gives you a chance to be on the inside of "big time" expertise.

Do your buying at the "low" periods in the cycles of interest for both antiquities and ethnic art.

If you can afford it, buy only from established, reputable dealers, or with their advice.

Bone up on the new scientific tests for age of various materials. Talking about them may inspire respect.

Thermoluminescence tests are made at Oxford, Tokyo, and Philadelphia. This is the most sure-fire technique of establishing the age of many objects, but is not readily available for small fry.

You are most vulnerable to being cheated when buying in the area where the antiquities and primitive art originate.

Foreign dealers unknown to you may guarantee quite freely, being sure that you aren't likely to make an expensive return trip just to exercise the guarantee.

Magnificent art books on antiquities and ethnic art are published in plentiful numbers. Art reference libraries and art departments of bookshops offer browsing opportunity to choose carefully before buying.

ARMS AND ARMOR

There is undoubtedly a mystique of arms and armor, accounting for the passionate intensity with which they are collected. Some of this is attributed to an elemental response to weaponry by the machismo-oriented male. Yet no one who is sensitive to quality and workmanship, much of it on the highest artistic level, can associate appreciation of finely wrought weapons solely with the primitive instincts of the chase and war. In addition to the technical and aesthetic attractions of superb mechanisms and splendid artisanship, there is the pull of history, a powerful force inviting attention to the dramatic artifacts of its tensions and explosions.

Winston Churchill's .30 Mauser semiautomatic pistol, engraved with his name and mentioned in his autobiography, brought almost $10,000 after his death. The flintlock fowling piece made for Louis XIII, bearing his crown cypher and the inventory number of his cabinet of arms, was sold for 125,000 pounds, in 1972. The fact that it had been in the fabulous Renwick collection did not detract from its value.

Under the martial heading of arms and armor, collectors subdivide into numerous regiments and platoons of their specialties. Bulletproof vests and underarm holsters used by famous gangsters are at one end of a parade which runs to Greek shields and Roman greaves at the other. In the unserried ranks between are collectors of coats of mails, suits of armor, crossbows, various states of the harquebus, and other early forms of firearms. Ambitious collectors with plentiful storage space are actually buying tanks and weapons carriers while some with smaller scope collect pocketknives. Swords, daggers, and dirks are included among edged weapons, and in this area antique examples are prized highly, with the lavishly jeweled ones usually most costly. Small sidearms of all periods appeal to the largest number of collectors, although antique rifles, muskets, and the like have an enormous following.

Some collectors specialize in military weapons, others in naval weapons, and still others in hunting weapons. Arms and armor of every country are pursued and studied. Persian, Turkish, Indian, and similar exotic examples, as well as English and Continental weapons intrigue beginners and advanced collectors alike. Very sophisticated connoisseurs have made the field of Japanese weaponry into a special cult with a world following.

According to Gerald Reitlinger in his *The Economics of Taste*, the armor of Henry V was sold for a little under three pounds in 1791. In 1921, when merchant princes used them for status symbols, Duveen sold a sixteenth-century suit of armor to Clarence Mackay for $25,000, a price that seems high even in the inflation-shrunken dollars of half a century later.

In general, full suits of armor gravitate to museums rather than private buyers when they make their comparatively rare appearances on the contemporary market. However, what has been called "knightly haberdashery" is quite popular. Elbows, gauntlets, stirrups, spurs, helmets, and similar paraphernalia of the joust or battlefield, appeal to those with a decorative purpose in mind, as well as to the serious collector of armor. Japanese tsuba, the sword guards of great artistic interest, have sold for as much as $3,500, and in an important sale, their prices ranged from $14 for one to $2,064 for another.

American guns are another highly specialized field in which experts show their appreciation for star quality by paying large sums for the products of Revolutionary gunsmiths and their successors, including Deringer, Colt, and Smith and Wesson.

Newsworthy highs have included $20,000 for an 1820 flintlock pistol, signed "S. North, Middletown, Connecticut." Purchased at auction as part of the splendid Renwick collection, it is described as "a D.B. over-and-under pistol, having browned barrels with single gold breech lines and vents with the lower barrel fitted with a swivel ramrod . . . the tang engraved with foliage and an American shield, the lock with V-shaped waterproof pans, roller frizzens, ring-neck cocks, push-on safety catches

. . . the lock plates also signed, with leaf borders . . . checkered walnut butt with oval silver escutcheon plates and spurred trigger guard decorated with foliage. . . ." Obviously there is much to know about fine guns.

INSIDERS ADVISE

If a vintage gun or edged weapon is sold in its original case with all accessories intact, the value may be as much as double what it would be for the same item without them.

Signatures and marks alone may be treacherous guides with arms and armor as well as in other fields. However, here too, with all other factors being equal, the marked, signed piece is more valuable.

English guns and edged weapons with silver or gold mounts usually bear hallmarks to aid in identification and dating.

Some weapons catalogues appear in several issues, each successive offering at a lower price. Since the most desirable material is presumed to have sold at the beginning, prices are lowered in the second go-round, and if there is a third, they are even lower.

Those who collect vintage weapons prefer to be identified as such and not to be confused with those who just like guns.

The number of arms and armor transactions conducted by mail makes the integrity and reputations of dealers most important. Some publications carrying vintage gun advertising are said to be alert to complaints and threaten to blackball dealers who renege on offers or otherwise behave unethically or dishonestly.

For the most part, experienced collectors exchange information about the advisability of doing business with dealers they do not know personally.

The Civil War centennial was celebrated with a spate of reproduction weapons made for sale as such. The usual "confusion" resulted in some being sold as antique originals. Kentucky rifles were thereafter also "reproduced" and they too have been sold as originals to inexperienced collectors.

Prices of authentic Revolutionary weapons and gear began to ascend before other preparations for that centennial commenced. Prudent collectors aware that fakes and reproductions would probably accompany the event went on the alert.

Collectors prize those fine, accurate flintlock rifles made in the early to mid-eighteenth century especially for use on the frontier. Adapted from the European model, but refined by native gunsmiths, it was known as the Kentucky rifle but was also produced in other colonies, particularly Pennsylvania.

Later percussion rifles have been altered as reversions to the earlier, more valuable flintlock. These are hard to spot but easy to accomplish, so inexperienced collectors rely on dealer experts.

The well-known classic types of arms and armor usually bring better prices than rare and off-beat oddities and are preferred for investment for that reason.

The famous Philadelphia gunsmith who in 1825 developed the short-barreled pocket pistol of large caliber known as the derringer was a man by the name of Deringer. The difference of an extra letter r is an accident that has become a convention. This is the kind of gun with which John Wilkes Booth assassinated Lincoln.

Conversions meant to deceive, such as percussion guns fitted with flintlocks, are undesirable, but "conversion types," which were army models redesigned by authorities after manufacture, are wanted by advanced collectors rounding out their series.

Serial numbers may help to fix the historical period when guns were made and used, although often obsolete weapons were used at the beginning of wars, before the start of larger scale armament production.

English guns bearing the mark "BGP" with crossed scepters are sometimes mistaken for American Revolutionary or Colonial flintlocks. This is a Birmingham, England, proof mark and was first used in 1813.

Often taken for antique flintlocks are Belgian guns made until quite recently for sale to African countries for hunting and warfare. Some can be identified by the "LG" which shows their origin in Liège, Belgium.

For a long time it was thought that "CP" meant "Continental Property" and was an indication that a gun with the authentic markings was probably used in the American Revolutionary War. It has been discovered that the meaning is "Commonwealth of Pennsylvania" and could not have been made before 1797.

Proof marks showing that a gun was checked as to function and mechanism (usually a V) and that it had been fired with heavy charges to prove its safety (usually a P) are generally found on English guns.

Although proof marks are not obligatory on American-made guns, they appear on those made for export in an effort to conform with customs or regulations of the country for which they were destined. However, the letter "P" on an antique American gun may indicate "Provincial" or "Pennsylvania" as well!

When in doubt, identify by comparing with weapons in an authenticated private collection or museum.

Uniform numbers throughout a gun mean all parts are intact and original rather than assembled from various pieces or a production line.

In general, short arms are considered a safer investment and easier to resell than rifles or other long arms, reflecting this in price.

All sets are *not* pairs of dueling pistols. Some are twin or ornamental sets, which are desirable, but not in the category of pairs of exactly matched dueling weapons.

Dueling pistols lack bright or overornamental decoration which might make them targets with disastrous consequences. Most attention was given to their perfect balance and the need to "come up" accurately when fired.

Although Samuel Colt was an American and his great pistols are considered a form of Americana, some of them were made in London between 1853 and 1857.

"Fine" in reference to a weapon indicates that it has a minimum of 50 per cent original factory finish, distinct markings, and is in perfect working order. In descending order, "good, fair, about good and poor" are used to define condition.

The description of arms or armor as being in "decorator" condition indicates they are suitable to be viewed from a distance, as over a fireplace, but will not bear close scrutiny.

Since many gun collectors are publicity shy, for various reasons, including aversion to tax assessors, visiting curiosity seekers, and possible thieves, many of the best collections are known within a comparatively small circle of friends, fellow collectors, and dealers.

Most armor collections include some for the horse as well as the man. In particular, chamfrets, the plate defenses for the horse's head (used from the fourteenth through the seventeenth centuries), appeal for their sculptural style.

Not all of the armor made during the period of its use was for military purposes. Jousting armor was especially made for tournaments. Parade armor, the most elegant and magnificently decorated, was intended for ceremonial glamour. Weapons and armor made for presentation for valor or as diplomatic gifts between potentates are usually highly prized for their splendor.

In addition to arms and armor, and impinging as specialties, are military prints, flags, drums, uniforms, and military buttons. Toy soldiers, miniature artillery, and powder flasks and horns are related popular collectibles in allied fields.

Not all armor is metal. Leather known as *cuir bouilli*, horn, wood, and lacquer are among other materials used.

"Maximilian" armor indicates a fluted form originating in the reign of the Emperor Maximilian I (1494–1519). It was made until the latter part of the sixteenth century, so the term refers to the crested, fluted style which is much admired. In 1926, the Metropolitan Museum paid $5,000 for a pair of Maximilian puffed sleeves.

Although the fine workmanship characteristic of quality armor of the period ending about 1700 would be almost impossible to reproduce in large units at any price, small bits and pieces purporting to be ancient armor have been made within this century and passed off as authentic.

Suits of armor are often assembled from many sources. It takes an expert to recognize that knee pieces, cuirass, helmet, and shield may even originate in different centuries.

Swords, dirks, and daggers are seldom assembled from cannibalized items, but sometimes the entire unit is a fake. Complete guns are also made as fakes, but more often are cleverly put together from parts of different old weapons.

"Guns from Turkey" at prices under $50, offered in retail mail order advertisements, may imply, but carefully do not explicitly state, that they are antiques. "Old style" brass-fitted flintlocks and blunderbusses made for the tourist and sucker trade will disappoint bargain hunters expecting vintage arms.

Until this century, personal weapons and armor were usually furnished by officers themselves. Knowing their lives depended on quality and design, they preferred to have them custom-made. The gunsmith and armorer were very highly respected craftsmen.

Neophytes are warned never to unload guns by firing. A gun that has not been checked for safety should never be fired. The cleaning and handling of guns comprise rituals that even experts respect.

Since old gunpowder retains its power for decades, it is urged that collectors remember to avoid smoking near open gunpowder or containers thereof.

If you restore or otherwise "improve" an old gun, keep a record of the replacement parts.

To avoid rust or other deterioration, do not store weapons in leather holsters or scabbards. Cloth or paper wrappings are also unsatisfactory.

Weapons are best stored on racks within cabinets, or suspended by slings if kept in individual boxes.

Historic association does increase the value of arms and armor, but it is more easily claimed than proved that an item belonged to, or was used by, a particular individual. Keep all documentary evidence about material in your possession safely intact. Don't pay supplements above the usual value for purchases unless the proof of association is impeccable.

The Complete Book of Gun Collecting, by Charles Edward Chapel, as well as this authority's other books, is outstanding.

Paul Martin's *Arms and Armour*, Richard Akehurst's *Antique Weapons for Pleasure and Investment*, and *Douglas J. Fyer's Antique Weapons*, together with publications of the Arms and Armour Society, are useful collecting aids.

Note and observe local, state, and federal laws regarding the purchase, sale, possession, and use of weapons. Individual variations cover antiques and vintage arms in some areas. Collectors unfamiliar with prohibitions and requirements for licenses have been embarrassed and inconvenienced, if not more seriously charged.

ART GLASS

Art Glass looks "artistic" and expensive, and while some may debate the former attribute, no one can deny the latter; prices of this ware are high. Largely ornamental, Art Glass expresses the range of glassmakers' technical mastery gained throughout the ages, culminating in the late nineteenth and early twentieth centuries in the United States and Europe.

Exploiting overlay, cameo cutting, enameling, frosting, gilding, painting, swagging, and quilting, plus flowing and exotic shapes, with colors that vary from subtle to explosive, craftsmen produced this luxury glass in unprecedented variety for a market that had an endless appetite for decoration.

Tiffany, Steuben, Frederick Carder, Thomas Webb, Émil Gallé, Daum, Loetz, and Lalique are among the names of producers now sought by dealers and collectors. Many pieces were numbered and signed, greatly adding to market value. Signed choice Tiffany lamps have brought over $30,000; less important pieces may sell for thousands of dollars.

Favrile, the much-copied iridescent glass made by Tiffany, Agata, Murrhina, Satin, Amberina, Peachblow, and Burmese are among the types that stand out in this period. Victorian Baroque, Art Nouveau, and at the end of the era, Art Deco are all represented in the glittering panorama of Art Glass.

INSIDERS ADVISE

Japanese and German collectors are buying Art Nouveau and other styles of Art Glass in European and U.S. markets.

Kits for etching forged numbers and faking Tiffany and other signatures are openly advertised.

Some of the late Tiffany glass, although authentic, is inferior in quality to certain very fine iridescent glass items made by Quezal, Victor Durand, and Steuben.

Authentic signatures are sometimes removed, so that "better" names can be forged in their places.

The small iridescent glass shades, made for gas and electric lights, are "converted" into bowls, compotes, and epergnes by inserting plugs and mounting them.

Factories all over the world are making Art Glass reproductions. Italy especially exports many types.

Pieces of fine quality, requiring painstaking workmanship, are least often reproduced.

Two outstanding books in this field are Ray and Lee Grover's *Art Glass Nouveau* and *Carved and Decorated European Art Glass*.

Another good writer on this subject is Albert Christian Revi, author of *American Art Nouveau Glass* and *Nineteenth-Century Art Glass*.

American Art Glass Price Guide, which is published by the bookseller, Hotchkiss House, is popularly consulted in the trade.

AUTOGRAPHS

The Good Humor man who collects contemporary autographs, and is known to celebrities visiting Manhattan for his brash persistence, has over 10,000 autographs and the kind of drive that makes formidable collectors. He gets two copies of each autograph; one goes into his permanent book, the other goes on to a file card. He has sold several thousand of his duplicates, including autographs of Presidents Truman, Eisenhower, Kennedy, and Nixon, some to dealers, thus confirming the diversity of the strands that tie into the knot that binds a trade together.

The urge to possess a tangible fragment of greatness, notoriety, history, science, or the arts, through the ownership of autographs, is a powerful one. The writer may be an important individual, or the material's content may be the magnet. For some collectors, a signature of Napoleon might be less desirable than a letter written by a simple soldier describing the Battle of Waterloo. Those who collect "sets" of signatures of U. S. Presidents, families of royalty, or football teams, find the primary factor is "who." Those who collect on the basis of a subject, such as medicine, literature, or music, find information on the specialty is the dominant or "what" factor.

Letters and documents relating to the Revolutionary or Civil wars, early industries, whaling, Indians, pioneer life, the Gold Rush, and similar aspects of American life are particularly desirable. Land grants signed by U. S. Presidents before 1834 are plentiful, numbering into the tens of thousands; signed presidential appointments until the time of Lincoln are also very common. As a result these prices are not particularly high, with some exceptions, namely, Washington, John Adams, Jefferson, and Lincoln.

The autograph of a President may be very common in one form and rare in another, reflecting itself in the price. A check written and signed by George Washington was priced at $2,000, hardly an insignificant sum. But at the same time, a letter written from Mount Vernon in 1799, in which Washington complains of having to borrow money, brought $7,500 at auction in October 1972; yet another Washington letter brought $27,500 in May 1973.

About the time that a newspaper article headlined the $3,300 paid for an unpublished letter from Edgar Allan Poe, in which he indicated that he was an autograph collector, the same newspaper carried an advertisement offering the signature of Lord Randolph Churchill, father of Sir Winston, at $5.00 and a letter from Sarah Bernhardt at $25. A manuscript copy of the first-known work of fiction, created in what is now the United States and written by two Princeton students in 1770, fetched $22,000 at auction in New York.

The market for important and costly autograph material is built around the dealer-experts. They sell principally through catalogues, some of which go to regular customers and special subscribers. A certain amount of business is transacted with clients in dealers' offices, but that seems to be the exception.

Autograph auctions are held at established auction houses in the United States and abroad, and individual dealers hold regularly scheduled auctions which dealers and collectors attend. Mail bids are also invited for these. Mail auctions are another popular sales method; these are usually variations on the catalogue system. There is also some amount of private trading between collectors, but it is believed that this rarely involves items of great value.

Aside from the important private collector market, autographs are bought by public, private, and university libraries, also by historical societies, historical restorations, institutions developing special collections, various sorts of museums, private corporations, and many professional people for their business offices.

Because the majority of prospective buyers have special interests, most auction lots, which include a number of items, are purchased by dealers. They are in a position to take a selection of autographs into stock and can more readily sell what they do not wish to keep than can the individual collector, librarian, or curator.

As an indication of the most popular subjects for autograph collection, the Universal Autograph Collectors Club membership application lists the following:

Theatrical	Politics	Civil War
Military	Authors	Supreme Court
Musical	Astronauts	First Ladies
Financial	Sports	World Leaders
Presidents	Artists	Scientists
Royalty	Religion	Medical
Statesmen	Lincoln	American West
Judaica	American Revolution	Aviation
	Kennedy	

INSIDERS ADVISE

Signatures of celebrities are the most commonplace units of the autograph market. They are usually sold for a few dollars and are rarely listed by dealers, although this type of "fan" collectible is popular with many people.

Autographs are not only signatures. Anything handwritten may be of interest to the autograph dealer or collector.

Abbreviations used in the trade indicate the variety and range of autograph combinations
    ALS   autograph letter signed
    LS   letter signed
    ADS   autograph document signed
    AMsS   autograph manuscript signed
    DS   document signed
    AQS   autograph quotation signed
    ANS   autograph note signed
    SIG   signature

Autograph musical manuscripts can be very valuable. The 75-page manuscript of Mozart's little opera, *The Impresario,* is said to have cost over "six figures" when acquired by the Pierpont Morgan Library in New York.

Fame alone is no guarantee of value, especially if the person was a prolific writer.

Authenticity guaranteed, on an unlimited money-back basis, is the backbone of the autograph-collecting trade. Prices as high as thousands of dollars for a sheet of paper cannot be generated unless a buyer trusts a vendor's integrity as well as knowledge.

The need for expertise is enormous. This field has always been, and continues to be, a target for forgers.

Problems arising in validating autographs may include the kind of paper, type of ink, literally, the dotting of i's, to say nothing of the content itself.

Value factors for autographs include condition, contents, length, date, name of the addressee, place where written, size of signature, kind of signature, clarity of signature, and postal strikings.

Age alone is of consequence if a European document dates before 1400, or an American one before 1675.

The autopen, a mechanism much used by public figures, produces an exact duplicate of the original signature. Experts spot it just because it is always identical.

Many documents are signed by a proxy, usually a secretary. Experts consider them professional forgeries, although not for profit.

President John F. Kennedy's papers were analyzed to show seven autopen signatures and 14 different secretarial signatures.

There are fewer than 20 important autograph dealers in the United States. About as many more function as part-time dealers in that they are also involved in stamps or rare books.

Fifty per cent of the retail list price is considered the average wholesale price the private seller can expect from a dealer. Less is offered when there is little demand, and the item is bought for stock and the long term.

More than half of the retail list price will be paid by a dealer only if the item is much wanted or an immediate sale is assured.

Only if the private owner has a signed authentication by an expert, and an appraisal, may it be possible to deal directly and profitably with a private collector or institution.

Experienced buyers always take material out of a frame to examine more closely and to check the back.

Much autograph material is sold on a decorative basis, in an attractive frame, often for gifts. This is like buying cooked, packaged food; it costs more because you are paying for a service.

Verify catalogue descriptions and photographs; mistakes are made, rarely to the buyer's advantage.

It is better to have several fields of special interest than to go only after a single one. Broadening your interests gives you greater freedom of action.

Verify the credit and bona fides of unknown persons and dealers before concluding transactions.

Use a dealer's catalogue as a model in concisely describing your material for an inquiry.

Refuse to allow your manuscripts, letters, or documents to be microfilmed, photostated, or otherwise copied, except for your own records. If such copies appear, even in one place, they will reduce the selling price of your originals by as much as two thirds.

Don't try to sell material right after the death of its author. This is when most sellers mistakenly bring autographs into the market. It is the very worst time, since the market is inundated and prices fall. Wait, or better yet, buy low, and wait for the recovery.

Don't ever try to repair autographs or documents yourself. Plastic self-sealing tape will stain and possibly later destroy the material. The tape discolors the paper; it also weakens the paper underneath and may be impossible to remove.

Tears, holes, mildew, broken folds, or other blemishes can be repaired, but only after professionals have been consulted, and preferably, employed.

If you are a beginner interested in collecting autographs, check with the Universal Autograph Collectors Club and the Manuscript Society. They are two leading organizations in this field.

Never ship your autographs to a dealer without having previously sent a list describing what you want to sell and having been invited to forward your material for examination.

When you mail, pack in protective cartons or between corrugated paper sheets plus heavy outside wrappings.

Remove glass frames, since material could be cut or otherwise damaged by broken glass in transit.

Keep autograph and manuscript material out of direct sunlight and do not expose to extremes in humidity or temperature.

Avoid storing material where it will touch newspapers, photostats, or engravings.

Do not frame with wood backing.

Insure autograph material under a Fine Arts policy.

Read *The Complete Book of Autograph Collecting*, by George Sullivan, Mary A. Benjamin's *Autographs, A Key to Collecting*, as well as *Collecting Autographs and Manuscripts* and *Scribblers and Scoundrels*, the latter two by Charles Hamilton who, like Mrs. Benjamin, is a leading dealer.

BOOKS

Dusty second-hand stores, dirty junk shops, and hodgepodge thrift shops are happy hunting grounds for book fanciers with unlimited time to browse and who have photographic memories for lists of titles, authors, and editions. Here, knowledgeable scouts search out the finds that secure them comfortable livings when sold to specialists for whom they cull the stacks and shelves. Most second-hand-book dealers sell whatever valuable material they amass directly to the bookseller who has a market for it. At this level, the book may move from dealer to auction to connoisseur; it has reached a zone where it is identified, appreciated, valued, and priced accordingly.

This is a world where dealers call themselves "bookmen" and advertise for "desiderata." With some connections in the autograph field through signed books, maps, and broadsides, they are organized into the Antiquarian Booksellers Association of America and also deal in more recently published fine and rare books of interest to collectors. Known as the ABAA, the purpose of this group is to establish and maintain standards for the field and to stimulate book collecting. It is a fraternity which includes some very distinguished scholars and experts.

Famous book collectors, such as Huntington, Folger, Morgan, and Newberry, were wealthy men, but private collectors include many people of modest means, often of intellectual bent, but not necessarily so. To collect old or rare books, including children's books, books on hunting, gardening, sex, travel, or beautiful limited editions, requires no degree of any kind. However, the activity may educate the collector in more ways than one, and if the collection should become a gift to a college or university, it might provide an honorary degree at that.

With some, book collecting is a passion. Sir Thomas Philips (1792–1872), the world's greatest collector of books, had an income of £8,000 per year, not an inconsiderable sum in his time, but insufficient to keep him out of debt while making his gargantuan accumulation. So far, forty-two sales at auction and private transactions, yielding over 5 million pounds to date, have dispersed less than half of the collection, which has not yet been completely examined and catalogued.

Lessing J. Rosenwald, the multimillionaire whose lifetime pursuit of collecting prints and illustrated books started in the 1920s, was still at it when in his eighties a half century later. Quoting one of the celebrated Rosenbach brothers, the great book dealers of Philadelphia, this collector stressed that Dr. Rosenbach would sometimes refuse to sell him an item because he did not think it good enough in condition or quality and would urge him to wait until a better copy came along. A dean of contemporary book dealers once topped some accolades to Mr. Rosenwald by saying of him, "He never bargains."

Books in the rare and antiquarian category are collected by educational institutions, historical and other research foundations, museums, business corporations, and private individuals. Although bookmen are happy to serve their private clients, a great part of their business is done with institutional buyers.

Whether or not an individual ever expects to become a book collector, few can avoid the hope that somewhere among their old books, in cellar, attic, or household proper, is at least one of those thrilling rarities that brings thousands, or at least hundreds, of windfall dollars to a happy discoverer. Lists of such wanted treasures are available in book form, both paperback and hard cover, and are in themselves best sellers.

A *Leaves of Grass* at $3,700, a first edition of *Moby Dick* at $2,500, or even a few of those little pamphlets about the West that fetch hundreds of dollars seem possible prizes and stir the imaginations of thousands who have little interest in their contents.

It has been noted by one authority that when there is a possibility of getting $25 or more for a book, owners consider selling. Dealers, who are bombarded by such eager private sellers who offer old Bibles, school readers, and the like, usually of little or no monetary value, and who themselves usually pay the wholesale market rate for valuable books, become jaded and often will not take the time or trouble to go over the lists submitted.

In an effort to lessen the waste of booksellers' time and private sellers' hopes, the ABAA has suggested a form accurately describing books offered for sale by a private seller to a bookseller. If the bookseller is interested, it is explained, an effort to send for the books, or to arrange to call, will follow.

Author:
Title:
Size: (give size of pages in inches)
Binding: (full leather, one-half leather, cloth, paper covers)
Publisher and place where published:
Date: (if no date on title, give copyright date on reverse of title)
Number of plates and illustrations: (plain or colored)
Condition: (inside and out, state if stains and tears are present)

INSIDERS ADVISE

A first edition is not automatically valuable. Most are not. However, first editions of the important works of American authors have greatly risen in value in recent times.

The key word is "important." This can be checked in catalogue listings and auction sale prices. It changes in different eras.

A growing interest in Americana has included books, pamphlets, and other printed documents published before 1880, which are concerned with exploration, pioneering, adventure, local history, transportation, trade, and military affairs.

The book collector's market is served largely by catalogue, either that of the dealer, with prices listed, or the auction catalogue, for which prices realized are available.

Book auctions are also attended by collectors, but the principal bidders are booksellers. Veteran traders claim the prices realized are about half of what they will be priced at retail to a collector.

Each transaction is subject to its own financial equation, but it is believed that the private seller can expect to get one third to one half of the listed retail price when selling to a dealer *if* the dealer has an immediate client.

When books are bought for stock, to be held until a buyer appears, the offer will most likely be 20 to 30 per cent of the listed retail value.

Old books are rarely in the "mint" condition that makes dealers drool and bombard the owner with offers to buy at top prices.

The state of a book or pamphlet and its binding are subject to every ill that paper, thread, fabric, glue, ink, and leather are heir to, and a few more for bad luck.

Every defect in a book's condition is costly in reverse, reducing the price. A perfect copy of William Cullen Bryant's *Poems*, 44 pages, published in 1821, is quoted at $1,000 in perfect condition. A rebacked copy is $85.

The celebrated Thomas J. Wise's "first edition" forgeries, which fooled the greatest experts in their time, are recognized for what they are and now bring fabulous figures from collectors.

Although the most famous book forgers are said to be motivated by ego rather than monetary gain, most forged books are costly ones. For this reason, high-priced books are usually sold through dealer-experts, whose reputations are on the line with every guarantee.

A book is in mint condition if:

Original covers are intact. (It has not been rebound.)

A perfect dust wrapper or jacket is included.

It is *not* a library copy showing markings.

The spine is original, has not been rebacked.

The original slipcase is included, not a substitute.

The hinges and joints are as new, not cracking or repaired.

It is not foxed, stained, browned, yellowed, or moldy.

It is not damp-stained or water-stained. (This often shrinks the pages.)

It is uncut, with fore edges untrimmed, and even more desirable if it is unopened; the uncut fore edges not having been cut apart.

It is not scuffed, gouged, rubbed, or otherwise worn.

Folding plates are intact.

It is not marked with any comments, unless of the author or a prominent associated person.

Every page is present in proper sequence, as known and recorded by bibliographers, including the fly, printed pages, plates, and errata slip, if any.

It includes its "point"—that particular characteristic (it may be a flaw) that identifies the edition.

It has not been subject to repair or reconstruction of any kind.

Not too many books that have been read, nor many that are old, can meet the definition of "mint." However, as each catalogue listing is presumed to exactly describe each book's condition, it can be seen that when scarcity and demand combine, half a leaf is often highly acceptable.

Dust books frequently; treat leather to avoid drying. Treat books with care; watch heat, humidity, and light. Never try to mend valuable books yourself; get professional aid.

Do not pull at the spine to take books down from shelf. Push the books at either side back, leaving your book free.

Have a solander case made to order for especially valuable books. More protective than an ordinary slipcase, it includes an internal and external folding wrap of cloth and board and looks like an elegant binding on the shelf.

As might be expected, the literature on book collecting is of considerable size. Especially concerned with book values are those of the very readable Van Allen Bradley. His *Gold in Your Attic, More Gold in Your Attic,* and *Book Collector's Handbook of Values* are intended largely for laymen, but are of interest to the collector as well.

American Book Prices Current, United States Cumulative Book Auction Records, and *Bookman's Price Index* are consulted by dealers and collectors.

J. S. Blanck's *Bibliography of American Literature,* in four volumes, is considered the definitive work. Another classic is *U.S.-iana,* by Wright Howes.

ABAA recommends the following books for laymen: *The Bookman's Glossary; ABC for Book-Collectors,* by John Carter; and *Primer of Book Collecting,* by John Winterich and David Randall.

BOTTLES

Most bottles are glass, but pottery and porcelain bottles are also dear to bottle collectors' hearts, and plastic bottles probably are already listed in some obscure bottle price guide. For years, Early American bottles and Historical Flasks were the two chief categories. While they are still important, they have been overwhelmed, if not superseded, by newer ones, including a group called "Contemporary."

Hundreds of clubs of bottle collectors have been organized, many by dealers. There are hundreds of specialties, with constantly added items enlarging the scope of what is still called bottle collecting. A recent addition is the glass insulator, which has taken on the aura of a cult object. Priced from a few cents to as much as $50 or more for rarities, they are catalogued by color, size, stamping, shape, age, and source.

Advertising items affiliated with bottles, such as Coca-Cola trays, leaded lampshades, knives, and lighters, are among other peripheral novelties. Bottle listings include Avon, which is also the singular object of clubs, publications, price guides, auctions, shows, and conventions. Others are Apothecary, Bar, Barber, Beam, Brooks, Beer, Bitters, Candy Containers, Decanters, Drugstore, Early American, Fire Grenade, Figural, Garnier, Historical Flasks, Inkwells, Luxardo, Miniature, Mineral and Soda, Nursing, Perfume, Patent Medicine, Poison, Snuff, Soft Drink, and Wine.

INSIDERS ADVISE

Collect more than one kind of bottle. Diversity of interest makes you less anxious to acquire and less likely to overpay.

Early American bottles, Avon bottles, and Historical Flasks are three groups that have been especially "infiltrated" by reproductions.

Reissues of rare bottles are common, so learn the variations of each issue. Watch ads addressed to dealers, import shops, and glass retailers, offering reproductions.

Color is a big value factor in bottles. Dark blue, green, and amber will often sell at a premium. For each kind of bottle, there is usually one outstanding color most sought by collectors.

Since some bottles are more valuable with original contents intact (Avon bottles among them), be sure that the closure is original too.

Bottle prices in guides allude to mint condition. A small flaw in a wanted item may reduce it only 10 per cent, but if a bottle is badly chipped, scratched, or rough, you may take off as much as 90 per cent.

Check the source of your price guide before using it when you buy or sell.

Cecil Munsey's *Guide to Collecting Bottles* and John P. Adams' *Bottle Collecting in America* only show the tip of the bottleberg. Each of the many subdivisions of the subject has its own studies, handbooks, manuals, and price guides.

Much in this field is privately printed and can best be located through glass, bottle, antiques, and general collecting publications.

Among those price guides generally available are Ralph and Terry Kovel's *Official Bottle Price List,* as well as the Hotchkiss House publication, *Bottle Collecting Manual with Prices.* There are also other price supplements to popular bottle books.

BRASS AND COPPER

This is a promising area for collectors with great taste and modest means. Except for the Renaissance and earlier periods in this field, one does not need large sums to acquire the best. The collector of brass and copper antiques will have many problems of identification, but on the other hand, will find many attractive and interesting objects to choose from.

Few immigrants to the New World brought silverware, but brass and copper were often included in the possessions that accompanied them to their new homes. Well-crafted brass and copper from any land makes a worthy collectible.

Although there are dealers who specialize in brass and copper, almost any kind of antique shop, junk shop, or flea market may be the source of something worth while and interesting.

INSIDERS ADVISE

If you want to collect in this field, you had better learn to detect casting, stamping, and spinning and to recognize hard hammering, planishing, and fine riveting.

A large number of concentric circles indicates spinning, a technique developed about 1800 for brass and after 1820 for copper.

Paul Revere worked in brass and copper, as did some other colonial silversmiths. Not too many braziers and coppersmiths are known by name.

Copper containers can be used for cooking and eating, but only if they are tin-lined, as the taste of copper is undesirable.

The most costly brass, for which museums compete, is called Mosan and was made in the early Renaissance in the area of the valley of the Meuse.

Horse brasses, now prized as wall decorations, were made from 1750 to 1920. Those from the middle period are the finest; much sought by collectors.

Old brass has a silky texture, due to polishing. While old reproductions may have it, modern ones do not.

Brass candlesticks with stems and sockets cast in one piece were made until the seventeenth century and again in the nineteenth century.

Brass candlesticks made in the eighteenth century usually had stems and sockets hollow-cast separately, and then brazed together.

Although the expression "dinanderie" is used in Europe for brass objects, it was originally used for brass from the town of Dinant, near Liège.

Recently India, and before that China, has been the source of mass-produced brass for decorative purposes, some of which reproduces antique designs.

Those who use lacquer finish on brass and copper had better keep track of the kind used, as only the proper solvent will dissolve it. Lacquer cannot be used on metal for cooking or serving food, as it will peel and discolor.

Wax or lacquer coatings keep normal patina from forming. This patina enriches brass and copper.

Patina does not include dirt or corrosion. Wash copper and brass with soapsuds and ammonia before polishing.

Engraved and embossed pieces should have slight shadows; do not overclean. Use salt with warm vinegar to make a paste. Apply with clean cloth. Wash off with warm, soapy water. Rinse, dry, and polish with soft cloth.

Copper patina is green, similar to that on some bronze. Some people find it admirable on weather vanes and elsewhere. It is a matter of taste. Many prefer the sheen of clean copper.

Two useful books are *American Copper and Brass*, by Henry J. Kauffman, and Geoffrey Wills's *Collecting Copper and Brass*.

CARNIVAL AND DEPRESSION GLASS

Manufactured from about 1910 to the early 1930s as the poor man's version of Tiffany glass and originally called Taffeta glass for its characteristic iridescence, this now popular collectible is known as Carnival glass. It is an interesting example of how a well-promoted and merchandised ware can make fortunes for dealers, within decades of its disappearance from the scene as a cheap staple item.

Originally plentiful, produced by various U.S. glass manufacturers in many patterns and color ranges, at wholesale prices as low as a dollar per dozen for rose bowls and $2.15 per dozen for berry bowls, these lines were phased out by the mid-1930s. During World War II, they began to reappear for resale, usually in less elegant antique shops, on the fifty cents and dollar tables. By the mid-fifties, this glass had developed a following of collectors and a gently curving arc of rising prices.

In the mid-sixties, an enterprising "combine" went to work digging Carnival glass out of the Canadian provinces. Scouts paid small cash sums for all they could get, and they found tons of it. Brought back into the United States by wholesalers, who paid a required customs duty on "imported glass," it was resold to now Carnival-hungry American dealers at substantial markups.

Before long, Carnival collectors' clubs, publications, shows, and auctions were regularly reported on in the trade press. Page upon page of advertising offerings to buy and sell, a deluge of books and price guides, regular spates of news releases, recording prices of $2,000, $3,000, and even more for "rare" items, formed a heavy promotional barrage surrounding the Carnival glass "boom." Whether or not there had been one, when it was first hailed, there eventually was the reality of something very like it.

Following on the heels of the Carnival phenomenon, another specialty of mass glass production, this under the name of Depression glass, seemed to be heading for similar success. Originating in the 1920s, but rising to heights of popularity in the 1930s as "glass dishes," inexpensively sold and also given as prizes for movie attendance, it was plentiful. Made in sets and odd pieces, in various colors, decorations, and patterns, Depression glass is much collected in series and sets. Well promoted, it is not uncommon to see it publicized in the collecting trade press. A photograph of a smiling dealer holding a piece of glass will be captioned, "Depression Glass Butter Dish Sells for $195." The buyer is rarely shown in such pictures.

More such forays into glass nostalgia are on the way, as Imperial, Heisey, Fostoria, and other popular trade names go under careful and clever scrutiny by dealers whose promotional know-how will collect profits as they create collectors.

INSIDERS ADVISE

Since old molds are still available, some manufacturers are helpfully "filling in" items in Carnival and Depression glass.

Although a limited number of items sell in the astronomical price range, the publicity that is generated helps the sale of lower-priced items.

Iridescence can now be "home made" with a small kiln and the proper chemicals. It is no longer a secret formula.

Home iridizing of unusual pieces can create undoubted rarities, but hardly the kind that collectors want to pay for.

When you are sold an "offhand" piece, check to be sure that it hasn't been iridized outside a factory.

If you buy this type of glass for investment or speculation, watch the manipulators who run up certain patterns or colors, dump them to the suckers, and then start a new "trend."

Sherman Hand's "Colors in Carnival Glass" books and Marion T. Hartung's several books on Carnival Glass are among the best known in that field.

Colored Glass of the Depression Era and *Price Trends,* by Hazel Marie Weatherman, cover much of this subject in detail.

CERAMICS

This subject is so vast, that collectors and dealers rarely know more than their own specialties. Yet even within these limits, they are more dependent on marks, but have less confidence in them, than any other group of collectors.

Anything can, and often does, happen in the world of pottery and porcelain collecting. A world-famous museum reportedly pays over a million dollars for a hitherto unknown and unrecorded Greek calyx krater from a mysterious source. An anonymous buyer pays $573,000 at auction for a thirteenth-century Chinese jar that had been unrecognized by the previous owner, who used it as an umbrella stand. A well-known price guide introduces a new category of ceramics into its pages. Made during the American occupation of Japan, the items which are listed at average prices of from $2.00 to $10, are further characterized as "attracting interest of many collectors."

Thus pottery and porcelain prices for collectibles range as widely as do taste, sophistication, and the means to satisfy collectors' desires.

POTTERY

Although, or perhaps because pottery has been made since prehistoric times, it continues to fascinate an enormous number of people to the point of making them obsessive collectors.

Whether hand-patted and sunbaked, shaped and coiled, formed on the wheel, or poured into molds, pottery has retained an appeal in all the myriad forms in which clay can reflect the skill and art of its makers.

Although outclassed in some aspects by higher-fired porcelain with its many virtues, pottery has its own qualities that continue to provide it with value and appeal. The glazed pottery types known as Hispano-Moresque, Maiolica, Faïence, Delft, and Slipware have had periods of market activity and decline over centuries. There seems to be a revival brewing, based on interest in both the antique and Art Nouveau forms of pottery.

PORCELAIN

At the highest level, those who collect porcelain have been called the aristocrats of all collectors. Fascinated with a ware in which quality and workmanship are always discernible, but rarely obvious, they venture fortunes upon slight and fragile pieces that a second's mishap may completely destroy.

The urge to reverse a piece of china to see its markings, may be condemned as poor taste by those concerned with etiquette, but has no detractors among those who deal in, or collect it. Although the marks are only one of many factors, they rate very high in the value quotient of porcelain. There are many fakes and forgeries and some fine wares which lack any mark, but most factories were so proud to produce quality wares, that some sort of identification is expected, although not always found.

First made in China, over a thousand years ago, often attempted, but never successfully made in the West until the secret was discovered in the early eighteenth century at Meissen in Germany, every piece of early porcelain was collected and treasured at the time it was made. Even today, fine porcelain is not taken for granted, and much that is collected is of recent as well as contemporary date.

INSIDERS ADVISE

Pictures are very poor guides for identifying ceramics. Comparison with an authentic piece is the best of all.

You, or anyone who chooses, can become an expert on any single type of pottery or porcelain; no one can identify every type.

It takes a more cultivated taste to appreciate values in simple pottery or porcelain styles, than in ornate examples. Just now the highest prices are paid for the simpler pieces; however, the pendulum may swing again many times.

Marks can be removed as well as added or changed. Be alert for indications that the glaze at the base of a piece has been tampered with. Usually this is excised with a file.

In addition to knowing the marks that factories painted or impressed, be sure to learn the markings used to indicate rejects. Sometimes they are indelible modifications or cancellations; usually they are shown over the mark.

Check lids and covers to be sure they are originals. These can be newly made to replace missing parts, or can be cannibalized from other units.

Look-alike marks are usually purposefully confusing. Neither Wedgewood, Wedgewoode, Wedgewoode, Edgwoode, or Hedgwood are really mistakes for authentic Wedgwood.

It's a wise buyer who carries a book of marks for verification, but only consults it to confirm an opinion.

Ultraviolet light will show repairs and restorations by a difference in color. Make sure the piece is checked while still in the dealer's possession, or it may be said that you damaged it before returning for a refund.

Tap suspected replacements or restorations with a coin; the sound is different than that of the rest of the body.

Old molds which are reused when they are worn will produce inferior ceramics with poor details. These are the kind of "reissues" which give the original a bad name.

Strip, or otherwise check, felted bottoms before making a purchase. Cracks and drilled holes may thus be concealed. Taped tags and stickers should also be lifted.

Unglazed pottery is the easiest to fake. Glazed pottery takes more trouble, but the fakers try harder too.

Careful old repairs on old pottery are considered a sign that the piece was valued in its own time.

Fakes of the beautiful antique tin-enamel glazed pottery of the Near East and Persia are spotted by skimped reliefs and details. Luster decoration also tempts the fakers going for larger stakes.

Italian Maiolica of the Renaissance is the model for very old as well as newer copies and reproductions. The later wares are usually prettified and use more exact perspective. In authentic examples, decorations accent the shapes in a subtle way.

For a while, the high prices of French Faïence attracted so many forgeries of Palissy ware that the bottom dropped out of that market. It is making a comeback after several decades, but the reused molds may be doing the same thing.

Delft is another tin-enameled pottery which is a classic collectible that is much admired, costly, and much faked and copied in reproductions. Be skeptical if the item seems heavy for its proportions. The original brownish body was light in weight.

Forgeries of English eighteenth-century pottery are plentiful, but misrepresentation of Victorian items in the style of Astbury, Whieldon, and early Wedgwood causes most confusion.

Watch out for copies of Pennsylvania slipware. Authentic pieces made with the scratched decoration bring hundreds of dollars, while copies can be made cheaply and easily. The copies are usually thinner, straighter, and more regular in shape, with smoother glazes and "cute" decoration.

White bodies on most types of pottery will be the giveaway that the pieces are modern.

Bennington is credited with much brown-glazed mottled ware that was made in other factories. The type is Rockingham ware. If it isn't marked Bennington, maybe it isn't Bennington.

Art Nouveau pottery is still available at reasonable prices for those who want to buy selectively.

Earthenware stains may be removed by bleaching with peroxide or scrubbing with a damp cloth dipped in salt.

Paste, glaze, form, color, and quality mean more in identifying china than do the marks.

Crazing does not indicate age in porcelain which is sometimes purposely made with a controlled crackle which may add to the value. Scalding water may cause a network of cracks in the glaze; this is undesirable.

Hard-paste porcelain, made of kaolin and petuntse, cannot be scratched with a steel knife or file. It is white and translucent, even if unglazed.

Antique soft-paste porcelain is very valuable because it preceded true porcelain in Europe. It is made of clays mixed with ground glass and is very translucent. The color is greenish and it is easily scratched.

English soft-paste porcelain is called bone china and continues to be popular. It includes ashes of calcined bones in its composition. It scratches more easily than hard-paste porcelain and is almost, but not quite, as white.

Stoneware is closer to porcelain than pottery. It is glazed and made into country wares such as pickle crocks and jugs because of its vitrification. However, it is also the material of Wedgwood's elegant, famous jasper.

No matter how elaborate the design, decalcomania ornament should not be confused with hand-painted decoration, nor paid for as if it were.

On the other hand, certain hand-painted decoration, while done by hand, results from assembly-line techniques, and such limitations should be noted.

Unglazed porcelain may be called bisque, biscuit, or parian. Its value depends on the origin and quality. American parian ware will bring higher prices than the equivalent type of English piece, also of Victorian origin.

Don't be impressed just because a ceramic is porcelain. It's the quality that counts. Some pieces are worth just a few dollars; others may be bargains at thousands. The basic material is never worth more than a few cents.

Very fine porcelain wares may show signatures and marks of painters and modelers, as well as of factories. That Meissen teapot which fetched $94,000 at auction, included the mark of the decorator.

Antique Meissen was the most expensive of all porcelains 50 years ago, then antique Sèvres overtook it. Now it appears that Meissen is about to forge ahead again.

Precious Chinese porcelains, which are thought to be entering a period of price appreciation, require special expertise. If you own such items, which you believe are valuable, take them for expert appraisal, as the average dealer lacks the knowledge to identify quality wares.

The firm of Samson in Paris was notable for making outstanding reproductions and fakes in a great variety of wares. If you have suspicions, look for a hidden S which sometimes nestles in the decoration.

There are tens of thousands of discontinued patterns of Haviland china, the ware made in France for the U.S. market since 1842. If you want to match your pattern, look for the dealers who specialize in just this.

So-called "limited editions" of commercial porcelains, be they plates, figures, or vessels, do not warrant prices higher than the quality of the item would bring competitively.

The Dorothy Doughty porcelain bird figures, issued by Worcester in the 1930s and 1940s for hundreds of dollars, have brought as much as tens of thousands because they are of fine quality and true scarcity. In one case, that of the Bob White Quail, just 22 pairs were made.

Damp salt is a helpful cleaning agent for porcelain with cracks in the glaze that hold dirt. Some suggest peroxide as a bleaching agent. On the whole, gentle soapsuds are recommended for all decorated porcelain.

Hot water is permissible; scalding or boiling water, never. Store china carefully, never piling. Use padding.

Whether or not you have a repair or restoration to be done, try to visit a china-repair shop and ask to see the kind of work they do. You will buy more carefully after that, recognizing that damaged pieces can be made to appear perfect.

Dealers pay less than private individuals for repairs, so you are unlikely to find it profitable to have an expensive repair done before selling. Good work is expensive at both retail and wholesale rates.

There are so many books on pottery and porcelain that dealers and collectors are almost compelled to specialize, studying in special areas to keep well informed.

Price guides continue to proliferate. Ceramic prices can be found in little privately printed volumes and are also well represented in listings in the larger, generalized price-guide publications.

William Chaffers' *Marks and Monograms on European and Oriental Pottery and Porcelain* is a basic and invaluable reference book.

Especially strong in English marks, but including marks from Europe, China, and Japan, is the John P. Cushion and William B. Honey work, *Handbook of Pottery and Porcelain Marks.*

Not as strong on marks, but especially helpful for descriptions and evaluation is *The Book of Pottery and Porcelain,* in two volumes, by Warren Cox.

Pottery and Porcelain of the United States, by Edwin Atlee Barber, remains the great American classic.

CLOCKS AND WATCHES

Antiquarian clock and watch collectors, who are interested only in timepieces made before 1800, comprise an elite group of specialists, who can keep their eyebrows in place when a little English clock made for Queen Anne, and signed by the great master Thomas Tompion, fetches over $62,000 at auction in London. They study Renaissance watches for unusual cases, movements, and rare shapes; understand what makes them tick (or if musical, play); and, in general, are experts in the complexities of horological science and history.

Another group consists of collectors more concerned with the nineteenth century, the period in which clocks and watches were no longer made only to order, but for what was then mass production. American collectors of this sort will cherish the desire for an early Simon Willard banjo clock or an Aaron Willard shelf clock in the $5,000 range, but will also appreciate clocks made much later in the century, which can be had for figures in the hundreds, or less. Watch collectors in this category are interested in the products of early Waltham, Elgin, and Hamilton—when numbered under 1,000—and others by pioneer makers.

Decorative Victorian watches, both men's and ladies', are usually sold by the antique jewelry trade, and here too the market is an active one, with specialist collectors expert in cases as well as movements. Fobs, chains, and watch papers are items of peripheral interest, and there are also collectors of watch keys and watch stands or holders.

Grandfather, or long-case clocks, the shorter grandmother clock, not exceeding six feet six inches in height, bracket, wall, and mantel clocks and carriage clocks form some of the categories. The largest group of clock and watch collectors can be called enthusiasts about almost anything that ticks, and while they do specialize, the range is limitless. They also collect by shapes, as in clock-in-the-stomach figures; by makers, Ansonia is a popular one; by materials, iron, china, or bronze. They collect musical clocks, schoolhouse clocks, cuckoo clocks, and more recently, "character" clocks and watches.

This is part of the nostalgia boom we have noted elsewhere, in which Disney characters, among other movie and comic figures, have taken on major collecting importance. Prices for such figure-decorated clocks and watches, in mint condition and with original boxes, have made hundreds of dollars at auction. The original purchase price was usually in the area of $1.00 to $5.00, and the publicity that resounds when a Mickey Mouse clock or watch sells for $200 reflects the fact that almost every adult who was a child in the 1930s remembers them well. However great the distance from the uniqueness of a masterpiece by a Tompion to the mass-produced child's cherished treasure, each has its meaning, value, and market.

INSIDERS ADVISE

Except for lantern clocks, there are not many out-and-out forgeries of rare antique clocks and watches. They would be too expensive to make.

The problems of authenticity involve alterations. As old movements needed complicated repairs, the construction of the works would be changed.

Back plates and front plates are sometimes the only original parts of old clocks offered for sale.

Sometimes escapements and other parts must be replaced; the ideal for an antique movement is for the part to be handmade exactly like the original. This is considered "restored," in the best sense.

If there are many vacant holes in the back of a clock, it is a good indication that the original train has been removed.

Read any present-day catalogue of clock and watch parts, and you'll see why any old clock or watch you buy may be only an old shell with modern replacements.

Note how they advertise, "Exact reproductions of old dials."

Old cases and movements, formerly separate, are sometime "married," resulting in a bastard creation.

Attractive or utilitarian old cases, bought as decorative antiques, should be paid for at "as is" prices, unless the original old works are guaranteed to be included.

If you buy an old clock or watch that is not in running order, be prepared to buy a new movement to fit it. If the present movement can be made to run at a reasonable cost, you have won a long-shot gamble.

Unmarked old clock faces are a temptation, and sometimes false signatures are engraved to fetch higher prices. Compare with known authentic examples.

Old cases were sometimes altered as fashions changed. An arch would be added to a square dial; a hood reconstructed to take an arched dial. This lessens value, but should not spoil one's pleasure in a clock.

"Character" watches and clocks have had a revival as part of the nostalgia boom and are made in reproduction.

If you are offered a bracket clock with shelf, check that it is the original shelf.

If the name on the case of a clock and the name on the movement are different, it may indicate that the clock movement was bought by the casemaker.

Choose your clock or watch repairman by recommendation. Sometimes your old clock or watch has just the part he has been looking for, and unless very ethical, he may take it to restore something of his own, replacing yours with a makeshift and leaving it cannibalized.

Old clocks must be moved very carefully. If the unit will fit into a box, it may be easier to carry it level.

When you set up your antique clock, be sure it is on an absolutely level surface.

Dust and humidity are the enemies of any movement. A regular cleaning averts trouble.

Buy clocks and watches in working order; sell "as is."

Ask for an explanation when a repair is required. It may help to give the impression that you know what it is all about.

Always tie the key or exterior pendulum to the clock when it is moved or repaired. The originals increase value.

Useful books on the subject are *Watchmakers and Clockmakers of the World,* by Granville H. Baillie, *American Clocks and Clock-makers,* by Carl Dreppard, and *Guide to Clock Identification with Prices,* by Robert W. Miller.

Watches, by Cecil Clutton and George Daniels, and *Investing in Clocks and Watches,* by P. W. Cumhaill, are also consulted by dealers and collectors.

CLOTHING AND COSTUMES

Immediately after the death of the American designer, Norman Norell, in 1972, the fortunate few who owned any clothes he had designed in the previous 25 years double-checked their closets, or other storage facilities, to ensure the safety of their treasures. Others were reported to have made thrift-shop forays in the hope they could find some.

Museums hold retrospectives of Balenciaga designs, and costume institutes constantly replenish and bring their accessions up to date on the assumption that what just went out of fashion is important to the history of fashion.

For a time, "antique clothing," from 30 to 100 years old, was the most up-to-date attire, as young fashion leaders of both sexes invaded thrift shops and flea markets for clothing that became costume and uniforms that became clothing. When that subsided, patches of distinctively printed old fabrics were sewn to strategic points of sportswear, and recycled old textiles were made into instant "antique clothing."

Concurrent with these two aspects of fashion collecting—one pretentious and costly, the other unpretentious and less costly—is the pursuit of antique fabrics, clothing, costumes, and uniforms by the serious scholar, aided by dealers and collectors. A white silk shirt, thought to have belonged to Henry VII, was sold to the Victoria and Albert Museum for $2,329, but they also had less formidable items and prices at Christie's annual auction of clothes and costumes.

INSIDERS ADVISE

Keep records of maker, materials, where purchased, and original labels.

Make sure peasant costumes are not tourist bait.

Only very old, rare museum material is justified in threadbare, torn, or soiled condition.

Don't alter to fit you unless the item is expendable.

If you buy very old furs, be prepared to store them far away from your other clothing. They have quite a strong odor. So do some old woolens like serge.

Sources are thrift shops, resale shops, auction sales, antique dealers, warehouses, theatrical trunks, lost-and-found sales, bankruptcies of fine old shops.

Old fashion magazines are collected as a corollary item and guide for this field.

Store purchases at about 60 to 65 degrees, with 50 per cent humidity.

Keep away from sunlight. Protect against moths in airtight bag with napthalene or camphor.

If washable, laundries can treat for preservation. But don't clean or wash rarities without expert opinion.

Don't store without cleaning. Don't fold into creases.

The Dictionary of Costume, by R. Turner Wilcox, and the two volumes by Alice M. Earle, *Two Centuries of Costume in America,* offer fascinating background for the collector.

The Wonderful World of Ladies Fashions, by Joseph J. Schroeder, and Millia Davenport's *The Book of Costume* are studied along with catalogues and old fashion magazines.

The Smithsonian Institution in Washington, D.C. and the Metropolitan Museum in New York are among the important repositories for collections of clothing and costumes.

COINS

All authorities agree that expertise on condition plays the single most important role in the successful collecting and marketing of rare coins. Since the value and price of the same coin vary enormously, according to this factor, every effort is made to take the judgment out of the subjective area and to make it objective.

The difference between conditions in an 1857 U.S. half dollar of the Liberty Seated type has been price listed as:

Good	$3.00
Fine	$6.00
Very Fine	$10.00
Uncirculated	$50.00
Proof	$750.00

The difference between conditions in an 1807 U.S. large cent of the Draped Bust type:

Good	$10.00
Fine	$20.00
Very Fine	$40.00
Uncirculated	$3,200.00

Obviously, such distinctions are worth knowing!

GOOD   really means not very good at all. Date and mint marks should be legible and major design distinguishable.

VERY GOOD   means much worn, but without serious gouges or other mutilations.

FINE   indicates a reasonable amount of wear with the basic outline still clear, but much fine detail worn away. All lettering legible. (Often used by collectors as space filler pending better example.)

VERY FINE   design is quite clear, with a slight amount of over-all wear.

EXTREMELY FINE   slightest signs of wear or rubbing, only at the highest points of design.

UNCIRCULATED absolutely without wear.

PROOF especially minted for collectors, with a mirrorlike surface. Absolutely perfect.

Expressions such as "debased proof," "cabinet worn," and "cleaned" are individualized descriptions, requiring careful scrutiny, and generally are used as warning signals.

A lot of wheeling and dealing in the world of coin collecting revolves about the tricks by which coins are made to look better than they are. Coin collectors are constantly improving and weeding out items, to replace them with others in superior condition; and as they become expert in detecting minute distinctions, they often try to mask defects.

Early strikes of regular-issue coins appear to be proofs, as new dies give perfect mirrorlike surfaces, but the highlights are usually not as sharp, and the coin is not perfectly centered, nor are the edges as sharply struck. However, they are sometimes passed as proof to the unwary. Attempts to fake proofs are often made by buffing uncirculated coins. Governments have been known to use old dies to strike new proofs years after their original issue. These too can be spotted by experts, but are passed as authentic original proofs to the less initiate who are disillusioned only when they try to sell.

Closely related to condition is the subject of cleaning old and rare coins. Orthodox dicta gives three pieces of advice. No, no, and never. Admitting that soap may remove dirt, they say it destroys luster. Polishes scratch, dips remove some of the metal. Certain reformed opinions admit to an occasional instance when cleaning might be permissible. However, as has been noted, a coin labeled "cleaned" has lost some virtue and some value. The sign of a barbarian in numismatic circles is holding a proof coin flat on the palm where moisture, dirt, and oil can defile it. Those who know better, grasp any coin on its edges, between thumb and index finger, although the owners of proof coins don't encourage this either. An entire industry has been built about display and care equipment for coin collectors to use in the war against wear.

Volumes have been written about the detection of counterfeit rare coins and, no doubt, more will be needed. Authorities believe that many gold counterfeits of the costliest American rare coins are made in Europe. They are said to be of the proper weight and fineness, made by a centrifugal molding process, and hard to detect. Silver coins are not as often newly forged, but they are altered by removing branch mint marks, adding or "sweating on" letters, and changing 8s to 3s and os. Nickels are gold-plated and passed as five-dollar gold pieces, and two coins joined to look like rare mint errors. Mint errors are copied, and lead-centered, copper-coated rare cents are well-known dangers. These and many other variations of fraud and fakery have plagued collectors and dealers, who have had to pit experience against technology.

Now, however, there is a scientific basis for judging the authenticity of coins, provided by the American Numismatic Association. It is a coin-identification service, in which a coin, either U.S. or foreign, is put through a series of sophisticated tests, employing reliable instruments such as high-powered electron microscopes, specific gravity scales, electron probes, and X-ray diffraction in the American Numismatic Association Certification Service laboratories in Washington, D.C. If genuine, a coin receives a printed official certificate to accompany the coin on its travels henceforward. Copies are kept on permanent file at ANACS headquarters as an immutable pedigree.

The cost militates against checking less important coins, although some of sentimental value have been sent by indulgent owners. However, when an 1894 dime sells for $50,000 and dealers and collectors speak of prices as "balmy, fantastic and astronomical," guaranteed authenticity would seem to be sensible and prudent.

If you speculate in bulk silver coins in bags or buy just any gold coins to have a hedge against inflation, you may or may not be successful in your goal, but you are not a coin collector or numismatist, you are a gambler.

INSIDERS ADVISE

Before embarking on collecting complete sets of coins, establish the numbers issued, so you won't be defeated by a combination of scarcity and high prices for certain units. Figure the ratio for possible acquisition.

Consider the slogan of a dealer, "Buy the book before the coin."

Don't be overwhelmed by the fact a coin is silver or gold. The 1776 pewter dollar sold for $1,500.

The principal value factors for coins are quality, condition, scarcity, and demand.

Study coins under 20-power glass and compare with authentic originals.

Question any "bargain" from unknown sources.

When in doubt, use ANACS testing service if practicable.

Swap or exchange with the same care as purchasing.

Avoid "junk" end of the grading scale as poor resale.

Build a collection, rather than an assortment.

Don't be taken in by phony high prices due to dealers' taking in each others "washing" for publicity purposes.

Check each piece carefully when buying more than one.

Compare dealers' offers; some may be overstocked on certain items and offer better buys.

Do the same when you sell; some offers may be better than others, for reason of overstock.

If you want to sell quickly, you should get 50 to 70 per cent of guide-book prices, with the exception of higher prices for great rarities and less for commonplace material.

Don't consign coins for sale. Never take payment in installments when you sell.

Avoid local club auctions for important coins; there is too little competition.

Check credit rating of auctioneers you choose.

Auction fee (negotiable 10–20 per cent) should include all costs, insurance, advertising, printing, mailing.

Beware of overstated promises regarding auction prices.

Draw cash advance. Require auctioneer to give settlement date in *writing*. Should be 30 days.

If costly and important collection, keep and show in vault. If you clean coins, do so only under expert supervision.

Whitman's *Red Book of United States Coins,* annual illustrated catalogue and retail price list from 1616 to the present, is often accompanied on the shelf by Whitman's *Blue Book of United States Coins,* also by R. S. Yeoman. The latter lists average prices paid by dealers.

The green volume, *Appraising and Selling Your Coins,* by Robert Friedberg, gives prices the seller can expect for paper money as well as U.S. and Canadian coins.

Standard Catalogue of World Coins, by Krause and Mishler; *Modern World Coins* and *Current Coins of the World,* both by R. S. Yeoman, are also popular with dealers and collectors.

An outstanding reference volume is the *Select Numismatic Bibliography*, by Elvira Clain-Stefanelli. Its scope is international and inclusive to 1965.

Coin Collecting in a Nutshell, by T. G. Wear, and *American Guide to U.S. Coins*, by Charles F. French, are helpful aids for beginners.

The American Numismatic Society, founded in 1858, continues to make outstanding contributions to the study of coins, and its Numismatics Museum in New York City is an aid to scholars as well as collectors.

The American Numismatic Association, with headquarters in Denver, Colorado, conducts a national convention annually, in August, in various cities of the United States. With about 30,000 individual members and hundreds of local club affiliates, it is an important factor in the numismatic market.

Riding the crest of a wave of nostalgia for the 30s, 40s, and 50s is the collecting market for comic books, magazines, and affiliated material of this period. Trade journals called "fanzines," an annual Comics Art Convention, numerous shops, and a mail-order market of huge dimensions characterize this phenomenon, which is dominated by adults who may pay hundreds of dollars for a wanted item.

An allied, but more contemporary, comic book and magazine market includes items with a decade's age on them; this is the domain of the eight- to sixteen-year-olds. Two-year-old issues of some comic books, issued at the newsstand price of twenty cents, are bringing $3.00 and $4.00 in the resale market where these newly dedicated junior collectors compete.

The more venerable Horatio Alger and Frank Merriwell cultists have been overwhelmed by the sheer numbers of adherents to *Dick Tracy, Little Orphan Annie, Captain Marvel,* and similar figures of their era. Some are attracted by a sense of nostalgia; some by the scent of profit. *Superman* ✕1, issued in 1934, is said to sell for $500 in mint condition, *Batman* ✕1 for $600. They are indeed golden glamour issues, with few overtones of the depression era when they originated.

Movie magazines, posters, sports, and horror categories, as well as science fiction are included in this market, which swings wildly as certain fads spring up, and often as quickly subside. However, the blue chips of the field, as the scarce and wanted classic issues are called, get the most attention.

The name of the game is the pursuit of a complete series; and while many issues sell for less than a dollar, others may rise to hundreds as scarcity and demand go on a collision course. Some collectors prefer not to advertise their needs, on the theory that the intensity of demand will encourage sellers to tailor the price to it.

New collectors who have some original material from their

own attic "libraries" can be quickly fleeced in swaps, and exchanges may leave them with many more issues, but without the prize rarities which they were too inexperienced to recognize.

It appears that dealers will offer about one third of the selling price when buying wanted material. This is borne out by comparing their "buy" and "sell" advertisements. However, when it comes to "star quality" material at very high prices, dealers will offer more for a quick turnover. Yet should one of them be lucky enough to find a treasure for a low price, it will still go to list price in a rising market.

Junior collectors sell entire collections when they need money for another project or when they outgrow the interest. Some are excellent traders and liquidate piecemeal at close to retail prices; others, in a hurry, sell all at once at the best price they can get.

Dealers' stocks of "golden age" comics and related material originate in backrooms of poorly run, small old stores, secondhand and junk shops, junk yards, cellars and attics of clubhouses, storerooms of all sorts, and overlooked warehouse and storage facilities.

The greatest part of this market is conducted by mail, but there are shops in most big cities. These dealers usually trade in both "golden age" and the more recent issues. Some dealers combine the comic book business with records of the same vintage; some with pornography; some with antiques; some with second-hand books.

INSIDERS ADVISE

Try to know your sources when you buy, not that recourse is likely, but to try to avoid fakes.

In this market it is smart to make a trend, but dangerous to follow one if large sums are involved. It is volatile.

Dealers' price lists are available and make excellent price guides if used with discretion.

Be prepared to take your punishment if completing a series requires great rarities.

The odds for poor condition are high, accounting for the prices of star items in mint condition.

Missing pages, torn covers, and taped tears are acceptable if the item is a scarce one.

Current revivals such as *Shazam* are being stockpiled by some against future demand.

Fakes and reproductions have become plentiful.

Careful collectors check for the exact original paper and even know the kinds of staples used in various comic books and magazines.

Guard against damp, heat, and light, just as for fine books.

CUT GLASS

Touted as an improvement on the diamond because it was larger, had more facets, and cost less, Brilliant Period cut glass, made from the 1870s to the 1920s, was a form of perfection available to many, if not all, who admired it.

For all the elegance and beauty of design of English, Waterford, and Continental cut glass of the eighteenth and early nineteenth centuries, there were problems with the material itself. Now much admired, the blue or gray tint created by chemical reaction of lead impurities was, in its time, considered a defect.

Therefore, when a new formula created a fine, pure, and clear glass, with a more reflective surface, just at the time when new wheels and abrasives were developed, designers were challenged to new heights of skill in extending all possible combinations of pattern and form. What they produced was flashy and ornate, but it was a period of ostentation, appreciating just this.

Hawkes, Dorflinger, and Libbey are the outstanding makers' names for this ware in the United States; there were many more, now unknown, here and abroad. Collectors and dealers study available catalogues, furnishing names and descriptions of the shapes and patterns, and differentiating quality.

Bottles, decanters, baskets, bowls, boxes, dishes, candlesticks, and items as small as knife rests and as large as punch bowls are priced according to pattern, scarcity, condition, and quality. On the average, collectors find prices are now 10 to 20 times what they sold for originally when they were new. The range of $3.00 to $300 listed in old catalogues, costly at the time, make the modern collector of cut glass nostalgic in more ways than one.

INSIDERS ADVISE

Top-quality Brilliant Period cut glass can be recognized by a clear ring, great refractive power and sparkle, clarity, sharpness of the cut, and heavy weight.

It is wise to check availability and price structure before embarking on collecting a particular pattern.

Examine every piece of cut glass in a bright light. Experts use daylight plus a magnifying glass.

Do not buy for top prices unless the condition is mint. Check for chips that have been ground down, this is the most common flaw, along with scratches.

The ring of the glass is a good test for flaws, but it is not a sure test. Visual examination should be thorough.

Some "cut glass" was made on pressed blanks that were fire-finished. The general outlines are similar to genuine cut glass, but the interior has slight ridges which are directly opposite the deeper incisions on the outside.

Genuine cut glass is smooth on the inside.

Consult *Cut and Engraved Glass,* by Dorothy Daniel, *American Cut and Engraved Glass,* by Albert Christian Revi, and *Cut-Glass Handbook and Price Guide,* by John F. Hotchkiss.

DOLLS

Among other accusations leveled against American collectors is that of raising the world-wide prices of dolls by their competitive stance and willingness to pay high prices. Whether or not this is true, it is undoubtedly a fact that the number of doll collectors in the United States exceeds that of any other country, and it must be admitted that they take a leading position in pursuit of the quarry.

Here too, doll clubs, doll dealers, doll hospitals, doll periodicals, books about dolls, plus the volume of advertising and the sale of doll reproductions reflect the tremendous size of this collecting market, involving women, men, and children, in that order.

Folk, character, storybook, historic dolls, and paper, rag, bisque, wax, and rubber dolls, make up a few of the categories that inspire collecting and research of a high quality. Perhaps because they so easily identify with the original owners, doll collectors tend to search out the historic and social backgrounds of their subjects.

Although there are collectors who have as many as 10,000 dolls, most collectors limit themselves and become expert in special areas. Black dolls and other ethnic types are presently in the limelight of research and demand.

Prices at auction and shows indicate a growing interest and commensurate rise. The exquisite early German models bring top prices and fine French antique dolls are also much sought. Prices of $250 to $500 are commonly advertised for 100-year-old authentic, finely dressed china dolls in good condition.

Like doll collectors, doll dealers tend to be emotionally involved with their subject, making for much enthusiasm. However, it must be observed that this never seems to inhibit the excellent business sense characteristic of this part of the collecting trade.

INSIDERS ADVISE

Beginning doll collectors might well study how to repair and restore old dolls, before buying expensive ones.

There are few collectors of pre-nineteenth-century dolls, because there are so few to collect.

The history of commercial dolls in the United States starts about 1858 in Philadelphia with papier-mâché heads made by Ludwig Greiner. They are rare, but occasionally turn up.

Any doll dating up to the 1950s is called antique by somebody.

Kewpie Dolls, Shirley Temple and various movie-character dolls, the Dionne quintuplets and other twentieth-century dolls are much sought by collectors.

Almost all antique dolls have been subject to some restoration. The question is how much, and how?

Overrestoration is the greatest problem in doll collecting. Find out what the market offers in the way of doll parts, so you can recognize substitutions.

Each category of doll has its ideal and rare examples which may depend more on scarcity than charm.

Books of doll marks are helpful in identifying, but pictures of dolls can be deceptive.

Most china doll heads are marked near the base of the skull. You can copy the marks by placing a piece of thin paper over them and rubbing with crayon or soft pencil.

Patent and trademarks were used largely in the nineteenth century. Usually the numbers indicate style or size rather than date.

Original doll clothes and hair styles help to date dolls, but are also readily copied. Painted hair styles are a better indication.

Reproductions of certain dolls are known to experts. If in doubt, verify.

Old dolls still turn up in attics and trunks, alertness pays.

DEP means the item has been registered. The doll may be German or French.

Dolls with sleeping eyes should be packed face down, with some paper inside the skull, so the eyes remain open. Be sure to discourage moths which especially like doll wigs made of mohair as well as any wool clothing.

If dolls are kept in plastic bags, be sure you have sufficient holes to prevent condensation and retention of destructive dampness.

Exposure to strong light is especially harmful to wax dolls, as are extremes of heat and cold.

Among the outstanding books on dolls is *Collector's Encyclopedia of Dolls,* by Dorothy, Elizabeth, and Evelyn Coleman. It covers the subject to 1925.

Twentieth-Century Dolls by Johana G. Anderton identifies the period from 1900 to 1970. This is also a large and handsome book. There are many less elaborate, but excellent books.

EARLY AND LATER AMERICAN SILVER

Considered by prudent colonial owners as the safest way to protect silver wealth in a handy, useful, and easily identifiable form, Early American silver is still much appreciated for its investment potential, as well as for its outstanding qualities of craftsmanship and beauty as an art form.

American colonial silversmiths developed a native tradition which was not dependent on guild regulations, but on sturdy pride and honesty and on standards of excellence beyond reproach.

In addition to those made in the important centers of Boston, Philadelphia, and New York, fine tankards, porringers, flagons, beakers, sugar boxes, goblets, and many other pieces were produced by provincial silversmiths. These are also much desired by specialist collectors and historical societies.

The enormous output of plated and sterling silver wares in the latter half of the nineteenth century expressed the fulfillment of that American dream, in which, for the first time in history, the masses might aspire to some of the material appurtenances that had hitherto been reserved for persons of wealth and power.

Silver, always in the past synonymous with such status, could now be ordered from a mail-order catalogue or bought from countless small and larger shops. A silver-plated cake basket was priced at less than $5.00, cruet stands with handsome bottles cost little more, while $50 bought a six-piece tea and coffee service with a huge tray to match.

Sterling silver and coin silver in rich and ornate forms were plentiful for those who could afford it in the many weights and qualities produced for a large market.

Dominating the early 1900s, Art Nouveau styling challenged silversmiths and silver manufacturers to explore the possibilities of the naturalistic, flowing line. Lost ladies with flowing hair, and sinuous botanical forms signal interested collectors to note

and evaluate flatware, holloware, and the many personal accessories, such as belt buckles and letter openers made in this style.

Never plentiful, fine-quality Art Deco silver of the 1920s
has already found its way into museums and collections. Discriminating collectors still hope that unknown and unappreci-
ated examples will somehow turn up, and they keep looking for
them at flea markets, rummage sales, and in thrift shops.

INSIDERS ADVISE

Don't expect to find important Early American silver except at
important auctions and specialist dealers, but keep looking; you may
be lucky.

Early American used to mean late seventeenth and eighteenth centuries. It has been stretched to 1835 and even 1850 for hand-wrought
silver. This is known as late Early American.

Silver was much more valuable than the labor in those days. Often
coins were brought to the silversmith to be melted down and shaped
into easily identifiable objects, as a form of safekeeping and insurance.

Except for Maryland (1814–30), Early American silver was not required by law to be marked, as was English silver, although American
silversmiths were proud to impress their names and marks.

Much Early American silver is sterling quality because of the integrity of the makers; however, it was 1868 before the sterling
standard of .925 parts fine and .75 parts alloy was officially adopted
in the United States.

After the Revolution, more silversmiths began to show the standard
of silver by marks. Coin, Pure Coin, Standard, Premium, and Dollar,
or the letters "C" or "D," were among the marks used to indicate .900
parts of pure silver and .100 parts of alloy.

Some American silver pieces made in the early nineteenth century
were marked with "pseudomarks," to give the impression they had

been made in England. These have been duly noted as American marks and are collected as such.

Peace medals and other special items made for presentation to Indian chiefs are much prized Early American silver.

Early American silver of top quality has been priced far beyond the reach of the average collector. However, the ubiquitous spoon is a family heirloom that keeps many in touch with a great tradition.

If you have reason to think that you have a piece of very old American silver, take it to a specialist or an important auction house for identification. The average antiques dealer would not be likely to recognize it.

Paul Revere was a very fine silversmith, but his standing as a patriot helps to fetch great prices for his work—$7,500 for a punch ladle and $25,000 for a gravy boat are worthy homage to a hero's memory.

About mid-century, the local silversmith became the local jeweler. He might continue to make coin-silver spoons to order, but he ordered his stock from a large manufacturer.

Collectors seeking sterling, coin, and plated silver of this period find useful information in old sales catalogues.

Victorian silver is often bought at lowest prices from elite antique-silver dealers who specialize in eighteenth-century material.

Some of the ugliest Victorian silver is the heaviest, so don't let weight alone influence your choice if you aren't paying break-up prices for bulk.

One quality judgment involves the weight of the silver in relation to its purpose.

Many of the names on Victorian silver were not those of the makers, but of the jewelers for whom the stock was made.

American electroplated silver originated in 1847, with Rogers Brothers of Hartford, Connecticut. This firm still uses the 1847 date as a trademark.

The markings Triple-plated, Quadruple-plated, AA, AAA, and AAAA refer to the amount of silver deposited on the base metal by electroplating and signaled the amount of wear a piece could take before wearing through to the base.

There is much quality variance in electroplated silver. Some of it is very fine, the body being made with care and detail, and with a heavy coat of silver which has achieved a patina by polishing.

Many kinds of base metal were used. Nickel silver was favored because of its own natural silvery color.

Silver electroplated on a copper base is not Sheffield plate, although some manufacturers call it that. The only "advantage" is that it imitates genuine Sheffield by bleeding pink when the silver wears off.

Railroad silver is heavy-duty silver-plated-nickel tableware made for railroads. Some carry the name of the train, some of the line. It is collected by railroad buffs.

The mark EPNS means electroplated on nickel silver; EPBM signifies electroplated on britannia metal; EPC indicates the ware is electoplated silver on copper. The latter is often called Sheffield; it is not at all.

Art Nouveau silver is still quite plentiful, so selectivity as to design and quality is possible.

Unger Brothers, a Newark manufacturer, was an important producer of Art Nouveau in both sterling and silver plate. Note marks indicating which.

Gorham's "Martele" line of Art Nouveau silver holloware exceeds the sterling standard. It is .950 fine, making it desirable to collectors on two counts.

Noel D. Turner's *American Silver Flatware* gives patterns and marks from 1837 to 1910.

Collecting American 19th-Century Silver, by Katherine Morrison McClinton, is highly recommended.

Between *American Silversmiths and Their Marks*, by Stephen Ensko, and *A Directory of American Silver, Pewter, and Silverplate*, by Ralph and Terry Kovel, you stand a good chance of finding marks and makers.

Graham Hood's *History of American Silver* and J. M. Phillips' *American Silver* are two fine classic works.

ENGLISH AND CONTINENTAL SILVER

Although the silver of each country of the world has its collectors, they are, for the most part, nationals of the country of origin. The exception that dominates the world scene and towers as the exemplar of workmanship and quality is antique English sterling plate, internationally prized and collected.

Usually mentioned as an investment which outperforms glamorous securities, it is a classic hedge against inflation and has taken on new market importance with the growth of inflation in Britain as well as throughout the world.

Hallmarked for over 500 years, by use of a simple code indicating quality, maker, date, and place, English silver has unsurpassed acceptance for its beauty and adherence to rigidly enforced standards. Yet within this over-all heading, there are many qualifications that comprise the canons of value. How good an example, the desirability of the period, the standing of the silversmith, questions of craftsmanship, rarity, clarity of the hallmarks, these and other factors go into the informed judgments of experts.

Just as Early American silver is most appreciated in the United States, so European silver, lumped under the catchall "Continental," is especially valued in each country of origin.

Museums and individual collectors cross national boundaries, as do dealers, for exceptions such as products of the Fabergé workshops in Russia, eighteenth-century French silver masterworks, and the great German silver of the fifteenth and sixteenth centuries. These, like antique English silver, fetch fine prices at auction anywhere in the world.

For the most part, American collectors may come across an occasional stray heirloom of modest importance, but unless they frequent the shops and galleries of important dealers with international clientele, they will rarely see important Continental silver outside of museum collections.

INSIDERS ADVISE

Pure silver is too soft for practical use. Copper, the most desirable alloy, in the right proportions, makes for the finest silver.

The sterling standard of .925 silver to .75 copper was set in England in A.D. 1300. This statute required that a leopard's head be marked on each piece to indicate that it was sterling quality.

For a short time (1697–1719) the English standard was raised to .9584 pure silver and .416 alloy. It was called the Britannia standard, and is marked by Britannia seated. It can still be used, but rarely is. Don't confuse new with old Britannia nor britannia base metal with the real thing.

The expression "solid silver" is not used by professionals. They say "English plate" to refer to English sterling or Britannia silver, and sterling or Continental as appropriate.

London-made silver was especially fine, but the provincial guilds of York, Exeter, and Chester were among those whose marks are also of importance. Irish and Scottish silver are much collected by appreciative connoisseurs.

Breathe hard on silver around marks. Lines of solder will show if the hallmarks have been taken from another piece and inserted.

Hallmarks are sometimes purposely worn down to indicate a piece is very old, or to confuse as to its exact age. If you have to guess, pay less.

Early silver that has been embossed, chased, or otherwise additionally decorated at a later date is less valuable. Usually the styles will clash.

If ornament or markings are removed by filing or hammering, that part will be thinner than the rest, and the whole less desirable.

Worn pieces are sometimes cut down to make smaller, "perfect" but less desirable items with good hallmarks.

Beat-up teapots are shorn of handles and spouts to make tea caddies.

At one time, falsely marking English silver was punishable by death. It is still illegal, but the penalties are less and the gains are much greater.

Pocket folders giving the basics of English silver hallmarks are often presented by dealers. Other small volumes are easily available to help decipher marks easily.

Almost every piece of English sterling plate is completely hallmarked. However, there are a few exceptions. Very tiny pieces and those so richly decorated that markings would deface are exempt by law.

English silversmiths were members of the Goldsmiths Guild and are often called goldsmiths. You can check their marks in the goldsmiths' directory.

Unless a piece of English silver is completely hallmarked, its value is much reduced. The marks should be clear, so they can be deciphered without equivocation.

Most antique Continental silver was made with more alloy than sterling quality. Much of it varies from .800 to .900 and it is only in the twentieth century that the .925 of sterling is approached.

In most European countries, provincial silversmiths continued to work by hand until late in the nineteenth century.

Almost every European country had a different set of silver standards as to content and quality.

Marks on Continental silver are harder to trace than English hallmarks, but by no means impossible.

Almost every country exalts some special silversmith and period as its best.

The units of measurement for silver quality in various European countries have been the denier in Latin countries, zolotnik in Slavic countries, and lod, or loth, in Germanic nations.

Some European countries use a different standard of silver quality for domestic and export ware.

Although silver marks in Europe have been controlled by governments for centuries, changing times have resulted in a great variation of standards.

Don't be overwhelmed by the mark "sterling." It indicates only the standard of the metal, not its weight, thickness, or workmanship.

Poorly made, thin-walled objects, "loaded" or artificially weighted with pitch or lead, carry the same "sterling silver" mark as do fine, high-quality wares.

When silver has been gilded, it is called "vermeil." The gilt areas should never be polished, only washed with soap and water.

Silver containers require washing immediately after service and should not be used to hold food or liquids for an extended period, unless provided with liners.

Patina is the fine finish resulting from years of careful polishing. Avoid hard-bristled brushes and abrasive polishes; they scratch and mar.

Don't rub silver too hard when cleaning and polishing; avoid pressure, especially on hallmarked areas.

Buffing may remove stains, but it also removes some of the silver and always destroys patina.

Rubber leaves permanent marks on silver. Rubber bands are the most likely causes of trouble.

Troy weight is the unit used for silver internationally. One pound avoirdupois equals 14.58 troy ounces. One ounce avoirdupois equals .91 troy ounce.

There is as much difference between hand-wrought silver and mass-produced stamped factory silver as between an original painting and a commercial print.

English Goldsmiths and Their Marks and *An Illustrated History of English Plate,* by Sir Charles Jackson, are two great classics. A handy guide is William Chaffers' *Hallmarks on Gold and Silver Plate.*

Der Goldschiede Merkzeichen, which is known to dealers as "Rosenberg," after its author, is the bible for German and European silver marks.

Poinçons d'Argent, published by Tardy in Paris, is used by dealers throughout the world to identify, to date, and to check the standard of silver of every country.

EXONUMIA

Not a new disease, but a word invented to describe collectibles other than government-issue coins, such as medals, tokens, scrip, commemorative materials, especially marked ingots, and even those famous wooden nickels, exonumia has become so important a branch of numismatics as to warrant its own national show. Along with paper currency, also growing in appeal, such specialties are gaining new adherents of both collectors and dealers.

Parallel with the normal growth of coin collecting as a hobby with investment advantages, a huge industry has developed its commercial aspects, promoting them as an investment activity, with hobby advantages.

Private silver manufacturers, legally using the prestigious description of their factories as "mints" and further preceding that with historically derived nomenclature, successfully produce silver, gold, and bronze commemorative medals in countless series and subjects, miniature silver ingots, and metallic plaques and silver plates etched with all sorts of subjects.

Limited editions, limited only by subscription deadlines, may run to unknown but huge quantities, most of them paid for in advance of their manufacture by subscription. An effort has been made to create a market in these items. However, experts and veterans are skeptical that many subscribers will ever show investment profits because quantities are huge and quality minimal considering the price of many issues.

INSIDERS ADVISE

Learn to distinguish the works of medal designers. Some are crude, while others are great.

Don't buy medals until you have seen the exact item that will be yours, and be sure it is perfectly struck.

Be prepared to know the historical background if your interest is in military memorabilia.

Verify so-called market prices by offering to sell the item in question elsewhere.

Distinguish between dealer-dominated clubs and associations and bona fide collectors' clubs.

By the time an item is promoted as a good investment, it probably won't appreciate much more.

Don't expect to collect notes of large denominations unless you are very rich, but you can collect paper currency on a modest scale with modest means.

Token collectors seem to have more fun for less money than any other numismatic collectors, or exonumists, for that matter.

The *Biographical Dictionary of Medallists,* which includes coin, gem, and seal-engravers and mintmasters, is an important reference work.

U.S. Military Medals and Ribbons, by Philip K. Robles, is generally considered a standard on its subject, as is *Paper Money of the United States,* by Robert Friedberg.

There are more articles than books on tokens, medals, scrips, exposition memorabilia, and even wooden nickels. These can be found in the numismatic press.

Numismatic journals publicize clubs and societies in the growing field of exonumia.

FINE ART

Dealers publicly infer that art at high prices sells like popcorn in a movie lobby on Saturday night, yet many privately complain that with only a few collectors and museums able to afford the quarter, half, and even several million dollars it now takes to buy Old Masters and important Impressionists, business in the "popular" $10,000 to $100,000 range isn't all that good either.

As each new high makes its headlines, whether of a $3 million Raphael or a $200,000 Eakins, there is hardly a word about the bargains bought, the auction prices that were lower than expected, or the good values that need seeking out, but can still be found. Japanese collectors invaded the American and European markets and were paying seemingly astounding prices for art, but not every dealer had Japanese clients, nor did the Japanese want to buy everything in sight. The astute collector, who knows how to ignore high asking prices and to wade in with a counteroffer that may have to be raised, is still with us and will continue to be, even in a bull market.

In certain circles, one might get the impression that those who buy art under $10,000 are "little people," hardly worth an important dealer's time and energy, although probably acceptable as clients having growth potential.

Yet thousands upon thousands, happily unaware of their insignificance, buy paintings, watercolors, drawings, and sculpture in three and four figure prices. Some of them collect fine-quality art, old and new, that may increase in value; others please themselves with commercial gimcracks or common daubs that are doomed to future oblivion. They buy them from artists, dealers, in galleries, department stores, antiques shops, flea markets, and from each other. And each one has the sense of being an art lover and the thrill of kinship with the collector who spends millions.

And this is right, because they do have common problems

and even mutual interests. At every level, he who naïvely ventures into an artist's studio may emerge with an unwanted purchase, made out of embarrassment and personal sympathy. When great art museums make "exchanges" with dealers which the art world considers sorry expressions of judgment on the one side and shrewd manipulation on the latter, then private buyers and sellers with large or small purses must learn to be wary and avoid the treacherous "swap."

It may be easier for the owner of a fine-quality and rare work of art to sell, than it is for the owner of an ordinary or mediocre work, no matter what the price level. Yet how to sell to best advantage poses mutual problems for all who want to sell privately owned art.

The art market has been likened to a jungle in which the dealers compete for the prey, who may be both clients and private sellers. When approached with a Picasso drawing, one gallery owner offered far less than the asking price because it was not a lithograph which would sell for more! When a Picasso lithograph was presented for sale on another occasion, this dealer regretted it was not a drawing, which would be more salable.

INSIDERS ADVISE

The price of art is not necessarily an index to its quality.

The market value of an artwork will depend on many factors, but the identity of the artist is among the first.

Strength of attribution also governs value. "From the workshop of—" "a scholar of—" or "attributed to—" are weak, and will lower price and value. A strong attribution says "by," and gives the full name of the artist.

Who makes the attribution is very important. It should be from a leading specialist-scholar, and in writing.

Former ownership, reliability of the vendor, and timing of a sale also determine price.

One period of an artist's work may be highly valued, another considered inferior and undesirable. Almost every artist who has had a full career has a cycle of this sort and a "best" period.

Condition of a painting is an essential element. Overcleaning is considered a form of damage.

A signed work is the more valuable, but signature alone is no guarantee of authenticity.

An item that has been offered to many dealers will seldom bring a good price at auction.

If it is known that an object is from a dealer's stock, it is less likely to bring a high auction price.

Modern paintings are favorably affected by being illustrated in an auction catalogue.

Dealers prefer that old pictures they buy at auction should not have been illustrated in the auction catalogue. They would rather the piece and price be less traceable by their clients.

Even topflight dealers do not expect to get first prices asked. Some of the biggest collectors are the shrewdest bargainers. There are some exceptions.

The greater the rarity of a work, the harder it is to estimate the price it will fetch at auction.

Imagine the anguish of the owner whose "little painting" was bought at an English provincial auction for $6,480 and which fetched $360,000 at a London auction seven months later!

An exhibition, a new book, an extraordinary find, or a promotional campaign can trigger a boom for an artist's work.

Unless artists are well established, they often pay for gallery exhibitions. This is in addition to the usual one-third commission taken by the dealer.

Artists who are under contract can sell only through the dealer or agent. If they sell privately, they jeopardize the connection. However, some may risk it.

The buyer who tries to circumvent paying the gallery price, by buying directly from the artist, is sometimes pressured by the artist's personal involvement and might find a more objective and therefore resistible atmosphere in the dealer's gallery.

Be sure you take advantage of all the customary courtesies when you buy art. You may ask that a piece be reserved for you for a short period, so that you can decide at leisure. You may also ask that a work under consideration be sent to your home for approval.

Do not feel obligated to buy just because you have had an item put on reserve or sent on approval. But do not make a practice of this, or refusals will result.

When a dealer or experienced collector remarks that an artwork doesn't seem "right," it means there is a doubt which can't yet be pinpointed, but which will be followed up.

Tastes change and opinions fluctuate, but bad art does not increase in value by aging.

Every classic masterpiece was once a modern picture.

If your credit is at all good, you will find that art dealers will be overjoyed to extend very generous terms, including installment payments.

Although modern science has made great strides in identifying fake paintings, it has also been used as an aid by the faker.

If all else is right, the truest test of a painting's authenticity is the distinctive brush stroke of the artist, as recognized by an authority on that artist.

Some collectors find that a black and white photograph tells a lot about a painting's quality.

Dealers often send color transparencies to colleagues and clients for a first reaction and opinion about a painting.

The number of casts, who made them, and the quality of each determine the value of sculpture except for original carvings.

Think twice about buying a crucifixion, flagellation, deposition, or other depressing subjects for resale. Light, bright, and gay pictures are more popular with buyers.

Art forgery is easier to detect in a later age than the period in which it was executed because the style of the time becomes more apparent in retrospect.

Some museum curators will act as private consultants for a fee, as will art historians.

If a museum's art is being sold, the reasons why the work is being "deaccessioned" should be noted by prospective buyers.

The stretcher and back of a painting often carry useful information, helping to identify the picture through a gallery or framer.

Once you know an artist's name you can look it up for further information in one of the biographical lists to be found in libraries and museums.

Constant exposure to bright light is bad for paintings, watercolors, and prints. Ultraviolet rays are harmful and can be screened out.

Never dust paintings with anything but a very soft brush, and then only very occasionally. Never use a cloth.

Incline oil paintings a few degrees from top, away from wall.

Most desirable temperature for oils and watercolors is 70–72 degrees. Most desirable humidity, 50 per cent.

Don't ever glue watercolors to a back. Use all-rag, special museum cardboard for backing.

The powdery pigment of pastels can shake loose and should be handled with great care.

The Art Crowd, by Sophy Burnham, gives some clues to the contemporary art market.

Duveen, by S. N. Behrman, refers to the days of the industrial tycoons, but it is a classic study of how a genius created markets for art.

Fakes, by Otto Kurz, and *The Art Game,* by Robert Wraight, are instructive.

FOLK ART

There is always someone to tell you whether or not an object can be rated as Fine Art, but you alone are free to confer the accolade of Folk Art.

As one of the most accessible, and possibly the most creative, forms of collecting, that of folk art spans time, place, and material, to indicate what is beautiful and admirable in the everyday objects characteristically made and used by societies simpler than our own.

Although rare and desirable items in this wide category often bring very high prices, because of the competition of collectors and museums, there are countless others that can still be bought reasonably because they are unrecognized or are still currently folk-made in rural areas of underdeveloped countries.

Folk art museums all over the world exhibit costumes, furniture, toys, baskets, textiles, needlework, prints, paintings, signs, and weather vanes. Whether the category be kitchenware, farm implements or tools, pottery, glass, wood, metal, plaster or stone, religious, political, medical, scholastic, cultural or domestic folk art, they are all acceptable, under headings of any nationality, as examples of popular, pioneer, or provincial art. To be a folk-collectible, the item may reflect folk taste and folkways as well as folkcraft.

INSIDERS ADVISE

Collect with a purpose and within controllable limits, as it is easy to get lost in this boundless field.

Folk art is valued for functional qualities, simplicity, modesty, earthiness, wit, design, color, and expression of personal style.

When a folk art is in touch with its roots, it will show more originality and sprightliness. When it becomes degenerate and commercialized, it will be repetitive and literally tired-looking.

In folk art, age is less important than individuality.

Dealers who are specialists may charge more, but they will have choicer selections.

Check on stocks of folk-import wholesalers and retailers. Sometimes you can still find excellent folk-art items. You will also be able to recognize the mass-made material if it is offered to you as authentic.

Explore the folk art of the lesser known sects as well as the Amish and Shakers. Try the Zoarites (1819–98).

Country auctions do offer folk-art items, but be sure you have examined carefully before bidding. This is a natural planting ground for fakes.

The farm, well planted with pseudoantiques, is another source of phony folk art. Pay little, unless you know a lot.

It is not crude, but loving workmanship that distinguishes fine folk art.

Don't restore old painted tinware, woodenware, furniture, or other objects where the finish is faded or worn. The piece is of greater value in "unimproved" condition.

Old baskets may be carefully washed according to instructions, but mending them at all is usually a mistake.

Shaker-style furniture was made commercially in the latter half of the nineteenth century. This is not the true folk art, handmade by the Shakers.

Have a look at *American Folk Art,* by Jean Lipman, *Early American Folk and Country Antiques,* by Donald Raycraft, *Pennsylvania Dutch American Folk Art,* by Henry J. Kauffman, and *Colonial Kitchens,* by Frances Phipps.

FURNITURE

Did you ever think that you might be engaged in aging and distressing fake furniture? Well, if you just happened to be dining in a restaurant to which a friendly "restorer" had loaned tables, chairs, sideboards, or other handy pieces, you might well be aiding and abetting the creation of a distressed finish with the authentic and logical signs of wear that some day might even convince you to buy them as antiques.

The very fact that there are recognized degrees of faking in the antique-furniture market is some indication of how the specter of fraud stalks in this field.

The wholly modern fake, made with modern antiqued wood, is the least convincing but possibly the most common. The modern fake made with old wood is a rival. Next is the piece of furniture made from several disintegrating parts of various antiques which have been cannibalized to make a newly designed so-called antique. A fourth technique is to enrich and ornament a plain authentic antique, possibly of country origin. By adding carving, veneers, or metal mounts, it is moved into the category of elegant and costlier antique furniture.

A serious challenge to collectors and dealers is the "restoration." This consists of less than half (and often even less than that) of an original, in poor condition, which is then repaired and restored into something fractionally original, in gorgeous condition. And, although the exact and absolutely perfect copy of a great antique piece is rarely made in these days of scarcity of fine workmanship, it too is sometimes produced for a suitably remunerative reward.

Occasionally an owner, wishing to sell an important family heirloom, will only do so on the condition that the dealer who buys it substitutes a perfect copy. When a dealer can make a good buy and then sell the original for several hundred thousand dollars, he may spur his cabinet shop to unprecedented heights of skill.

The very size and bulk of most furniture makes it awesome as a collectible. Lacking storage space on a suitable scale, the average person has to live at close quarters with a purchase. Accordingly, utility is a major factor, one which incorporates condition as well as use, and since furniture reflects the decorative level of a household, the difficulties are multiplied. Add to this the inhibitions attending the outlay of comparatively large or great sums, which may be involved, with the questions of value and authenticity, and it is a wonder that a market exists at all.

But it does for a French eighteenth-century desk with Sèvres plaques at $415,800, as well as for an American lift-top pine lap desk at $50. Connoisseur collectors buy beauty and quality according to their circumscribed period interests; decorators buy for rich clients, according to size, style, and utility; lovers of antiques buy for authenticity, charm, and rarity; homemakers buy for suitability and value, as related to prices for new furniture.

The publicity that attends the sale of an American corner chair for $85,000, a Newport block-front chest at $110,000, and signed French pieces in the $200,000 and higher range excites both imagination and cupidity. Prices of antique and old furniture of good quality, and some of merely ordinary quality, seem to rise in a sort of misplaced empathy. Thus all who are interested in acquiring old furniture might well arm themselves with as much information as possible.

INSIDERS ADVISE

Old carving is never sharp-edged. Cleaning, dusting, and rubbing smooth the edges.

Fake wormholes are straight, nearer the surface. Real wormholes meander and go far into the wood.

Finely made wood dowels are an indication of age, but not necessarily a proof.

Rough, crude, and careless workmanship does not increase in value with age.

Handmade nails have been reproduced, so in themselves are not an indication of age.

Dark stains on undersides of furniture often disguise new wood.

Old wood is heavier than it looks; new wood is lighter.

Check all moldings to see they "agree." Assembled pieces often show differences.

Don't consider buying Fine French Furniture unless you are rich, rich, rich.

If you are buying rare and costly furniture, be sure to get a guarantee, with a full description, from an established and reputable firm. Buy at auction with counsel.

Look for discrepancies between type of framework and the outside decorations.

Check metal mounts with a penknife or magnet to see that they are not electroplated or lacquered modern castings.

If marquetry is bright orange, it's probably a Dutch reproduction.

Genuinely fine antique furniture may be rich and ornate, but the decorations will flow naturally into the form.

Although it should look graceful and lightweight, elegant antique furniture will be strongly constructed and heavy.

Marvelous reproductions of English and French eighteenth-century furniture were made during the mid-Victorian era. It takes an expert to spot them, so take an expert.

Avoid veneered antique furniture recently brought from abroad. Change of climate from damp to very dry causes cracks, checks, and splitting of veneers.

Best quality faking nowadays is done in England, Italy, and Spain.

Really old gilded furniture will show some brighter areas, since surfaces where dust collects have darkened.

Painted finishes that are genuinely old, show some flaking. If condition is too "perfect," beware.

If an old piece has been repainted, as some need to be, some of the old paint will show beneath if probed for.

If you are going to use antique furniture, make sure it is sound and strong enough for your purpose.

Pull any piece of furniture out into the center of the room before you buy, to view from every direction for flaws.

A piece that has been over 30 per cent restored has had its value even more drastically reduced than that percentage.

Bona fide repairs and restoration of less than 30 per cent may be acceptable.

Although the fad for stripping furniture makes it attractive to many, pieces without patina have diminished value as antique collectibles.

Always get your estimate *beforehand* if you buy with the intention of refinishing, repairing, or reconstructing.

Good old nineteenth-century reproductions are valuable, but prices should be in proportion to cost of originals.

Just because a piece of furniture comes from a big and important collection, it is not automatically authentic.

Be sure to buy average-quality pieces at less than average prices, because there is no great demand for furniture in this range, as you can see by going to auctions.

If you are crazy for Queen Anne antique furniture and can't afford it in the American form, try the English; it's lower priced, though not cheap.

English and American Victorian furniture has suffered several false starts in market popularity. If you buy for investment, be discriminating and look for outstanding quality only.

By now you have missed the boat for bargains in Art Nouveau furniture. If you want to collect this style, get a good background in advance, because a piece should be in the mainstream of naturalistic design importance to justify the high prices asked.

Look in your attic and cellar for Art Deco furniture. It is selling at the kind of prices it is better to receive than to give. However, those who see this budding of modern art in furniture design as the last gasp in elegant craftsmanship may be right to collect.

Mission oak, as an aspect of Americana after the turn of the century, is being taken seriously by collectors who look for Stickley Craftsman and Hubbard Roycrafter mission styles.

Old brass beds "stretched" to modern queen and king sizes, or otherwise rearranged as twin beds, are particularly popular with young homemakers.

Rolltop desks are being imported to the United States in response to a revival, which includes every age and price category. The ugliest oak old-timers are usually stripped of all finish to give a "new" old look.

Oil finishes should not be waxed, as the characteristic patina is then lost.

Fine veneers should be hand-rubbed with hard-paste wax about every six months.

Boiled linseed oil in combination with equal parts of turpentine and vinegar is good for solid rustic furniture. It may darken, but enriches the wood.

Don't use linseed oil on gold leaf or painted furniture.

Never use a damp cloth on lacquer.

Dampen wicker and cane occasionally. Coat rush with white shellac; never dampen.

Lubricate marquetry decorations with a drop of olive oil on cotton dab. Remove without touching adjoining veneers.

Painted furniture may be slightly waxed. Oil darkens it. If necessary, wash small section at a time with mild soapsuds and damp cloth. Rinse and dry thoroughly. Rewax.

Furniture Treasury, the American masterwork by Wallace Nutting, consists of three volumes of splendid research.

The Complete Guide to Furniture Styles, by Louise Ade Boger, and *The Encyclopedia of Furniture,* by Joseph Aronson, are classics, as is *American Antique Furniture,* by Edgar Miller, Jr.

A Short Dictionary of Furniture, by John Gloag, and *English Furniture Styles from 1500 to 1830,* by Ralph Fastnedge, are two useful English guides.

Antique Furniture, Guide for Collectors, Investors and Dealers, by L. G. G. Ramsey and Helen Comstock, and *The New Antiques,* by George Grotz, contain helpful tips.

Two handy standard books are *Field Guide to Early American Furniture* and *Field Guide to American Victorian Furniture,* both by Thomas Ormsbee.

Price guides for furniture are particularly inadequate because no two handmade pieces of antique furniture can be properly compared without complete details.

GLASS PAPERWEIGHTS

Glass paperweights of the mid-nineteenth century, from the French factories of Saint Louis, Baccarat, and Clichy, are the most highly prized and highly priced. A Clichy weight of a rare design, one of three known, brought over $20,000 at auction. Prices for a fine specimen of one of the "big three" firms will usually hover in the thousands. There are English and American paperweights also in this league, some carrying dates and signatures, as do choice French examples.

The jewel-like character and convenient size of glass paperweights make them eminently collectible. In addition to the fortunate few who can afford the finest, there are many collectors who enjoy a wider, if less costly, range.

Millefiori (made with glass rods), overlays, latticine, sulphides, bubbles, swirls, cut glass, various types of Art glass, and mosaics make up some of the many variations of fine paperweights wanted by collectors. Both antique and modern weights have won followers, and commemorative and limited editions are widely promoted.

Great collections are usually sold at auction. An important sale was the dispersal of the deposed King Farouk's collection in Cairo, in 1954, for prices which then seemed high, but are not so in retrospect.

INSIDERS ADVISE

Dated Baccarat and Saint Louis paperweights prior to 1849, have the dates set off center. Dead-centered dates for this period are to be viewed with suspicion.

Attempts at identifying authentic paperweights by using refractive index tests to verify lead content and thus credit to certain factories, have been inconclusive.

In the 1930s, dealers sent fine old paperweights to China to be copied. Experts recognize them principally by their lack of brilliance.

Baccarat and Saint Louis are still making fine paperweights, these are signed and dated, and are sometimes limited editions.

Copies of quality antique paperweights are collected as such.

Initials or signatures can be forged, either on the inside or outside of a paperweight.

Among the most valuable American paperweights is the famous "Millville Rose," made in New Jersey by Barber, between 1907 and 1912.

Old weights of quality were usually cared for and rarely show scratches. Modern fakes are often "aged" with scratches.

To bring top prices, paperweights must be absolutely perfect. Even the most subtle repairs will reduce value greatly.

Some rare paperweights have the star cut into the base; so do some reproductions.

Clever recutting has been known to hide the crack in a paperweight.

Objects made by techniques similar to those used for glass paper-weights appeal to many collectors. Wigstands, doorknobs, vases, bottles, and inkstands are in this category.

Italian, especially Venetian, reproductions of glass paperweights are plentiful.

Books about glass paperweights written by either Paul Hollister, Jr., or Paul Jokelson are sure to be of interest to collectors and dealers in the field.

Glass Paperweights of the Bergstrom Art Centre, by Evelyn Cloak, is a volume devoted to the fine collection shown in the museum in Neenah, Wisconsin.

GRAPHICS

An avalanche of fakes, forgeries, reproductions, and restrikes have come out of the woodwork where graphics are stored and hung, in response to an unprecedented boom market.

Lithographs, etchings, engravings, woodcuts, mezzotints, and similar expressions of art, which are printed from a master image, may be called graphics or prints; they have always been valued and appreciated by collectors, but never before invested and speculated in, as in recent times.

The boom originated in the enormous prices that took big-name modern paintings out of the reach of art-minded but status-geared buyers. Unable to compete for the paintings, they found the usually colorful, important-looking prints, signed with names such as Bracque, Matisse, Chagall, and Miro among others, as desirable substitutes. Until the early 1960s they could be bought for $100 to $1,000, with the latter amount the price of an important rarity.

Nudging aside the collectors of limited means who had been motivated by a love for the beauty of the print form, the new buyers were soon met by new dealers who viewed the graphics market as a speculative investment exchange. One firm of dealers was reputed to have over $2 million in Picasso holdings alone. A Matisse black-and-white lithograph, "Le Renard," done in 1929, was sold for $9,000 at auction. A few years before, it had been priced at $750. Similarly star-quality prints of other artists soared to new highs. A Miro, published one year at $700, was sold the following year for $8,000.

Some of this could have been the result of manipulation and promotion, with prices hiked artificially, but most veterans believed that the rise was due principally to speculation as part of the art-investment syndrome. Sharp practices followed the high prices. Old plates were recut, then restruck to print garbage-quality "originals" for which good prices were asked and received. Prints were made after paintings and credited to artists who neither made the plates nor signed their names to the work. It became a market in which only the very knowledgeable could hold their own. Others were cheated unless they bought from honest and reputable dealers, or unless they were smart enough to forego the big names and buy some of the very beautiful prints that were produced by less well-known artists for sums well under $100 in most cases.

Japanese prints outpaced the big-name race. This delightful popular art of the eighteenth and nineteenth centuries had long been collected in the West, but it took the competition of Japanese-tycoon collectors to raise the price of Hokusai's "Great Wave" from $1,250 in 1969 and $4,100 in 1970 to $13,500 in 1972. Utamaro's much-admired portrait of the waitress Ohisa brought a world-admired record price of $37,500, till then the highest ever paid for any Japanese print.

Audubon engravings, unique and magnificent, have fetched $260,000 for a portfolio of the first impressions, numbering 435 of the "Birds of America," with $9,000 paid for a single engraving at a Sotheby Parke Bernet auction. A recent four-volume, 250-edition reprint of the work priced at $6,960 was selling at a goodly pace shortly after issuance, with most of the buyers expecting the value to rise with the years.

Valued more as social history than for sheer artistic merit, Currier and Ives are collected as Americana, as are other prints reflecting a sort of pictorial journalism. Here, too, prices for rarities can go very high, but there are areas and categories which are still reasonably priced and offer great scope to the creative collector.

INSIDERS ADVISE

Missing margins, either torn or cut, will diminish the value of a print. Be alert for the replaced margin which can be added by pasting the cut print together with new edges, over a lining.

Published research on the various states, conditions, variations in color and texture of paper, and other details of authenticity have also furnished fakers with useful information.

"State" refers to a single impression or group of impressions that have been pulled at each of various stages in the making of a print. Because Rembrandt made numerous alterations to his etchings, some have as many as five states.

Usually the earliest state is the rarest, although not necessarily the artist's ideal. Late states are sometimes reworked plates, pulled by other than the artist.

Every kind of plate has its maximum number of ideal strikes.

Restrikes are made from plates supposedly discarded. In order that they may be used, they are usually reworked, losing the special quality that made the impression artistic.

Unless restrikes are sold as such, they are a form of forgery.

French graphics marked "épreuve artiste" for artist's proof, or H.C., meaning "high commerce," or prenumbered plates for the artist to sell personally should only be few in number. However, sometimes large numbers of them are pulled before the numbered edition commences.

The print as a valuable work of art results from the creation of a master image, by the artist alone, on the plate, stone, woodblock, or metal.

Either the artist himself or someone following his exact directions must execute the print considered original, pulling each one and carefully examining it.

Approval of the finished product must be by the artist, preferably shown by penciled signature in the margin.

A signature in the print itself is not considered an indication of the artist's approval of a print.

Paintings by one artist, converted into an image by another, may or may not be fine art, but must be recorded as being by another hand.

Old Master prints, covering the same time span as Old Master paintings, multiplied 30 times in price over a two decade period from the 1950s on.

A magnificent impression of a Rembrandt print, "The Agony in the Garden," brought over $70,000 from a European dealer when auctioned at Sotheby Parke Bernet in 1973.

Some Rembrandt restrikes are barely worth $25, although they are usually sold as "originals" and for much more.

In a properly made quality edition, distinctions are not made on the basis of lower or higher numbers. As each print is an individual work of art, it should be judged as such.

A smaller edition usually indicates great concern for quality.

Prints are identified by subject, accurate measurements, states, watermarks, flaws, quality of impression, and color.

The only absolutely sure method of showing up a dubious print is to compare it with an authentic version of undoubted authority in a great collection.

You can consult catalogues showing the prints made by better-known artists, indicating the dates, sizes, paper, colors, number of impressions per editions, number of editions and signatures used.

Some dealers reproduce a better impression in their catalogues than the ones they are offering for sale. Collate the two.

Dealers' adjectives describing quality should usually be discounted by two degrees.

The quality of the paper influences the richness and precision of the impression.

Avoid graphics with weak printing, cracks, stains, and scratches.

Note condition and what repairs, if any, may have lowered the value of a print.

The paper used for prints can be analyzed and dated by experts.

Do not bond print to backing board which should be all rag.

Never trim margins. Never use plastic mending tape.

Keep a distance between the transparent cover and the print.

Avoid washing frame, glass, or plastic cover with flowing water. It might seep in.

Keep prints away from hot- and cold-air vents.

Use cardboard tubes for mailing, boxes for storage.

Experts can clean, bleach, mend tears, repair holes, remove varnish, uncrease folds, or remove curls. Amateurs are advised to get professional help.

Important galleries form complete catalogues of the prints of the artists they feature, and they may be consulted there.

Published collections of graphics range from inexpensive to costly issues, the latter owned mostly by important collectors. However, they may also be consulted in museums and art libraries.

Although print dealers' catalogues show their list prices, discounts may be available on inquiry.

Auction catalogues showing the prices realized for prints are widely circulated in the trade.

Print collectors have organized clubs in some cities. Their newsletters and similar publications offer useful perspective on the market and prints, print production, and printmakers.

An excellent basic volume on graphics is *The Book of Fine Prints*, by Carl Zigrosser.

JEWELRY

When Mrs. Astor was asked about the propriety of wearing diamonds in the morning, she replied, "Only if you have them, dear." Collectors similarly queried about wearing museum-quality ancient Greek, Roman, or pre-Columbian jewelry could give the same reply. In addition to being few, elegant, and, lately, quite fashionable, they are also probably rich, as indicated by prices such as $29,980 for a Byzantine gold pendant, $4,680 for a seventh-century-B.C. Rhodian-gold breast ornament, and $3,120 for a fourth-century-B.C. plaited-gold Greek necklace.

Renaissance jewelry and that of the seventeenth and eighteenth centuries is occasionally seen on fortunate females, but this fashion, too, is limited by cost as well as taste. When an internationally famous society beauty is reported to be wearing her eighteenth-century diamonds with cashmere sweaters, not too many are in a position to follow her example.

Most of the antique jewelry popularly collected and worn is mid-Victorian and late Victorian, the product of an age when ladies of any means were considered to be undressed without their earrings, brooches, necklaces, rings, chatelaines, chains, watches, and on grand occasions, jeweled hair ornaments.

Custom and costly handmade jewelry was produced in the Victorian era by Castellani in Italy, Tiffany, Ball, and Black in the United States; Garrard in England; and Fabergé in Russia, to mention some of the internationally important jewelers. However, much that is admired and collected today was factory produced and sometimes, not always, finished by hand. Prices thus could be low enough for good-quality real gold and real stone jewelry to flood the market and, as treasured heirlooms, remain for today's collector to accumulate and enjoy wearing.

INSIDERS ADVISE

Wherever you buy antique jewelry, be sure that you ask the right questions. Is this an original piece with all the original parts? Has the stone been tested?

"Real gold" can vary from less than 10 to 24 carats. The so-called "garnet gold" is the former and often used for garnet settings.

Variations of gold plating are called gold washed, rolled gold, gold filled, and gold plated.

Pinchbeck is a valued gold substitute. Shellware is a thin shell of gold which may be weighted.

If you make it a policy to ask to be shown "the repair," you may be surprised at how often one turns up.

Whenever you see an exact duplicate of a piece of antique jewelry, be alert for more. Reproductions usually show up in fairly close order in shops and at antique shows.

When in doubt, imply that you know the piece is a reproduction. Many dealers are relieved to admit it.

Larger pieces of old English silver jewelry are often hallmarked, showing place of origin, age, maker, and content.

If the Fabergé marks are very clear and strong, check most carefully. They were usually quite fine, to match the work.

Hungarian enamel, Indian precious stone, Czech garnet, and other jewelry still made in traditional styling, are often sold for antique.

Really exquisite workmanship is a good test of quality, although not always of age. There are still very expert artisans, especially in Italy, who can hand copy fine old pieces quite perfectly.

Until the eighteenth century, real stones were often backed with foil to "improve" their color and brilliance. Make sure that you aren't getting later items which are fakes.

Watch out for doublets. One stone is pasted over another, to give the impression of greater size and depth. The thin layer of the precious stone often departs down the drain when water dissolves the glue. There are "triplets" too.

Until the nineteenth century, diamonds were usually set in silver to enhance the color. For a time thereafter, till white gold appeared, the silver was used at the front only, with gold used for the backing.

Mine diamonds have the fewest facets, rose diamonds from 24 to 36 facets, and brilliant-cut diamonds, which appeared in the eighteenth century, 56 facets.

There is less antique brilliant-cut diamond jewelry than mine or rose-cut available, because the brilliants were thought worth resetting for their greater value and beauty.

From the nineteenth century on, real stones were usually set in claws so the light could display the advantages of the improved cutting.

Don't redesign if you expect to be soon selling your jewelry. It is unlikely that you will retrieve your investment.

Visit a jewelry-findings resource and learn to recognize the "antique" replacement parts available.

Don't brush vigorously when cleaning jewelry.

Check clasps and links at regular intervals, along with stone settings, to verify they are secure.

For storage and travel, separate various units of antique jewelry in different compartments. Abrasion causes most damage.

Jewelry Through the Ages, by Guido Gregorietti, is a museum without walls, handsomely illustrated and well written.

Values are considered in *Antique and Old Jewelry Price Guide,* by Astron, *Investing in Antique Jewelry,* by Richard Falkiner, and *Antique Jewelry,* by Ada Darling.

Margaret Flower's *Victorian Jewelry,* Joan Evans' *History of Jewelry,* and Mona Curran's *Collecting Antique Jewelry* are informative and helpful.

MUSICAL INSTRUMENTS

Even the lady who in the 1940s bought a quartet of Stradivari—two violins, a viola, and cello—did not answer to the title of musical instrument collector, but rather of music patron. Actually, some of the finest antique instruments were billed to the accounts of titled patrons who had them made to order for musicians to play.

Old and rare musical instruments of all sorts are still collected, as the extraordinary Crosby Brown Collection in the Metropolitan Museum of Art testifies, but it is a special and limited market. Even investors seldom frequent it, despite the sale in 1971 of the great "Lady Blunt" Stradivarius at over $200,000, in London.

Late nineteenth-century musical instruments, mostly made in Germany and the United States, are still fairly plentiful, and those who collect them have the advantage of many catalogues by which to trace and identify them. Price reflects demand, which is moderate.

Music boxes, automata, player pianos, nickelodeons, and other mechanical musical instruments comprise a much more active market. Nostalgia for the sound of the tuned steel comb, bells, reed organs, drums, castanets, and similar tinkling or clarion calls produced by cylinder or disc continues to grow, depite, or perhaps because of, the most modern advances in sound reproduction.

The largest dealer in automated musical instruments, who buys outright or on consignment, has showrooms on both East and West coasts and warehouses and repair shops in Belgium and Denmark.

Although the steel-comb music box was invented in 1796 in Geneva, it was 1820 before production became widespread, mostly in Switzerland and, until 1875, mostly by individual artisans in their homes. Mass production began after 1880. The disc instrument was developed in Germany with large boxes and more varied tunes. Symphonion and Polyphon, those great complex and vibrant machines, were made for noise and status seekers. They are now in great demand, and depending on condition and rarity, sell for thousands of dollars.

Small, exquisite musical mechanisms in gold or silver snuff-boxes, others in clocks, bird cages, or figures also fascinate and charm, usually with price tags to match their appeal. These too may sell for thousands of dollars, although the collector with smaller means and simpler taste can also be accommodated.

Many music box collectors happily accumulate contemporary examples, without reference to age or rarity.

"Wanted, cylinder and disc phonographs with outside horns, Victor, Edison, Zonophone, Columbia Gramophone," reads an advertisement often repeated in the columns of antiques and trade publications. Horns and parts are also listed, as are new and old catalogues and reproductions of old catalogues. Not only the older generation, which recalls these early phonographs from domestic scenes, but young enthusiasts for the talking machine are involved in collecting this pioneer material.

Recently, a category of "early electronics" has been added to include vintage wireless, radio, and even television, as foresighted collectors presage future interest and profit.

Condition and completeness of original instrument, or machine, are leading price factors, along with the rarity-demand equation. When asked how prices were set by the seller in an area where auctions were the exception rather than the rule and two identical items were seldom on the market at one time, a dealer smiled, "That's what makes it easy."

INSIDERS ADVISE

For decades, Stradivari labels were standard equipment for cheap European fiddles.

Check old paintings of musical subjects for date, method of playing, and type of instruments.

Decoration of old instruments is often clue to identity.

Banjos catapulted back into popularity because of a song in the movie *Deliverance*. Not only new, but old banjos were sought.

Instruments that seem to be unusual, very old, or exceptionally well crafted should be checked by experts for value.

Fine instruments need special care and atmosphere control.

Decorative use of antique instruments accounts for much of the market, and those who buy for that purpose do not require perfect condition.

About the same time, one Stradivarius violin fetched $200,000 at auction; another brought $42,000. Quality told.

Music boxes handmade before 1850 are the choice specimens that connoisseurs seek. These are usually key-wound types.

When you acquire a music box, listen to every tune in the box, not just what the vendor plays for you.

Check that each tune is played singly. Sometimes two tunes play at once; this is a serious defect.

Be alert if the music box plays a tune over again. It may be set to do that and to skip a dud or ruined one.

Rust ruins sound. A badly rusted comb is useless; however, light rust may be cleaned off.

Broken teeth on combs can be repaired, but if teeth at base of comb are broken, this is hardest to repair.

Cylinder pins should all be at the same angle to the cylinder. If too many are broken, it may not pay to repin.

If you find gray powder in the box, check for oxidation of lead weights. This is a poor prognosis.

Be careful when playing a music box for the first time. You might catch a finger or hand in it and be badly hurt.

Play several discs to check out an instrument.

Music boxes can be repaired, no matter how bad the condition. However, the cost must be reckoned.

Repair is not enough; restoration to approximately the original mechanical condition is required by fastidious collectors.

Player pianos that need repair must be considered to be pigs in a poke. They had best be bought by those who can do the work.

If you want to hear an antique musical instrument played while you look at it, you can do so in the André Mertens Galleries at the Metropolitan Museum of Art. The sound comes from an electronic system which picks up the music in a headset from each display as you approach it, in whatever order you choose.

Value factors of old phonographs are type of machine and model, condition, presence of accessories, such as horn brackets and reproducers, and of course, rarity.

Size and type of horn determine appeal to collectors. The morning glory horn, colored horns, and those with unusual designs are most wanted.

Beware the machine assembled from unrelated parts.

Check for original decoration, because fake labels and designs are not uncommon.

Phonograph catalogues and advertisements are very important to collectors.

Age alone does not determine price. Some early models are quite plentiful and priced modestly, as low as $50.

The first phonograph to bear the Victor label may bring as much as $2,000, but desirable and scarce machines in good condition can be bought for $250 and less.

Repair is very costly. Most collectors become good at it for this reason and also to be sufficiently expert to buy with confidence.

Read *The Glory of the Violin,* by Joseph Wechsberg.

Musical Instruments of the Western World, by Emanuel Winternitz, and *The History of Musical Instruments,* by Curt Sachs, are classics.

For information on music boxes, *Collecting Musical Boxes and How to Repair Them,* by Arthur Ord-Hume, is recommended, along with *Musical Boxes,* by David Tallis, and *The Curious History of Music Boxes,* by Roy Mosoriak.

For player-piano fans, or those that want to be, *Put Another Nickel In,* by Q. David Bowers, *The Player Piano Treasury,* by Roehl, and *Player Piano,* by Arthur Ord-Hume, make valuable reading.

Catalogues of specialist firms, such as Lyon & Healy of Chicago, are helpful to collectors of phonographs, as are those of mail-order firms and of the manufacturers themselves.

The Fabulous Phonograph; From Edison to Stereo, by Roland Gelatt, traces the history of the instrument and the men who made it.

NEEDLEWORK

Except for the sampler, that primer for young females, and the patchwork quilt, needlework of previous generations has appealed largely to specialist collectors. The few dealers who serve them also count as their clients certain museums, where interest and scholarship combine to rescue this very personal expression of skill and social history.

With so many devotees working in needlepoint today, it would seem that there might be an upsurge, if not a revival, of collecting examples of old needlework in the near future. Although the craft goes far back into history, examples of work earlier than the eighteenth century are unlikely to be hanging about unrecognized. However, nineteenth-century needlework of all countries is still available for collecting, much of it still in the hands of family heirs.

INSIDERS ADVISE

Even fragments of fine work are valuable.

Every country has its heritage of fine needlework in peasant styles and on a more sophisticated level.

Lack of perspective does not detract from value. Some of the most appreciated work, like the English stumpwork of the seventeenth century, is not based on developed perspective.

Much fine embroidery originated in the Near East. Both Persia and Turkey contributed to development of European stitches and designs.

Japanese and Chinese embroideries have long held high positions as important antique arts.

There are many kinds of samplers besides the alphabetical types which are the best known, but not the earliest.

Samplers from the seventeenth and eighteenth centuries stress a variety of stitches including some which utilize only darning stitches.

As a rule, brighter colors indicate later samplers.

Name and date do not guarantee exact authenticity. Even if not faked, many pieces were worked by two or three generations, the last dating it by the first.

Victorian ladies were addicted to needlework. Pincushions, book-bindings, mirror frames, antimacassars, and myriad other examples of their work are fine collectibles still available at comparatively low prices.

Early Victorian needlepoint has light backgrounds; mid-Victorian work is quite garish; late Victorian is more subdued, more geometric.

Collectors prize embroideries designed as a substitute for tapestry by William Morris in England in the 1870s.

Old crewel matching sets of bed hangings, coverlets, and cushions are much sought.

Encyclopedias of embroidery show every kind of stitch, and some tell when and where it was used. Almost every country has its scholars on the subject.

Victorian Embroidery, by Barbara Morris, *Samplers and Tapestry Embroideries,* by Marcus B. Huish and the *Dictionary of Needle-work,* by S. F. A. Caulfield, are useful to help identify many types of work, as is *American Needlework,* by G. B. Harbeson.

Old-Time Tools and Toys of Needlework, by Gertrude Whiting, covers the auxiliary materials which some collectors call "sewing tools."

ORIENTAL ART

Collecting oriental art has been an occidental preoccupation for centuries. Ceramics, jade, carved glass, enamel, paintings, bronze, lacquer, and silks continue to please connoisseurs and collectors as well as ordinary folk, with variations of fashion and taste accounting for changing prices and values.

One collector points to a Japanese kakemono, purchased in 1935 for $75, the value of which has merely doubled in that interim; however, within a shorter period, some Chinese treasures in his collection of about 200 objects have escalated over 1,000 times the price he originally paid. Chinese porcelains and Japanese prints have shown the greatest recent rises; but archaic bronzes, lacquers or T'ang terra cotta figures may take their turn another day.

The modest collector may start with netsuke, which may be bought for sums from $10 to thousands of dollars. Carved teak or lacquer furniture, brass, pewter, and ivory are also available in great variations of quality, and for every purse. The art of Asia outside China and Japan does not have as well established a market. The wars in Indo-China have destroyed and uprooted objects as well as people. In many cases, objects have fared better, finding themselves safely in Western settings.

Twentieth-century oriental commercial products, made for Eastern and Western bazaars and souvenir shops, continue to find a way into auction rooms, shops, and shows, satisfying many purchasers with their general appearance of distinction. A recent addition to the lists of collectibles, "Nippon" hand-painted, gold-decorated porcelain delights many who consider it artistic, and who might be disappointed in a small, undecorated peachblow vase that would merit an entire case in a museum.

INSIDERS ADVISE

For centuries, oriental craftsmen and artists have exactly copied the marks of their predecessors to show respect for them. This is why dependence on marks alone is dangerous.

The Chinese government does not permit export of pre-nineteenth-century antiques.

Japanese collectors are competitively buying oriental treasures of their own and other countries.

Those bronze hands and heads you see for sale were mostly looted from Indo-Chinese temples.

If you have oriental objects you don't know how to identify or value, get a line on them before selling.

Few, except experts, understand oriental art values, giving them a great advantage in trading with the average dealer.

Connoisseurs in this field follow the oriental custom of studying a single object for long periods of time. This alone could be a reason for their taste and expertise.

Recent excavations in Chinese tombs have increased knowledge and added value to antique objects, especially T'ang-period material.

Just because an oriental piece has an elaborate stand or mounting does not prove it is of great value. Depend on your appreciation of the object itself.

Many ordinary oriental objects are attractive without being particularly valuable.

Soapstone, imitation ivory, plastic lacquer, and wood carvings are commonplace and easily recognized as such by experienced buyers; however, they do impress some.

European *chinoiserie,* after the oriental style, should not be confused with oriental art, although fine examples are collected and highly valued.

On the other hand, Chinese export wares, especially ceramics and enamels picturing Westerners, are highly appealing to them and bring very high prices in Europe and the United States.

Oriental art has a long and venerable history with an enormous literature, so you can find a study on any subject you wish to learn about.

Among experts on oriental art, whose books are highly regarded, are S. W. Bushell, Hugo Munsterberg, William Willetts, and Lawrence Binyon.

Arthur and Grace Chu's *Oriental Antiques and Collectibles* discusses market values and reproductions.

ORIENTAL RUGS

According to ancient Near Eastern custom, it was a sin to sell a carpet. The vendor received a gift of money and, in exchange, gave a gift of merchandise. One wonders if that "buyer" had to be as careful about the value of the acquisition as buyers must be today.

For people who buy one or two precious carpets for utility and decoration, it is a "blind" item, as it is for most who sell privately. Since the trade is as interwoven as a fine rug, the problem is to find objective counseling. If the purchase involves large sums, an individual collector might be the best choice for the task. The private seller who is disposing of precious rugs may either consult such a collector or have the item appraised by a dealer "for insurance purposes," asking for both retail and wholesale replacement costs.

Insiders warn against "bazaars" at resorts or elsewhere. Long-established, rather than transient, auctions are more likely to offer bona fide quality merchandise. Paradoxically, in this trade, new carpets are sold as "used," to give the impression they are more valuable. Special meaning is attached to description of age in oriental rugs. "Antique" is used to designate rugs woven before 1860, with fibers colored with vegetable (not aniline) dyes. "Semiantique" refers to rugs made between 1860 and 1914. Oriental rugs are "old" 25 years after their manufacture.

Although they have fluctuated in fashion favor, handmade oriental rugs have always had world-wide currency as valuable collectibles. Lately, there has been renewed appreciation of their now irreplaceable craftsmanship and a new approach to their purely aesthetic value as an art form.

Prices depend on rarity, pattern, weave, fiber, color, age, history, and condition, in manifold and subtle variations. In no other field are there more angles to be watched, nor greater possibilities of trickery.

A handsome rug may be bought for $1,000 or $2,000; a precious rarity will fetch many tens of thousands. A rich Mughal carpet of the early nineteenth century, woven for the Emperor Shah Jehan, builder of the Taj Mahal, was considered an outstanding purchase for $33,600 at Sotheby's in London.

INSIDERS ADVISE

If you are going to acquire oriental rugs, plan to buy them only from well-known sources until you have some experience. Then you will continue to buy them from established firms.

Don't look for bargains in the Near East. Fine oriental rugs are more cherished and higher priced there. Tourists are usually preyed upon.

Value judgments are made on pattern, color, material, structure, and condition. Quality is more important than age, as a rule.

Dates knotted into some rugs usually refer to the Moslem calendar. However, if the maker, or client, is Christian, the Christian calendar may be used.

If a date is in mirror image, look out for a rug that is a copy. The knotter, being illiterate, knotted the inscription backward.

If a knot is removed and the wool can be smoothed out straight without curling back at once, it cannot have been very long in the knot.

Very fine old carpets, especially silk carpets, were seldom used underfoot, and therefore should not be heavily worn.

Intentional aging, by rubbing away the pile or burning it, can be recognized because the interior of the fabric remains untouched. Usually the selvage and plain surfaces are left out of such "treatment."

Most of the old large carpets are roughly twice as long as they are wide. After 1880, most were made for Western-sized rooms, and are only 20 to 30 per cent longer than wide.

Nomad carpet designs are unaltered by tradition and are equally valuable if made in the eighteenth or nineteenth century.

Small holes can be spotted if the carpet is held against a bright source of light and viewed from the underside.

Small repairs are entirely acceptable to collectors. Large areas of restoration are allowable only for historical antiques.

Partly worn rugs are sometimes cut down to the intact areas. Check to make sure that original bands and sides are not missing. Design will be the clue.

Compare the pattern on the upper side and underside. If the rug has been painted with a design, they will not be the same.

If the carpet is darker "at the roots," it has been bleached, a look admired by some decorators. This will reduce the useful life of the carpet by 8 to 12 per cent.

Rub the pile firmly with a damp cloth to see if the cloth picks up any color. Rugs are often "restored" by painting.

The direction of the light can greatly alter the appearance of a carpet. Compare by daylight and electric light. Note difference nearer windows; also check from several angles and move lamps.

Make sure that rugs lie evenly and well. They can be restretched, but it may be looking for trouble to require it.

Don't beat rugs. Vacuum, following the pile.

Snip, don't pull ravels. Clip charred ends.

Move and change position, to distribute wear.

Use slides or coasters to protect from furniture legs.

Have the slightest damage professionally mended at once, to keep it from spreading.

Expert cleaning and mothproofing are annual requirements.

The Book of Carpets, by Reinhard G. Hubel, *Check Points on How to Buy Oriental Rugs* and *Oriental Rugs,* both by Charles W. Jacobsen, are recommended as practical guides.

There are many excellent books on various types of oriental rugs; many are well illustrated. However, do not depend on photographs to compare quality, color, or other values.

PAPER COLLECTIBLES

Frilly valentines and bloodthirsty broadsides seeking bandits "Dead or Alive" fall into the range of those who collect paper memorabilia.

Not necessarily low priced, most paper items are still within the reach of a modest budget, while the growth of interest in Americana has proved a stimulating force encouraging collectors to examine the life styles of the past.

Book, autograph, and print dealers were originally the most important traders in the paper-collecting field, but more recently, specialist dealers have opened shops and developed mail-order and catalogue operations. Few are able to stock all the types of paper collectibles and most stress some particular kinds, attempting to show assortments in depth.

A rare valentine may sell for as much as $20, World War I Liberty Loan posters for $10 to $15, and a copy of the November 3, 1948 Chicago *Tribune*, with the headline, "Dewey Defeats Truman," brought $275 at auction a quarter century later.

Prices for old postcards start at a penny; a souvenir postcard of the 1933 World's Fair brings $2.00. An 1887 Hostetter's Almanac is listed for $2.50, an 1874 Overland Almanac for $25. Like dealers, collectors must specialize to be able to trade in a field where values are as delicately balanced as a sheet of paper.

Matchbook covers, matchbox labels, and all sorts of business trade cards are collectors' delights. Much paper is collected in the nostalgia syndrome, and baseball cards and bubble gum inserts prices indicate that here, too, rarity is costly when combined with demand.

Frivolous as playing cards may seem to some, they are serious matters to an international band of collectors. The exhibition of antique playing cards held at Yale, in 1973, indicated the scope and depth of the field, together with its scholarly implications.

INSIDERS ADVISE

The older the paper, the better chance it has for survival, because it was probably made from rag stock. Modern paper disintegrates quickly.

Reprints of old playing cards are common, and many are collected as such. However, inexperienced buyers often mistake the reproductions for originals.

Facsimile packs of rare antique playing cards are sold for $3.00 to $30 and more and are well worth the price to collectors. A pack of sixteenth-century Italian cards fetched about $500 at a London auction.

Advertising cards of the early 1800s are the most valuable, although the stock cards that were printed later in the century are much in demand.

Size is not a factor in the price of posters; as a matter of fact, most collectors prefer a smaller sheet.

Newspaper reprints are deceptively like the real thing. Tests for distinguishing reprints are explained in *Early American Newspapers,* by James E. Sheldon.

Postcards that have been through the mails are not shunned, but, in general, unused postcards are preferred.

Postcard collectors compete for sets complete as originally issued.

Steam gently when removing any material from old albums. Do one item at a time.

Keep paper items in print cases or flat in cabinet drawers.

Interleave paper items with tissue paper; line storage area with rag paper.

Dust is the greatest enemy of paper, with competition from damp and heat. Safe storage requires temperature of about 70 degrees, humidity of 40 to 50 degrees.

Never mend with plastic tape; do not trim margins. Never cut, fold, or crease paper collectibles.

Check for mildew. You can smell it before you can see it.

The Complete Book of Paper Antiquing, by Adelaide Hechtlinger and Wilbur Cross, covers much of the field.

J. R. Burdick's *American Card Catalog* and all his definitive work on postcards are required reading for all who collect them.

A History of Playing Cards, by Catherine Hargrave, and *Collecting Playing Cards,* by Sylvia Mann, are good introductions.

Prices on many paper collectibles are listed in *Official Guide to Paper Americana,* by H. L. Cohen. The general price guides also include some prices of paper items.

The Poster, by Harold Hutchison, is an illustrated history from 1860.

PATTERN GLASS

Thoroughly researched by pioneers, especially Ruth Webb Lee, the field of American pressed pattern glass got a head start as a "people's collectible," back in the 1920s and 1930s. Pattern-glass collecting involved more modest folk than had ever in history indulged in the luxury of collecting anything and served as a model for much that followed in the United States.

Pressed pattern glass started with the industrial era, in 1829, as a mechanical and therefore cheap substitute for luxury cut glass. Today, the first lacy stippled flint glass made at Sandwich will bring higher prices than its original cut-glass model. It was the first of a series of pattern-glass developments that crested in 1900, after more than 2,500 listed patterns had been made in countless unit multiples.

Once the dominant single item collected in the United States, it is still an important staple in many antique shops, but an enormous output of reproductions and fakes requires that the collector be alert and prudent.

INSIDERS ADVISE

Commercial reproductions of clear glass, milk glass, and colored pattern glass have been listed in various publications, but still they keep coming in different variations.

Watch the gift and glass markets to catch the fakes.

Pattern-glass values are well known and easily checked, so it is most unlikely that bargains far below market price will turn out to be authentic.

Prices in this field have followed the general inflationary trend, but have fluctuated to lower levels at times.

Some patterns that could not be traced to American factories have been identified as French pressed glass of the nineteenth century.

Find dealers who specialize in certain patterns. This makes it easier both to buy and sell.

Study the work of the late Ruth Webb Lee in this field. Her books furnish the rules for pattern-glass collectors.

PEWTER

Pewter worth collecting is handsome, looks important, and is of superior design and workmanship. Quality of the metal is reflected in its appearance. As a rule, the more it looks like silver, the finer it is. Touchmarks of the great pewterers of Britain and the United States bring high prices. The splendid, dramatic, yet simple American eighteenth-century and early nineteenth-century pewter that collectors seek is in short supply, as the ware was usually melted down when worn.

A pair of New York pewter chalices of 1780 has fetched $8,250 and a William Will Philadelphia tankard of 1790 made $4,250 at a New York auction. As a rule, American and British examples are more costly than their Continental counterparts.

Mass-produced pewter of the nineteenth century continued to follow the classic and conservative styles of the earlier period, but usually in the lighter britannia metal, which could be spun. Attractive and collectible, it brings much lower prices than the earlier pewter.

INSIDE GUIDE

Hammermarks on old pewter indicate top quality. They were intended to reinforce strength. They add luster and sheen.

If touchmarks indicating origin are faint, try using an ink eraser to bring them out more clearly.

Dates in old pewter touchmarks indicate registration date for the mark, not the date the item was made.

American pewter was often modeled after the British, even the touchmarks employed similar symbols, such as birds, flowers, and later, initials.

American pewterers sometimes marked a piece "London" to indicate it was as good as if made there. It was.

Continental pewter also influenced American styles, but only for a short time, after which the English wares were the models.

The form of pewter called "britannia," developed in England after 1800, included less lead. It could be spun and was thinner, lighter, and had sharp edges.

After 1840, britannia metal was used as a base for electroplated silver. EPBM means electroplated on britannia metal.

Unmarked pewter may be British as well as Early American, although dealers like to imply it is the rarer and more costly American ware.

The classic antique styles of pewter have been reproduced for about a hundred years in both Britain and the United States. More recently they have also been made in Italy.

Avoid acquiring corroded or "sick" pewter. It cannot be restored.

Keep pewter away from the heat of stoves or fireplaces. It also dents easily and should not be banged or bruised.

Do not use chemical cleaners to remove tarnish. If necessary, use very, very fine steel wool, with a little olive oil or fine emery powder.

When clean, keep pewter that way by washing with plain soap and water.

American Pewter, by J. B. Kerfoot, and the three-volume *Pewter in America,* by Ledlie I. Laughlin, are leading works on colonial and later pewter.

The Pewter Collector, by H. J. Massé, and *Pewter,* by John Bedford, include English and Continental wares.

A standard work is *Old Pewter; Its Makers and Marks in England, Scotland and Ireland,* by H. H. Cotterell.

PHOTOGRAPHICS

After decades of exposure to merely amused condescension, old family photographs, daguerreotypes, and tintypes are being re-examined for artistic and historic value and reappraised as contributions to an important aspect of our culture.

Antique slides, magic lanterns, stereoscope viewers, various kinds of vintage photographic equipment, albums, and other pioneer material in this field, from its mid-nineteenth-century beginnings to the 1930s, are now being classified and collected, forming another branch of the arts and incidentally another market.

Specifically, there are several areas on the expanding horizon. The equipment itself comprises one. Cameras, tripods, glass plates, plate holders, hand-painted slides and similar paraphernalia, including original catalogues listing the old equipment, are bought, sold, and traded at growing prices and in greater depth as collectors become more expert.

The photographs themselves form another branch. Some are valued as pioneer examples, showing the development of techniques. Subject matter, outstanding quality, and sheer artistry add other dimensions. London's National Portrait Gallery paid $72,000 for 258 calotype prints made by two Scotsmen, Gill and Adamson, who collaborated from 1843 to 1848. The first photographically illustrated book, published in England in 1844, *The Pencil of Nature*, which sold for $100 in the early 1950s, brought $6,500 ten years later and $16,000 ten years after that.

The third aspect of the boom is seen in the appreciation of the contemporary photograph as a work of art. Some dealers now specialize exclusively in photographs; other galleries are partially involved. Leading art museums have permanent photograph galleries, which they use for display of outstanding prints and for one-man and group shows. Photographers are rated as stylists and creative innovators and are judged as artists.

Twenty-five dollars is usually the base price for the work of "unknown" photographers, with the median between $40 and $75 for those who are not yet established. Promotion and fashion play the usual roles in making reputations and setting prices. A signed print originally selling for $100, the usual base price for established photographers, has been known to go to $500 or more within a few years, if the artist has made it into the winner's circle.

INSIDERS ADVISE

As original paintings and fine graphics have moved beyond the purse of most people, the $100 photograph has become the dealers' much-needed popular staple.

Not all photographers are under contract to dealers; some may be interested in selling at a discount privately.

Signed prints are sometimes numbered as well. If the photographer did the darkroom work, the print is more desirable and will bring a better price.

Portfolios and collections command comparatively better prices than do single photographs.

Sotheby Parke Bernet in New York has instituted photographic auction sales, indicating that a market has been established.

Museum shows often push up the price of a photographer's work. Museum employees sometimes buy up photographs before a big show and later sell at a substantial profit.

The publication of a book is sometimes a prelude to greater appreciation of a photographer's work.

Museums have been known to sell off duplicates when they buy large collections. Having helped raise the price, they can thus recover the original cost of the collection.

Daguerreotypes will fade if left for long in a strong light.

The Calotype, invented in England in the 1830s, is rare. It is a type of negative-printed picture greatly treasured by collectors.

The old photos on ruby glass or milk glass are called ambrotypes. This type of photograph was made on thin-coated glass.

Tintypes were still another photographic form, processed on japanned metal.

Great finds of old photographs are still being made. The earliest-known photographic images of the United States capitol and White House, taken in 1846, were found in a San Francisco flea market. Of seven bought there for $18, six were sold for a total of $12,000.

Found recently (in the National Archives) were photographs of Indian chiefs and warriors taken from the mid- to the late 1800s.

Twenty photos taken long ago by Thomas Eakins, the admired American artist, were discovered in an old house near Philadelphia, in 1972.

Alexander Gardner, E. Muybridge, Matthew Brady, William Henry Jackson, Eastman, Ives, Niepce, and of course Louis Daguerre are early photographers whose letters, notebooks, journals, and autographs are being collected and classified.

Don't sell photographic equipment that dates before 1930 to any but specialists who appreciate its value.

Carte de visite photographs of well-known persons bring good prices from autograph dealers who use them in conjunction with autograph material.

Those who have interesting old photos to sell will do best to check advertisements of dealers who offer to buy according to subject matter.

The case often determines the price of the daguerreotype, although the image itself may be of greater value.

The international bibliographic guide is Boni's *Photographic Literature,* an invaluable reference work, found in most large library reference rooms.

Photography and the American Scene, by R. Taft, *The Daguerreotype in America,* by Beaumont Newhall, and Floyd and Marion Rinehart's *American Miniature Case Art* contribute to the collector's knowledge.

The George Eastman House, a museum in Rochester, New York, is a mecca for collectors in this field.

PORNOGRAPHY

Collectors of pornography, to be distinguished from mere buyers of pornography, will probably continue to be with us and in all likelihood to proliferate, despite the swinging pendulum of censorship, moving alternatively between rigid and permissive laws and social standards. However, in times and places of greater latitude, the value factor of rarity, in itself titillating, becomes diminished if not destroyed.

As in other fields of collecting there are standards of quality and connoisseurship. "Feelthy" pictures and postcards, produced for the naïve tourist and adolescent youth, are unlikely to interest the serious collector. "Dirty" books published in editions of hundred thousands and even millions will hardly rate as the gems of a collection which includes costly rarities in luxurious limited editions.

Overlapping in other fields are not only books and pictures, but phonograph records, tapes, films; limited edition medals and graphics; sculpture and painting. These are only some of the areas in which collectors of other material may acquire pornographic examples along with other conventionally acceptable types of collectibles.

A vogue for collecting furnishings and equipment of Edwardian and Victorian bawdy houses is fairly recent, and such items as bawdy-house tokens, those famous brass checks indicating services forthcoming, illustrated bordello brochures, and similar red-light paraphernalia are now considered more colorful than off-color.

Antique and period pornography, often dubbed "erotica" and once considered the exclusive province of exquisites, required not only special tastes, but especially generous resources. The private buyer acquired the books, sculpture, paintings, prints, figurines, watches, music boxes, or any of a multitude of forms employed to present "improper" sexual material, under disadvantageous circumstances, due to the need for privacy in the transaction. The dealer, on the other hand, could exert these same pressures in reverse when buying privately. Neither force is of the same consequence today as in the past.

The pornography of one period often becomes acceptable and conventional in another, while the natural expression of an earlier age might be considered beyond the pale of propriety in still another. Certainly primitive art of ancient or recent times, with its emphasis on reproductive organs, has more religious than hedonistic meaning. So-called "artistic" pornography is sometimes the most vulgar, and that created with libidinous purpose can be truly artistic.

A visitor to the superb sculpture galleries of the Vatican Museum, questioning the authenticity of the fig leaves sported by every nude, was told by a helpful guide, in poor English, that all had been added in the name of religious "prurity." Whether purity, propriety, or prurience was intended, the error was felicitous indeed. It should be noted that the Vatican Library, said to contain one of the finest collections of great pornography, much of it in original Latin and Greek, is, to its credit, above tampering with such manuscripts.

Whether there is presently a private collection of pornography of the quality, range, and size of that of the late King Farouk of Egypt is problematical. However, it must be remembered that it was all sold to other eager collectors, so it is certain that there are numerous collections.

With few exceptions, dealers will buy salable pornographic material in their own fields, and almost every one knows which customers are eager to see and purchase such items. Specialists in pornography, formerly under wraps, now show their material more openly, and the collector, who in times past had to deal entirely under the counter, may shop and compare price and quality of this material, as of other merchandise and collectibles.

INSIDERS ADVISE

Most ivory nude reclining figures aren't pornographic. They are originals or copies of Chinese medical dolls, on which the female patient pointed out her ailments to the doctor. Only those that are explicitly erotic merit the interests of collectors of pornography.

Steins and other drinking objects with bawdy decoration were once considered pornographic; now they are shown in most collections with hardly a leer.

Erotic books and prints of the late nineteenth century have the status of art these days.

Sophisticated collectors are the hardest to interest in pornography, but they are amused by some of it as camp and kitsch.

Bawdy cloacal, or scatological, material isn't properly pornography, but passes as such with some who pay too much for it because they can't tell the difference.

Finely wrought pornographic collectibles will probably always have a market for workmanship if not for subject.

Sexual freedom may or may not continue, but an interest in erotic art is likely to.

While fine art featuring erotic subjects has never been pornographic in the same way as poor art of this ilk, both kinds find collectors with tastes to match.

Museums and libraries are not always averse to being offered fine-quality pornography, antique or modern. However, if they buy, they usually pay less than private individuals.

If you buy pornography, do not buy furtively. Be sure you examine your purchase in a good light and with care.

There is a *Dictionary of Erotic Literature,* by H. E. Wedeck, and a three-volume *World History of Erotic Art* by various authors including Robert Melville and Philip Rawson.

QUILTS AND COMFORTERS

For decades, quilts and comforters were staples of American country antique shops and were usually kept at the back of the premises, more or less carelessly folded and stacked. Many handsome ones were priced about $25. People who hadn't inherited quilts bought them if they had colonial antiques in their bedrooms. Occasionally a sophisticated decorator would use a dramatic quilt or comforter as a color source, to develop an interesting room design.

Riding a boom of popularity, quilts and comforters have moved out of their limited provincial settings into the modern world where the creative design and historical context are newly appreciated. More than a few dealers now specialize in them; a great modern museum has given them a glamorous show; as an American art form, quilts and comforters are catalogued, hung, attributed, dated, and priced accordingly—in the hundreds of dollars.

The idea of layering fabrics and stitching them together for greater warmth has a long history. Plain, dark woolen quilts were standard in the seventeenth and eighteenth centuries. Cotton fabrics quilted in large designs together with plain fabrics of the early eighteenth century are much valued. However, the pieced or patchwork quilt, made in the late eighteenth century and thereafter in countless thousands through the nineteenth century, has the greatest popular appeal.

Pieced or patchwork quilts are made from scraps or remnants of material, sewed into pattern into a patched top, which is later quilted by stitching to wool or cotton batting and then backed. Tops might be individually made or as a group effort. The quilting was often a community activity, known as a quilting bee.

Appliqué quilts were made by applying cutout designs to the cotton base. Patchwork or appliqué comforters were not quilted, but tied together with knots at short intervals, a less arduous task. After 1800, classic geometric block quilts, made in units of blocks, offering literally unlimited combinations of color and pattern, dominated the scene, and it is this type which is so much admired.

INSIDERS ADVISE

Quilt collectors judge them according to uniqueness of design, interpretation of the pattern on which it is based, and as pure graphic art.

Interesting fabrics and extraordinary borders are also points of value.

American Indians made patchwork quilts. Seminoles are known for their outstanding designs. Collectors find many in Oklahoma and Kansas.

Patchwork quilts are handsome wall hangings and when considered as abstract art, an excellent value, according to the galleries that sell them for $500 to $1,000.

Although most dealers say that about $100 is where the interesting quilt prices start, they do have them for less.

The silks in Victorian quilts are said to be quite perishable because so often silk was stiffened with shellac.

Some dealers say holes are worse than stains, while others say the opposite. In general, neither adds to the appeal, and never to the value of a quilt.

Old tops that were never quilted are used to make tablecloths.

The best quilts have fine, even stitches.

Most American work has a simple running stitch.

English and European quilting is done with the backstitch.

Look for prints unique to the period.

Date about ten years after latest fabric remnant.

Look for signatures and dating, either embroidered or written in India ink.

There should be generous fluff between quilting stitches.

Fancy silk and velvet remnants made into "crazy quilts" are usually late Victorian, even early twentieth century.

Only those made of *pure* cotton, muslin, and wool materials are authentic old quilts.

Recently made quilts are composed of synthetics and Dacron.

Presentation quilts, with each block signed by an individual maker, are desirable Americana.

Analyze fabrics before deciding on a cleaning process.

If the item is to be washed, handwashing in a nylon bag is recommended.

Sewing machines were used after mid-century to piece together patchwork tops, and may not diminish value.

Cottonseeds in the batting do not prove a quilt was made before invention of the cotton gin in 1790. Unprocessed cotton was sometimes used until the 1870s.

Fine quilts were often carefully handled and little used. Poor condition is not an indication of age.

Design originality, quality of workmanship, historical interest, unusual materials, and color combinations are all important value factors.

Sizes range from child's crib quilt to ample double-bed proportions. Corners were made clipped to fit four posters.

Verify that a small quilt is not a cut-down from a larger damaged quilt. This would be less valuable.

Salvageable small pieces are made into pillows, and even framed, if they are especially fine and attractive.

When you buy, check condition carefully. The item may not be torn, but on the verge of shredding, which is worse.

If quilts are mended or repaired, be sure no modern materials have been used and that stitches concur.

If you are going to collect quilts, learn how to make one.

American Quilts, by Elizabeth W. Robertson, *The Romance of the Patchwork Quilt in America,* by Carrie A. Hall and Rose G. Kretsinger, and *American Quilts and Coverlets,* by Saeford and Bishop, are among many excellent books on the subject.

RECORDS AND SHEET MUSIC

Collectors of records, sheet music, player-piano rolls, and music-box discs fall into two categories, there are those who cherish the subject and those whose principal drive is to own the object. The latter have been known never to have heard the item played, but are satisfied with possession and potential profit.

Most of the shops dealing in old and rare musical material are in metropolitan centers; for the rest, catalogue and mail-order merchandising services this often esoteric, faddish market.

The record buff may be collecting old-time comedy records, pioneer jazz, golden-age opera, symphonic, or theatrical material. "Anything with Melchior" is how one young record collector described his collection. Some look for the artist, some for the music, some for the quality of the performance, others the quality of the recording. Then there are those who cherish the rarity above all.

Although early Caruso recordings, such as a 1902 G & T, may sell for more than a hundred dollars, others, plentiful because of his great popular appeal and the huge sales of his records, are not costly.

Record albums of old Broadway shows that were not hits, and therefore were pressed in limited numbers, are particularly popular with collectors. Albums of *Hazel Flagg*, *Flahooley*, and *Green Willow* are scarce, hence have sold for as much as $75 to $100 in good condition. Many now collect original-cast albums and movie sound tracks of the past two decades in an urge to document the stage and screen of the era.

In addition to the great ragtime piano rolls, also collected by ardent fans, classical rolls, made by such artists as Paderewski, Hoffman, and other great virtuosi, by a process in which the exact finger touch and sound were reproduced, delight collectors. Among them, Welte rolls, made for the automatic piano of that name, were outstanding, and Duo Art and Ampico libraries for the player piano achieved distinctions also appreciated in a revival of interest.

Sheet music is collected according to many musical approaches. However, in addition to the song, the artist, the composer, and the style of music, the artist who illustrated the cover is also a factor. Some of Toulouse-Lautrec's lithographed covers for popular songs of his era have sold for hundreds of dollars.

Music-box metal discs, so necessary for the enjoyment of the disc machine, are especially wanted by dealers who offer them with the instruments as a package sale. Collecting them is tricky but challenging for the music-box owner who wants to add tunes to the repertoire of the instrument.

INSIDERS ADVISE

Some claim that reissues of rare old records must hurt values; others believe that reissues popularize the originals and make them more desirable.

Cylinder recordings deteriorate with every playing. It is best to play once and record.

Old 78s are sometimes variable, making between 70 and 80 RPM. Get professional advice as to turntable and needle; otherwise the record may be severely damaged.

Collectors of vocal records are the most intense and dedicated, identifying with the artists in a personal fashion.

Estates of record collectors quickly attract dealers and collectors, so heirs are advised to get expert help if they decide to sell.

Don't exchange records until you have learned something about prices and trading skills.

Some "oldies" of the 1950s have recently brought a hundred times more than their original cost of $.79. Radio stations buy them for their libraries.

The records that have the shortest life span on the market, often become the stars of collectors' catalogues, as few of them were produced.

Modern recordings of old music-box and piano-roll music are collected by some who bypass the originals.

When you buy records by mail, "scratched on outer third" is instructive only if you know the record.

The biggest snobs in record collecting are those who collect acoustical material—to 1926. Yet most of them have fine libraries of later recordings as well.

The greatest rarity in the record world is probably the 14-inch disc, issued by Pathé as No. 1. On it, Liszt's pupil Bernhard Stavenhagen played "My Joys."

Records must all be carefully handled. There is a special aluminum container for the transport of fragile 78s.

Some collectors spend a lifetime searching for records or rolls that were assigned catalogue numbers, but, for some reason, were not issued.

Certain original piano rolls of great classical pianists, on the appropriate player piano, offer exact reproductions more precisely than do old phonograph records.

The research that goes into jazz and classical discographies, player-piano rolls, and sheet music is a credit to collectors who produce them and a joy and asset to those who use them.

A badly worn record is usually dull-colored and has nicked grooves. Cylinders that are cracked or chipped are also almost worthless. If only soiled, warm water and detergent can revive to the original, shiny finish.

Cylinders are wanted in their original tubes. Among the rarities are speeches by eminent personalities.

The Diamond Disc records, produced by Edison, dating from 1913 on, are practically unbreakable, and therefore many are still available.

Victor Red Seal classical records which had enormous circulation were very sturdy and are extant in goodly quantities, except for a few which are rare and costly.

Dealers say the most collectible of the older records currently are popular songs of the 20s and 30s, made by movie and early radio artists.

Dealers' catalogues are the best indication of current prices and values.

Grace Notes in American History, by Lester Levy, and *Early American Sheet Music* (to 1870), by Harry Dichter and Elliott Shapiro, are useful books.

SHEFFIELD SILVER

Made originally as a lower-priced competitor to genuine silver plate, Sheffield plate, which required less silver, is not now considered a poor cousin, but rather a different kind of silverware, of interest to those collectors who value it for its own sake.

Mostly of English make, with an occasional item of French manufacture turning up, it is collected widely, especially in the United States and Britain. Huge quantities were imported into North America before the demise of the process in 1840, but there is now a two-way traffic of antique Sheffield, since some is exported back to England.

Named Sheffield for its place of origin, it was also produced in Birmingham and London until cheaper electroplating displaced it in 1840. Much Sheffield was a factory-made product and, therefore, is not associated with the names of great silversmiths; except for those of Thomas Boulsover, its inventor, and John Hancock, an early manufacturer, few names stand out as value factors.

INSIDERS ADVISE

Sheffield plate was made in England between 1740 and 1840. It has its own set of marks, differing from the hallmarks of silver plate.

Good-quality Sheffield used an ounce of silver to a pound of copper. The silver was fused to the copper sheet, and the sandwiched piece was worked like sterling, except for the edges, which showed copper.

Where the copper edge showed, it was covered with sterling silver wire or sterling decoration.

When the silver wears through to show the layer of copper beneath, a piece of Sheffield is said to "bleed." To a degree, bleeding is acceptable on an old piece.

Electroplating to cover the bleeding depreciates the value of antique Sheffield.

The first period of Sheffield is from 1740 to 1772. Some manufacturers began to use marks resembling the hallmarks of sterling, so all marking of Sheffield was forbidden.

In 1784, makers were required to register special Sheffield plate marks. The great period of fine Sheffield is that of 1784 to 1820.

Any piece marked "Sheffield" is not antique Sheffield plate, but more likely an electroplated modern piece.

Electroplated silver over copper does not come within miles of being true Sheffield plate. It is of much lesser value, and while it may be attractive, should be bought for less.

Sheffield Silver Plate, by G. Bernard Hughes, and *Old Silver and Old Sheffield Plate*, by Howard P. Okie, are on the bookshelves of most who deal in Sheffield.

STAMPS

Philately involves more people than any other form of collecting, albeit some very briefly. Many have gone through the phase of desultory or impulsively made stamp acquisitions. This soon phases out, leaving a partly empty album as the souvenir of a good intention. For others of all ages and life styles, it is a delightful hobby, offering an enjoyable activity which can be tailored to chosen expenditures of time and money, with hopes of long-term value appreciation. And then there are the avid and semiprofessional dealer and trader types, who see the stamp market as a lucrative and absorbing avocation, promising both short- and long-term profits. All of these, together with thousands of dealers, form the philatelic market.

The first adhesive postage stamps, as we know them, originated in 1840 with the famous Penny Black and Two Pence Blue, engraved with young Queen Victoria's portrait. Now at least 5,000 new stamps appear annually, some in huge quantities. An annual U. S. Christmas stamp issue has numbered over two billion. U.S. commemorative stamps which have limited sales periods have run to 120 million for an average issue.

Stamps worth collecting may be purchased for a few cents or for huge sums. In 1967, Guyana issued a five-cent stamp reproducing the famous 1856 British Guiana, considered the world's rarest stamp. The latter fetched $280,000 at auction in 1970. Now the former is also a desirable addition to many collections.

Not only stamps, but covers, as envelopes are known, postal cards, letter sheets and wrappers are included in the philatelic specialty. The story of the smuggled moon covers, sold by a German dealer for over $1,500 each in 1971, hints at the kind of intrigue that colors a value structure of extraordinary complexity.

Stamps can contain great value in small bulk; a fact that has proved most useful for political refugees who have smuggled life-saving fortunes in this guise. Sales of fine collections have also rescued pensioners and retirees from the dismal prospects of living entirely on limited incomes. Extraordinary increases in the value of certain stamps are much publicized and encourage those seeking inflation hedges and profits to invest in stamps. It also encourages makers and sellers of reproductions, fakes, and forgeries.

INSIDERS ADVISE

Hoarding is not collecting. Those who buy panes of stamps to hold are often left holding the bag.

Plate-number blocks have a place in albums, but holding large quantities is not creative collecting nor an original idea.

If you try to sell low-cost common stamps, you may find no purchasers, or if brokers or dealers take them, they may do so only at a discount off face value.

When stamps for an album are acquired, a few extra should be put aside for swapping with other collectors.

A mint stamp will have the original gum back, and it will be well-centered, with complete perforations on all sides.

If a gummed stamp has a hinge, or shows signs of having been hinged, it is no longer mint. Watch out for regummed stamps offered as mint.

Used stamps should be well-centered, preferably with a faint cancel, or one that just barely touches a corner.

Other placement of cancellations is acceptable on desirable first-day covers.

Facsimiles are imitation stamps, made to defraud collectors. To make the risk worth while, they are usually rarities.

Counterfeit stamps, usually of high-cost face value, are made to defraud the post office.

As collectors put more emphasis on errors, and prices for these errors rise, they tempt the faker. The famous 1918 upside-down $.24 airmail, of which only 100 are known, has fetched $31,000.

The many types of "doctoring" include color changes, impressed surcharges and overprints, cleaning, and trimmed perforations to pass as imperforate stamps.

Some governments have canceled remainders, or even current issues, to sell at a discount to dealers. These may have the original gum washed off to make them appear to be normally used stamps.

It is possible to identify the gum on the back of a stamp to distinguish original issue, later printings, and regummed stamps.

Stamps "thinned" or damaged by loss of thickness in peeling from envelope or hinge are less valuable. Soak stamps away from envelope, one at a time.

The patterns, letters, or figures incorporated as watermarks are useful in identifying stamps.

Perforation gauges should be fine and exact, or they only confuse.

Classic issues of the nineteenth and early twentieth centuries have had the best records for value growth. Fewer stamps were issued in those days.

Small countries have sometimes contracted with commercial stamp-producing agencies to exploit the possibilities of issuing stamps almost entirely for the collecting market, rather than mail use.

Collectors whose specialties are involved in these "blackmail" issues are almost compelled to buy them.

Beware of bargains you can only get by accepting "approvals." If approval prices are full catalogue value, you are probably not getting a bargain.

In general, dealers undersell the catalogues. The listed price is not a retail selling price, but a sort of reference point.

If no prepaid addressed envelope is included with unordered approvals, you are not required by law to return them. Many people return them to the Post Office Inspector, with a complaint.

Do not consign stamps. Sell for cash at time of sale.

Although stamp auctions are conducted by licensed dealers, some have better reputations than others.

Auction commissions are in the vicinity of 20 per cent of the price fetched at auction. This should include all costs, including billing.

Always arrange with the auctioneer, in advance of the sale, the exact date of the settlement.

Dealers and collectors use *Scott's Standard Postage Stamp Catalogue* as a bible. In three volumes, its annual publication is awaited with great interest as it lists prices along with illustrations. It includes the stamps of the United States, the United Nations, Great Britain, and the past and present nations of the Commonwealth in Volume I. Countries listed as "A through I," appear in Volume II, the balance in Volume III. The Scott's U.S. specialized catalogue is a separate publication.

The Nineteenth Century Postage Stamps of the United States, by Lester G. Brookman, and *American Philatelic Dictionary,* by Harry M. Konwiser, are much consulted for historical and technical information.

A small pocket volume, *New York Times Guide to Collecting Stamps,* by David Lidman, is an excellent introduction for beginners.

TEXTILES

This somewhat neglected field includes pre-Columbian feather robes, bits of linen from Egyptian tombs, richly woven cut velvets of Renaissance Venice, damask and tapestry made for Versailles, as well as the simple linsey-woolsey of colonial America. In an economy such as ours, in which cloth as such is so plentiful and comparatively cheap, many are startled to discover that some collectors find the textile remnants of the past worthy of interest and investment.

Put into the perspective of thousands of years of development of one of the most basic expressions of man's culture, the products of the weaving craft are fascinating and even exciting. Some collect by subject matter, some by historical period, others by basic materials, still others according to the technique. Not only hand-woven, but mechanically woven fabrics are being collected and classified.

Old textiles are so perishable and were often so thoroughly used that comparatively small quantities are available, but those who collect in the field rip linings from antique church cupboards, scrounge into old trunks, and pursue peasant petticoats.

INSIDERS ADVISE

Church vestments are a primary source for antique fabrics.

Collectors trace the influence of Chinese silks on Italian fabrics from the thirteenth to the eighteenth centuries.

Fragments of old textiles are eagerly sought, although larger pieces are the ideal.

Heraldic symbols are an aid to identifying antique textiles, as are the types of weaving craft.

Tapestries which were out of fashion for decades are now appreciated again, especially if dimensions are suitable for smaller scaled interiors.

Early American woven coverlets and hooked rugs repay study, as they are still fairly available, although prices reflect the growing demand.

A Stevensgraph, a Jacquard-loomed silk picture of the 1870s, brought over $500 at one London sale. Also made as bookmarks and valentines, they are much prized by collectors.

If you recover that horsehair loveseat, hang on to the horsehair. Don't discard old and interesting fabrics before checking their values.

Bands are sometimes stitched onto contemporary fabrics that are going to be artificially aged so that some parts will be more worn than others, indicating antiquity.

American and European itinerant weavers often signed and dated their handicraft; check for this in the weave.

Craft weavers today are producing textiles worth collecting as works of art as well as examples of fine loomwork.

Careful framing, completely sealed, is a safe form of storage for textiles. Strong light, excessive heat, cold, and damp are destructive.

Make as few folds as possible when storing. Change the folds periodically. Roll linens on poles.

Get specialists' directions before cleaning old textiles.

Handbook of Weaves, by G. H. Oelsner, *Textiles in New England,* by Catherine Fennelly, and *Printed Textiles, English and American,* by Florence M. Montgomery, are a few of many fine books dealing with textiles.

TINWARE

Only in most recent times has tin been subject to contempt, as in "tin can," although not by dealers, collectors, and those who have learned the revived art of decorating tin. A scarcity of desirable authentic antique objects in this metal has boosted prices for even items that are in less than first-rate condition.

Tin food containers, or cans, originating in the early nineteenth century are much wanted by collectors, and since many carried advertising material, this whole field has been broadened on that account. In addition to the early examples, tin containers for such items as Prince Albert tobacco, Camel cigarettes, Log Cabin syrup, and Grape Nuts cereal are listed and priced at startling figures.

Country or kitchen tinware and its more elegant relation, tôle, are valued according to condition and decoration. A revival of the art of decorating tin has created greater interest in the material.

INSIDERS ADVISE

The most desirable early nineteenth-century tinware is actually made of sheet iron which is tin-plated.

The wares made by itinerant tinkers were usually undecorated except for pierced designs.

Country or kitchen, tin appeals to those interested in folk art. It may be pierced, plain, or painted.

Tôle describes more elegant tin. It has a painted background, and the shape and decoration are usually more formal.

Commercial tin was used for packaging. Stencils, lithographs, transfer prints, and paper labels distinguish it.

Some tôle is French, some Italian, some American. A lot of it is new, and with a few signs of wear, passes for old.

Look for hand-soldered seams. Turned edges also characterize desirable old tinware which is heavy and well finished.

Mexico is a source of much modern reproduction tinware. However, some of the original handcraft designs might be properly collected as Mexican folk art.

Old biscuit tins in unusual shapes are valuable collectibles. Some early pieces were hand-painted; most are lithographed. Prices for rarities are as high as several hundred dollars.

Wash tinware very gently. Don't use pressure or very hot water. Keep away from heat and cold.

Test carefully for reaction to turpentine. If no paint comes off, you can clean off dirt by wiping gently.

If piece is purely decorative, apply a thin coating of clear wax.

Good books are *American Country Tinware*, by Margaret Coffin, and *Antique Tin and Tôleware*, by Mary Earle Gould.

More recent collectibles are discussed in Tom Polansky's, *Advertising Tin Containers* and *Advertising Trays*. Also Ernest L. Pettit's two volumes entitled, *Collectible Tin Containers*.

TOYS

Toy collectors and traders haunt residential attics and cellars, barns, church bazaars, thrift shops, flea markets, and especially backrooms of likely old stores, in searching for playthings of the long distant and nearer past. In addition to these grass-roots sources, many recently established antique-toy specialists, as well as alert antique dealers, offer more accessible finds but at prices reflecting the degree of selectivity represented.

F. A. O. Schwarz, known for over a century as a toy retailer, pioneered a toy flea market in its Fifth Avenue store at one time, selling old, antique, and "tired" toys, thus coming full circle, since many collectible items, now sold as treasures, had been sold there when they were recently manufactured novelties.

Wheel toys, paper toys, child-size toys, primitive toys, railroad toys, mechanical banks, still banks, pull toys, motor toys, military toys, and many sorts of games are a few of the subdivisions and specialties in this category. Some of these can be characterized as early examples, some as later ones, but there is no doubt about the vintage of Walt Disney, Buck Rogers, Howdy Doody, Lone Ranger, Superman, and similar material, since a nostalgia-ridden generation has barely had time to grow up, earn, and collect.

Prices range from twenty cents for a marble to $200 for an 1890s trolley car and to as much as $2,000 for certain rare mechanical banks. There are plenty of price guides, but clever collectors are still hopefully scouting the boondocks for bargains.

Neither those who collect old toys nor the many who collect later toys are keen about any toys that show the effects of play. Condition is such an important element in toy value that a collector's dream of Golconda is to find a cache of unused toys in their original cartons. Toys are described as "playthings, not in human form," but signs of too much play are abhorred by collectors.

INSIDERS ADVISE

Prices for toys are quoted as "mint," "as found," and "restored."

Be wary when issuing lists of "wants." Series collectors have been held up for high prices after disclosing their needs.

If you are a beginner, don't rely on the knowledge of general dealers. Only specialist dealers know the value of toys and games.

Old toys can be found in the storage rooms of hardware stores, electrical-appliance stores and repair shops, candy stores, and even jewelers who may have sold toys at Christmas time in the past.

Paper material such as old catalogues, trade journals, boxes, and guarantees is valuable to toy collectors.

While true-factory condition is the most desirable, simulated-factory condition is the most undesirable.

If the paint is flaking, do not even brush a toy. Never repaint, remove paint, or paint over. Wax, polish, or wash with utmost care, and avoid even that unless expert.

Completeness, meaning all parts are present and none unaccounted for, is a toy collector's standard.

Replacement of parts is considered criminal by some collectors, although others condone it when it is done like a museum restoration, to show clearly.

A toy in working order appeals to collectors, but they rarely exercise the characteristic. Even if a toy is perfect in this regard, toy collectors prefer not to demonstrate.

Since most replacement parts are made with non-ferrous metals or even plastic, collectors go over toys with a magnet to check for hidden replacements.

Beware the "improved" item sold by a collector who has found one in better original condition and doctors the lesser piece to make it more salable.

Catalogues are important to check against made-up toys. Sometimes front and back ends of two incomplete units are put together, creating a bastard unwanted by experts.

It is a great gamble to buy an incomplete toy, hoping to find the missing parts.

Collectors say that even worse than repairing toys yourself is allowing them to be repaired by professional "fix it" shops.

Reproducing old toys has become a modern business. Send for catalogues offering reproductions, so you can recognize them if they are offered as originals.

Start collecting toys now, with your eye on two or three decades in the future. Toys bearing obvious errors, and those released in small quantities due to design changes or structural defects, will be particularly desirable.

On the basis of past experience, toys representing contemporary personages, contemporary events, such as space travel, and continuing series based on older toys have good investment potential for the long term.

Toys and Banks, by William P. Hopkinson, describes, and lists, prices. The Dafran House paperback, *Curios and Collectibles,* is another source for prices.

An outstanding work is *The Toy Collector,* by Louis H. Hertz, who gives the subject new dimensions. *Antique Toys and Their Backgrounds,* by White, and *Dictionary of Toys Sold in America,* by Earnest A. Long, are useful.

Later Toys, by Bill Feeney, *Illustrated History of Toys,* by Fritzsch, and Robert Culff's *The World of Toys* are on many collectors' shelves.

VINTAGE WINES

Putting away wine for future enjoyment is a very old specialized form of collecting that has widened in appeal as wine prices have risen, and a growing number of wine lovers find themselves unable to afford the great vintages as they mature to their highest potential palatability.

When a 1959 Lafite, which sold for $50 the case in 1960, reaches over $1,000, many talk about private persons buying wine for investment, and a few are tempted. Lesser wines have not risen in these crazy proportions, but *have* doubled and tripled in a few years, with even higher prices forecast from the French vineyards.

Yet collecting wine for pleasure is more practical than collecting wine for profit, because it is illegal to buy or sell wine without a license in the United States, and only retailers can get such licenses. Those who might buy would expect bargain prices to reflect the risk.

If sold abroad, the expenses involved in shipping, handling, consigning, and commissions would not make such a venture worth while unless it were a sizable one, ruling out all but those who wouldn't need the money anyhow. Most wine experts are basing their advice to wine collectors on a $1,000 cellar, hardly a funnel to future wealth. There are no equivalent great wines now selling at such low prices that they can be projected into enormous profits.

Of all spirits, Scotch is the most fashionable for investment, with about forty brokers competing for U.S. clients' business. The whiskey, aging in a bonded British warehouse, changes hands in the form of receipts, very much as do other commodities. Success stories of money doubled in four years have attracted many, not all of whom have had the same fortunate experience. Like all other collectibles, the quality of the item and the reliability of the seller are of paramount importance. Business experts warn of chicanery and fraud.

INSIDERS ADVISE

While French wine prices are rising, some shippers are shrinking their bottles by as much as 5 centiliters per bottle. This comes to almost a full bottle per case.

Inflation, fluctuations in international currencies, higher costs at the vineyards, world-wide competition for fine wines, limited production, and higher profits are the reasons for higher prices.

Decide on wines to put away according to what you can afford. Even if you are sure that a certain wine will double or triple in price, note that $720 buys only 12 bottles at $60 each.

Do not buy wines for profit unless you can afford to drink them should you not be able to sell.

The wines that appreciate most in price are the most famous and costly. They are also the wines that must be held the longest to be at their peak. So you must invest a lot for a long time, possibly ten, twenty, or thirty years.

If you drink a wine before it has matured, you are pouring away potential pleasure as well as value.

If you hold a wine too long, you have wasted it.

Each vintage has its own rate of maturity and will stay at its best for different lengths of time. Even experts do not always agree on the time spans involved.

If you buy wines to put away, be sure they are insured and that you have a controlled atmosphere in which to store them.

Sometimes you can buy the same wine more cheaply in the United States than abroad because the wine was bought early from the wholesaler.

You must know the vineyard and the owners of every section of it to be able to compare prices and quality of burgundies from the many vineyards that are split into parts.

The main reason for buying young burgundies of good vintages is not only price, but because they disappear soon after the first appearance on the market.

Wine and spirits merchants' prices differ greatly; compare when possible.

Some Scotch sellers have registered with the SEC, providing buyers with a prospectus.

You might have to drink some of your vintage wines, so it would be wise to choose them with that in mind.

The books that can best equip you to buy are *Wines of the World*, by Andre L. Simon, *The World Atlas of Wine*, by Hugh Johnson, and *The Encyclopedia of Wine and Spirits*, by Alexis Lichine.

Current retail wine prices appear regularly in the catalogues of the superior shops in the United States, but London winesellers prefer to quote only on a daily basis in a fast-rising market.

WORKS OF NATURE

It has been observed that the works of nature bring less at auction than do the works of man; a fact sustained by a review of the prices fetched by minerals, fossils, butterflies and shells when they are sold on the basis of rarity, form, color, condition, and aesthetic appeal.

However, a revival of interest in natural curiosities is reflected by rising prices and the mounting number of retailers who sell decoratively oriented natural objects. Some of this may derive from the return to nature of a generation fearful of the growing destruction caused by technology. Based partly on appreciation of these objects as marvels of nature and partly as marvels of beauty, they are becoming established aspects of the fine arts market.

Sculptural masses of minerals, some in the form of geodes, are especially fashionable decoration, although scientific buffs still form the base on which this commerce rests. Fossils are also entering a decorative phase; fossil fish, wood, shells, eggs, plants, and bones of animals are enjoyed by many who know little or nothing of scientific classification, but see them as interesting and individual forms, often reminiscent of modern art.

A promotion of lepidoptera, an order of insects comprising butterflies and moths, as limited edition works of art, noted that they are captured in strictly limited numbers, to protect their species. Priced from $20 to $30 per plexiglass box, some were even offered "signed."

A historic high price for a mounted bird was the $21,600 for a specimen of the now-extinct great auk, Alca impennis. It was also the all-time record in the field of Natural History, occasioned by great rarity and a special set of circumstances. It was purchased at Sotheby's in London, the money raised by public subscription, for the Icelandic Museum of Natural History.

Shells, once a staple ornament on the Victorian whatnot, in intervening years of interest largely to the scientific collector, have returned to the living room, this time on the polished chrome and glass *étagère*. Their prices fluctuate with the harvest of a particular season and also with newly developed dredging techniques. It is not beauty that is reflected in the price of shells, but rarity. Many superbly formed and colored specimens are common, and thus reasonably priced.

INSIDERS ADVISE

Hobby publications carry advertisements of firms specializing in the various fields of natural history.

The best place to check market prices of works of nature is in the catalogues of the firms selling them.

If you have a specimen you want to check, try the public library for books that carry classifications.

Antique shops and second-hand stores sometimes have bargains in this field, because they usually price such items without reference to their market value.

They also overprice for the same reason, so you must know how to check value.

Define the price you are paying for the object as separate from the price of the stand or mounting.

Minerals chip easily; handle with great care.

Mounted birds and animals are best kept under glass; dust and dirt are their mortal enemies.

If you beachcomb for your own shells, boil the live specimens to kill the animals inside, extract them, then polish the shells with baby oil.

In the past few years the annual reports of international auction sales have begun to carry prices for works of nature.

The Shell; Five Hundred Million Years of Inspired Design, by Stix and Abbott, is in itself a work of art.

Rocks, Minerals and Gemstones, by I. O. Evans, *The Mineral Kingdom,* by Paul E. Desautels, and Carroll and Mildred Fenton's *Fossil Book* are recommended.